The Encyclopedia of
DREAM CARS

The Encyclopedia of
DREAM CARS

A CELEBRATION OF CONTEMPORARY AND FANTASY CARS

Chris Rees

HERMES
HOUSE

Continental R

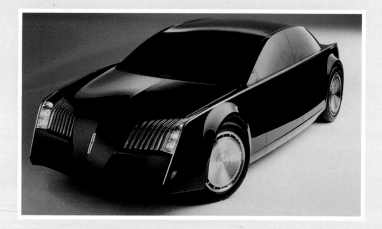

Produced by
Anness Publishing Limited
Hermes House
88-89 Blackfriars Road
London SE1 8HA

A CIP catalogue record for this book is available from the British Library

Publisher: Joanna Lorenz
Editorial Manager: Helen Sudell
Editorialt Assistant: Emma Gray
Designer: Alan Marshall

Printed and bound in Singapore

© Anness Publishing Limited 1998
Updated © 2001
1 3 5 7 9 10 8 6 4 2

CONTENTS

INTRODUCTION

Everyone knows a classic car when they see one, even if they can't actually tell you what makes a car a "classic". Most people associate advancing age with classic credentials, but that ignores the existence of "living classics" and future classics.

The first section of this book starts at 1976 and ends with the cars of the future. The 1970s was a difficult time for motoring, with oil crises, escalating congestion, pollution issues and industrial troubles. Yet a true golden age of cars began at this time, reaching full bloom in the late 1980s and 90s, as cars became more rewarding to drive, leapt ahead in technical terms and grew in design appeal.

There are few, if any, pieces of hardware as emotive as the car. The second section aims to chart the evolution in dream-car design over 60 years. With the birth of car *designers* rather than pure engineers, the door was open for them to express their visions of the future. These cars are celebrated here as we look back at what fired the imaginations of yesterday's creative minds and look to future creations, which will address the current issues of congestion, energy consumption and pollution.

The story of classic and dream cars charts the progress of our own history and experience, and this book is a celebration of that progression and a recognition of the value and importance of these cars in our lives.

SECTION ONE

A–Z of Classic Cars from 1976

This book brings future classics to life from 1976 to the present day, and identifies the cars that have had the impact necessary to qualify them as genuine classics. Every car included is great in some way. Perhaps, like the Peugeot 205GTI, it was viewed as the best car in its class. Perhaps, like the Renault Espace or Audi Quattro, it changed motoring life and the way we look at cars. You won't find just sportscars or super-luxury coupés in this book, for many affordable "cars for the common people" are every bit as classic as the great Ferraris and Porsches of their era.

ALFA ROMEO

■ ALFA ROMEO GT/GTV

This smart sports coupé was launched in 1974 as the Alfetta GT. It was based on a shortened version of the Alfetta saloon floorpan, so it shared its racing-inspired rear-mounted gearbox. Perhaps the car's best feature was its superbly clean

■ RIGHT *The 1980 GTV6 brought fuel-injected power to the Alfa, and there was also a major face-lift.*

ALFA ROMEO GT/GTV (1974–86)	
Engine	4/V-six-cylinder
Capacity	1570–2934cc
Power	109–186bhp
Transmission	5-speed
Top speed	111–140mph (179–225kph)
No. built	136,275

■ LEFT *All Alfa GT/GTV models handled superbly, and the best of the bunch was this late-model GTV6.*

■ ABOVE *For a coupé, the GTV was very practical, with four full seats and a proper opening tailgate.*

■ ABOVE *The 2.5-litre V-six engine in the GTV6 delivered 160bhp – enough for a top speed of 127mph (204 kph).*

styling by Giugiaro. This was also a very practical car thanks to its hatchback rear opening.

The interior was very distinctive: only the rev counter (tachometer) was sited in front of the driver. All the other gauges were stacked in a central binnacle. There was more room for people than in most coupés in the GT class.

Initially, there was only one engine, the Alfetta 1.8, but by 1976, 1.6 and 2.0-litre units were added, the latter called GTV. There was even a very potent turbocharged model, but this was sold in tiny numbers (around 20). In 1980, the 2.0 GTV became the only model sold and got a face-lift, featuring larger bumpers and a more conventional instrument layout.

The best GTV of all was undoubtedly the GTV6 of 1980. Into the familiar body Alfa Romeo fitted a fuel-injected 2.5-litre V-six engine. Performance was now extremely high, and suspension changes and a limited slip differential made it handle superbly. Yet this was not the quickest GTV of all: that honour goes to the GTV 3.0 produced in Alfa Romeo's South African factory. Like other GTV models, this boasted considerable success on the race-track, as well as being a very satisfying car to drive on the road. Today, it is the most desirable of the classic GTV family.

■ BELOW *The 164 was responsible for reviving Alfa Romeo's reputation for making desirable large saloon (sedan) cars.*

■ ALFA ROMEO 164

Traditionally, Alfa Romeo produced rear-wheel-drive sporting cars and was generally most successful with its smaller saloons and coupés. Its track record with larger cars was not very good, the 1970 Montreal and 1979 Alfa 6 being complex, poor-selling, problem-ridden machines.

That all changed with the 164, the first Alfa to emerge following Fiat's 1986

take-over of the group. Not only was the 164 quite the most handsome saloon (sedan) car of its day – thanks to Pininfarina's master hand – but it had sharp front-wheel-drive handling and, most importantly of all, it was built up to a quality that rivalled Germany's best. The interiors looked as if they had been designed by an architect.

The floorpan was shared with three other cars: the Fiat Croma, Lancia Thema and Saab 9000. However, Alfa installed its own range of engines, which was always the marque's best feature. The range started with a two-litre Twin Spark (two spark plugs per cylinder) and culminated in a three-litre V-six. All engines were capable of reaching 125mph (201kph). The ultimate Q4 model had four-wheel drive, six speeds and a 230bhp Cloverleaf engine.

If there was one criticism of the 164, it was a tendency to suffer from torque-steer, which means pulling right or left

under acceleration. Alfa Romeo addressed the worst of the problem early on and also developed a Super version with longer body-coloured bumpers and chrome strips.

The 164 undoubtedly led a renaissance at Alfa Romeo, and re-establishing confidence in the marque. It left production in 1997 after a distinguished career.

■ FAR LEFT *Pininfarina's styling was widely admired for its crispness and distinctively Alfa Romeo character.*

■ LEFT *Pininfarina's extraordinary sculpted dash was a work of art, but the profusion of switches was criticized as confusing.*

ALFA ROMEO 164 (1987–97)	
Engine	4/V-six-cylinder
Capacity	1962–2959cc
Power	114–230bhp
Transmission	5/6-speed manual
Top speed	125–152mph (201–245kph)
No. built	248,278 (to end 1994)

■ BELOW *Technically, the 164 borrowed its floorpan from Fiat/Lancia, but added its own engine range and sports-tuned suspension.*

ALFA ROMEO

■ ALFA ROMEO SZ/RZ

Italians coined a new phrase to describe the amazing Alfa Romeo SZ: "Il Mostro", or The Monster, and it is easy to see why. In no way could the bodywork be described as handsome, but if you were looking to make a visual impact then this Alfa supercar was king. Although Alfa Romeo announced the birth of this amazing new model under its internal type designation of ES30, production cars were known as SZ.

The design house responsible for the SZ was Zagato, which has always had a strong association with Alfa Romeo. Zagato also produced the SZ for Alfa at its Milanese factory. The time it took for Zagato to develop and produce the SZ was a remarkably short two years. To

■ ABOVE *The striking SZ made its debut at the 1989 Geneva Motor Show where it created many headlines.*

■ LEFT *Even more desirable among Alfisti was the convertible RZ model, only 241 of which were made.*

3.0-litre V-six engine was given even more power thanks to integrated fuel injection/ignition systems, new camshafts and modified manifolding. Maximum power was now up to 207bhp.

Since the SZ weighed only 2822lb (1280kg), performance was deeply impressive: a top speed of over 152mph (245kph) and 0–62mph (0–100kph) in only seven seconds was quoted. The SZ was quite capable of handling all this

make the bodies, Zagato elected to use plastic composites (a mixture of thermosetting resins and glassfibre), mounted on a steel chassis. The result may have looked spectacularly ugly but it was surprisingly aerodynamic: its Cd (co-efficient of drag) figure of 0.30 was superior to that of many other cars.

Underneath that extraordinary coupé bodyshell was basically the mechanical package from the racing version of the Alfa Romeo 75, including its layout of longitudinal engine, rear transaxle and rear-wheel drive. The familiar Alfa

■ RIGHT *Underneath the exterior lay what was basically a racing car. This made the SZ feel very much like a circuit racer on the road.*

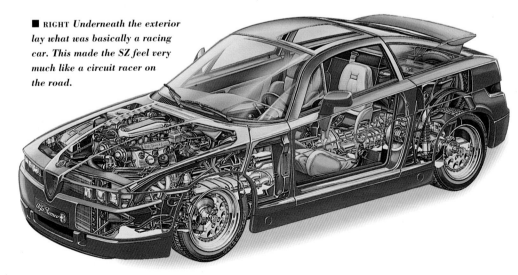

power thanks to its sophisticated suspension and asymmetric Pirelli P-Zero tyres. One interesting feature was hydraulic adjustment for the rear suspension, which was occasionally needed to overcome ramps and other . obstructions because ground clearance was just 2.4in (6cm).

Inside, the Alfa 75 driver would have felt immediately at home, since the instruments and much of the switchgear came from this humble saloon (sedan). Luxury was not overlooked, though, as standard equipment included leather seats and electric windows.

At the end of 1992, the SZ was joined by an open-topped model called the RZ. This was more than just a roofless version of the SZ, as it incorporated a number of detail changes like a shorter front spoiler, thinner body panels, lower windscreen and reshaped sills. The chassis was considerably stiffened to compensate for the loss of the roof, and in consequence its weight went up by 220lb (100kg).

■ ABOVE *The three-litre V-six engine under the bonnet (hood) was familiar, but it was tweaked to give 207bhp – enough for a 150mph (241kph) top speed.*

■ ABOVE *Milan-based coachbuilder Zagato was responsible for the design and construction of the SZ.*

■ TOP *Perhaps the most flattering view is from the bird's eye.*

■ ABOVE *Luxurious leather seating contrasted with humble switchgear from the Alfa 75.*

ALFA ROMEO SZ/RZ (1989–94)	
Engine	V-six-cylinder
Capacity	2959cc
Power	207bhp @ 6200rpm
Transmission	5-speed
Top speed	152mph (245kph)
No. built	1,035/241

As planned, Zagato built just over 1000 examples of this exceptional sportscar, despite the fact that Alfa Romeo had received 1600 orders for the model, almost before it had even been seen by the public. An additional 241 copies of the RZ drop-top model were made in 1992–3. That means the SZ and RZ will always be among the rarest and most sought-after Alfa Romeos of all.

ALFA ROMEO

■ BELOW *The brand-new 1994 Alfa Spider was a startlingly fresh design created by Alfa Romeo's own Centro Stile in collaboration with Pininfarina.*

■ ALFA ROMEO SPIDER/GTV

The name Spider in Alfa Romeo's vocabulary dates right back to 1955, and the most famous incarnation of the model – the one driven by Dustin Hoffman in the film *The Graduate* – lasted 18 years in production. At the Paris Salon in September 1994, Alfa Romeo not only used the name for its exciting new roadster, it also revived another famous name from its past for a sister coupé model – GTV.

■ ABOVE *The classic Alfa Romeo Spider dynasty began back in 1966 and ended with this model, the Series 4, in 1994.*

The most striking feature of this new sportscar couple was the styling. The elegant and dramatic wedge shape recalled the 1991 Proteo show car and, if anything, the production cars' styling was even more adventurous than the

■ BELOW *If the Spider's handling was affected by its non-rigid bodyshell, the GTV was the opposite: taut, sure-footed and rewarding.*

show car's. A collaboration between Alfa Romeo's own Styling Centre and Pininfarina, the body made full play of the famous Alfa triangular grille. Other features included a plastic clam-shell bonnet (hood) with cut-outs for the high-intensity headlamps, an uncompromising rising belt-line indentation, tapering rear flanks and air intakes at the front, which were strongly reminiscent of past Alfas.

However, Alfa Romeo departed from its sportscar traditions by opting for front-wheel drive. If anyone was in doubt about how well the new car would handle with this set-up, a simple test drive dispelled all such concern. A unique multi-link rear suspension system allowed for a degree of rear-wheel steering, and in terms of steering response and grip around corners, the new Alfa could hardly be surpassed. There was a big difference between the ultimate abilities of the fixed-top GTV and the open Spider, though: the loss of rigidity in the body structure of the Spider let it down compared to the super-sharp GTV.

The GTV also differed from the Spider in another important respect: it had two seats in the rear, although they were so tiny that only very small children could ever be comfortable.

Performance was a definite strong suit. In Italy, there was a choice of three engines: a brand new 150bhp 2-litre 16V Twin Spark engine with variable valve timing, a 200bhp 2-litre V-six Turbo unit (GTV only) and a 192bhp 3-litre V-six. In Britain, only the Twin Spark engine was offered. All engines

■ ABOVE *Alfa's sportscar twins took a healthy share of the market, and have already become living classics.*

provided acceleration to match the sharp styling.

The cockpit was a triumph of clean design and classic feel: shrouded circular dials, sculpted steering wheel, pleasing upholstery and a profusion of Alfa Romeo badges. The driving position was unusually good for an Italian car, too.

For their price, there was little to touch Alfa's new sportscar twins in the desirability stakes. Perhaps it was the ineffable magic of the badge, or the strikingly bold shape, or the class-leading levels of handling and response. Whatever the appeal, the Spider and GTV have already passed into the realm of instant classics.

ALFA ROMEO SPIDER/GTV (1994–)	
Engine	4/V-six-cylinder
Capacity	1970–2959cc
Power	150–200bhp
Transmission	5-speed
Top speed	130–146mph (209–235kph)
No. built	Still in production

■ RIGHT *The front end of both cars was a triumph of styling: an adventurous clamshell bonnet with cut-outs for the high-intensity projector headlamps.*

■ BELOW *The Spider was an exciting car to drive, even if some testers criticized the lack of rigidity in the bodyshell.*

■ ABOVE *The name GTV (last used in 1987) was revived for the fixed-head two-plus-two sister of the Spider, which was perhaps even more striking in its presence.*

ASTON MARTIN

■ ASTON MARTIN DB7

Aston Martin is part of a rich tradition of British coachbuilt sportscars. Its place is unique as a purveyor of brutally powerful, finely handcrafted, traditionally finished grand tourers. The "DB" dynasty of cars stretches back to 1947, the letters DB harking back to Sir David Brown, who owned Aston Martin from 1947 to 1972, and who helped design the DB7.

Ford became the new owner of Aston Martin in 1987. As well as giving the company the backing of a large

■ RIGHT *There is no doubt that the two Aston Martin DB7 models made an extremely strong pairing: elegant, powerful, luxurious, meticulously crafted and rich in character.*

■ BELOW *The most handsome car in the world? With the DB7, British designer Ian Callum created one of the great Aston Martin shapes.*

■ LEFT *The sumptuous interior reflected Aston's very British heritage and its tradition of hand-built quality: Connolly leather, tasteful British burr walnut, yet with plenty of modern electronics.*

organization, it instituted a new model programme, reviving the DB name on a new car that was designed to slot in below the existing Virage range. To develop this important newcomer, it turned to Tom Walkinshaw's TWR organization to do its best on the aging platform of the Jaguar XJS.

The DB7 was the supremely elegant result. In style it was a classic, two-plus-two, front-engined, rear-wheel-drive car with superbly integrated, flowing lines designed by Ian Callum. Some were tempted to call it the most beautiful car in the world.

It was powered by a new 3.2-litre six-cylinder engine, which looked back to the past to boost its horse power: an Eaton supercharger helped it develop a

ASTON MARTIN DB7 (1994–)	
Engine	6-cylinder
Capacity	3239cc
Power	335bhp @ 5750rpm
Transmission	5-speed manual 4-speed auto
Top speed	155mph (249kph)
No. built	Still in production

■ RIGHT *The DB7 Volante immediately made an impact in sales terms, especially in America, boosting Aston Martin's production levels to an unprecedented high.*

massive 335bhp, enough to take the DB7 to a top speed of 155mph (249kph), with acceleration to match. Technically, the DB7 was very sophisticated, having sequential fuel injection, four-piston brakes and specially designed tyres.

This was a superb car to drive, sharp enough to cut it as a sportscar yet refined enough to make a convincing grand tourer. The chassis was pure magic.

Inside, rich Connolly leather upholstery was standard, as was traditional British burr walnut for the dashboard and centre console. Standard equipment included electric front-seat controls, air-conditioning, electric roof and Alpine sound system. There may not have been much room in the rear seats but at least they were there, and they could always double up as extra luggage space.

If the coupé looked seductive, the Volante convertible was the ultimate temptress in markets such as the US where up to 80 per cent of Aston Martin sales were of this model.

This was certainly not a cheap car, especially in Volante convertible form, and some people questioned whether it

was worth paying the extra for the DB7 when the Jaguar XK8, launched shortly after, looked and behaved so similarly and cost so much less. The Aston Martin was very much more exclusive, however, since a maximum of 700 per year could be built at the factory, and the badge carries a special set of qualities.

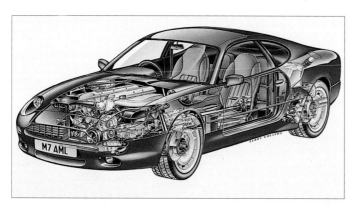

■ ABOVE *It may have had a mere six-cylinder engine, but supercharging and sophisticated fuel injection gave it 335bhp. The rest of the package was equally well engineered.*

■ ABOVE *Everyone who drove a DB7 was deeply impressed by its chassis, which provided keen handling, entertaining controllability and an accomplished ride.*

■ LEFT *A new Volante full convertible was presented ready for a 1996 launch. The hood (top) stacked under a tonneau cover in the British fashion.*

ASTON MARTIN

■ ASTON MARTIN VIRAGE

By 1988, Aston Martin had been relying on its mighty V-eight model for no less than 20 years, and it desperately needed a new car to tempt supercar owners. To design its car, it took the unusual step of asking several independent British car stylists to offer proposals, including Richard Oakes and Aston Martin veteran William Towns. The winner was John Heffernan's elegantly understated design, realized in aluminium by Aston Martin's skilled craftsmen.

The new Virage was unveiled at the 1988 Birmingham Motor Show and was greeted as the latest in a line of great British sportscars from the Newport Pagnell firm. It might have cost a six-figure sum, but its sumptuous specification, tremendous performance and hand-crafted quality were certainly appreciated by devotees.

■ ABOVE *Vast swathes of leather completely cloaked the cockpit; what it missed was covered with deep-pile carpets or polished wood.*

■ ABOVE *Even more muscle-bound was the later Vantage version, its twin supercharged engine boasting an incredible 557bhp.*

■ LEFT *For such an imposing, heavy and dimensionally grand car, the Virage managed to retain a certain elegance.*

■ ABOVE *When its V-eight engine kicked in, the Virage really flew. Its most impressive characteristic was almost limitless quantities of torque.*

ASTON MARTIN VIRAGE (1988–)	
Engine	V-eight-cylinder
Capacity	5340cc
Power	310–557bhp
Transmission	5/6-speed manual 4-speed auto
Top speed	160–186mph (257–299kph)
No. built	Still in production

In true Aston Martin tradition, each engine was hand-built and the name of the builder was placed on a plaque on the engine block. The familiar 5.3-litre V-eight engine was given a four-valves-per-cylinder head, developed by the American tuning company Callaway Engineering. Now power was up to 310bhp, and even more impressive was the torque figure of 340lb ft (461Nm (Newton metre)).

That all spiralled up to new heights with the pumped-up Vantage model of 1992. Twin superchargers raised the power figure to 557bhp and torque to just about the highest figure of any road car: no less than 550lb ft (745Nm) at 4000rpm. It was quicker than just about anything else on the road.

The most popular Virage model of all was the Volante, the convertible member of the family. Further choices were Shooting Brake (estate/station wagon) and Lagonda (four-door saloon/sedan) versions, a special 500bhp 6.3-litre engine and a version simply called V8 Coupé with Vantage-style wide bodywork and "only" 350bhp.

■ RIGHT *A mere 50 coupés was the plan, but a further run of convertibles brought the total of Aston Zagatos up to 89.*

■ ASTON MARTIN ZAGATO

All Aston Martins are rare but the 1986 Zagato was guaranteed to be one of the rarest of all. When Aston Martin released pictures and announced that it would be building only 50 cars at £70,000 ($117,810) apiece, buyers came

■ RIGHT *Aston Martin revived an old relationship with coachbuilder Zagato to create the fastest, most exciting production Aston yet in 1986.*

■ FAR RIGHT *There was only space for two passengers but they were treated to an Italian-styled cockpit trimmed to the highest standards.*

ASTON MARTIN ZAGATO (1986–90)	
Engine	V-eight-cylinder
Capacity	5340cc
Power	310–432bhp
Transmission	5-speed
Top speed	157–190mph (253–306kph)
No. built	89

rushing and all were pre-sold before any had been made. Speculators forced the price up as high as £500,000 ($841,500).

So what was all the fuss about? Italian coachbuilder Zagato had an illustrious history with Aston Martin stretching back to 1958, and this was to be a modern equivalent of the immortal DB4 Zagato. In addition to being a special-bodied Aston, it would be the company's

quickest ever car. An already mightily powerful Vantage V-eight engine was tuned even further to give over 430bhp, and Aston Martin quoted a top speed of 190mph or 306kph.

This was essentially a special-bodied, lightweight, short-wheelbase Aston Vantage with two seats and an Italian-designed interior. Zagato not only designed but also built the car. There was some concern that the finished article did not look much like the drawings that had convinced buyers to hand over deposits, but there was no doubting the brutal nature of the drive. Acceleration was explosive at 0–60mph (0–96kph) in under five seconds and handling was certainly more incisive than other Astons.

It was decided that the exclusivity of the coupé would not be harmed by adding a limited run of 25 Volante convertibles to the roster, and the

prototype drop-top was shown at Geneva in 1987. In fact 52 coupés and 37 Volantes were made in total, the last one being produced in 1990. Controversial it may have been, but it was also the ultimate in Aston exclusivity.

■ ABOVE *The performance was brutal. A top speed of 190mph (306kph) was claimed, and you could do 0–60mph (0–96kph) in under five seconds.*

AUDI

■ AUDI QUATTRO

The idea of four-wheel drive as an aid to fast road driving rather than pure off-roading may not have been new (Jensen introduced the FF supercar in 1966), but Audi certainly pioneered the art-form in the real world. The 1980 Quattro was the first mass-produced performance car to feature permanent four-wheel drive.

■ FAR LEFT *The Quattro Sport was a strict two-seater with a 300bhp engine – expensive and a very rare sight.*

■ LEFT *Safe and forgiving, the Audi Quattro became the handling benchmark of the 1980s.*

The four-wheel-drive system rewrote everyone's definition of handling limits. It certainly made it probably the safest car to be driving in wet or icy conditions. Reports in some journals even seemed to suggest that the Quattro was invincible around corners whatever the road conditions; in fact of course every car has its limits, and the Quattro's were simply much higher than other cars', but unfortunately dozens of owners found this out the hard way by asking too much of the car, and ending up in a ditch.

The body was based around the recently launched coupé, with suitably bulging wings and a deeper front spoiler. Audi was not above adding gimmicks to the package, notably a dubious digital talking dash.

Power was also very high thanks to a turbocharged 2.1-litre five-cylinder engine. There was mighty turbo lag (the time it took for the turbocharger to cut

■ LEFT *Not only was the Quattro grippy, it was very quick too, thanks to its five-cylinder turbo engine. This is a 1988 20V version with 220bhp.*

AUDI QUATTRO (1980–91)	
Engine	5-cylinder
Capacity	2144–2226cc
Power	200–220bhp
Transmission	5-speed
Top speed	135–142mph (217–228kph)
No. built	11,452

in), but when it did, the Quattro simply flew: 0–60mph (0–96kph) in 6.3 seconds was stunningly fast for 1980. Braking was criticized for having too much front bias, but Audi soon corrected this with standard anti-lock brakes.

This was not a cheap car by any standards: it cost more than a Jaguar XJS or Mercedes-Benz SL, but then it did offer a completely new class of driving experience.

■ OPPOSITE *The Quattro Sport was homologated for rallying and continued Audi's dominance in the sport for many years.*

■ BELOW *It was on slippery surfaces like snow-bound mountains that the Quattro really shone, gripping the road where others wandered.*

■ ABOVE *Because of its superior traction the Quattro was a runaway success in rallying, where it dispensed with the rough stuff and scored dozens of victories.*

The Quattro permanent (full-time) four-wheel-drive system also turned the rally world upside-down. Audi swept the board with its newcomer, and very soon everyone recognized that they weren't going to win anything unless they, too, adopted an all-wheels-driven strategy.

Later models got a bigger engine and more power, and the ultimate Quattro was the short-wheelbase Sport model launched in 1983. This limited-production homologation (production-recognized) special had a 300bhp 20V engine and was capable of 155mph (249kph). At three times the price of a standard Quattro, it was strictly for rich would-be rallying stars.

When Audi announced that Quattro would soon be axed, there was an outcry from enthusiasts and the production run was extended, the model finally bowing out in 1991, after 11 years of service. For many people, this superb Audi was deserving of the title "car of the decade".

OTHER MAKES

■ AC
Thames Ditton-based AC started life in 1911 as Autocarriers and, post-war, AC progressed through ever-more powerful sportscars, culminating in the legendary V-eight-powered, Shelby-developed Cobra and the Frua-styled 428. By 1973, AC needed a new model and the ME3000, with its mid-mounted Ford V-six, was shown in 1973 but not actually produced until 1979, and then in tiny quantities. The project went to Scotland in 1984, and was modified to become the Ecosse, but ended in bankruptcy. Bryan Angliss's Autokraft revived the Cobra and in 1986 showed a new Ace model (scrapped by new owners Ford in 1987). Ford sold out again to Autokraft in 1992, and an all-new Ace model was produced. Today, AC produces the Ace and a new version of the Cobra called Superblower.

■ AUTOBIANCHI
Part of the Fiat empire since 1955, by the 1970s Autobianchi was firmly established as the "character" wing of the small-car department with models like the 500 Giardinera and Fiat 127-based A112. In the 1980s, Autobianchi was allied to the Lancia brand, producing the Y10. When the Y10 was replaced in 1996, subsequent products were badged as Lancias, and the Autobianchi name sadly died.

■ AVANTI
Raymond Loewy's swoopy Avanti was produced by Studebaker for just two years (1963–4), but a private consortium took it over and continued to make it right up until the present day. The styling was very un-Detroit, the bodywork glassfibre, the interior very luxurious and the price exorbitant. Avantis have a small but fanatically loyal band of followers.

■ ABOVE *The road-car interior was extremely well designed, if a little sombre.*

BENTLEY

■ BENTLEY CONTINENTAL/AZURE

In the 1950s, the name Continental represented the very pinnacle of superior transportation: with such a badge on your Bentley, you were assured of absolute opulence combined with effortless touring power, and everyone else could be assured that you were driving quite the most expensive car money could buy.

That was Bentley's golden age, at least in post-war terms. After the great Continentals were retired by the parent company, Rolls-Royce, Bentleys became merely badge-engineered versions of Rolls-Royce products. By the 1970s, Bentley represented a mere 5 per cent of

all Rolls-Royce group sales. A great name was being squandered.

Luckily, the management at Crewe realized this fact and began a steady renaissance of Bentley. First came the Mulsanne Turbo, basically a much more powerful version of the Rolls-Royce Silver Spirit, which also benefited from being less ostentatious.

■ ABOVE *A fabulously evocative interior with milled aluminium made the Continental T feel very special. Note the red starter button in the centre console.*

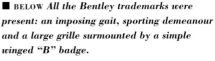

■ BELOW *All the Bentley trademarks were present: an imposing gait, sporting demeanour and a large grille surmounted by a simple winged "B" badge.*

■ ABOVE *The addition of a T to the Continental name meant a complete transformation: fat wheels, short wheelbase, 400bhp engine – an upper-class hot rod.*

BENTLEY CONTINENTAL/AZURE (1991–)	
Engine	V-eight-cylinder
Capacity	6750cc
Power	385–400bhp
Transmission	4-speed auto
Top speed	155mph (249kph)
No. built	Still in production

The sporting heritage of the Bentley badge deserved more, however, and in 1991 it got it. The Continental name was revived for a model that had no Rolls-Royce equivalent: here was a true-blood Bentley that lived up to the provenance of its name.

The new car was actually christened the Continental R, the R nominally referring to Roadholding. This was a handsome and imposing two-door coupé, some 17ft 6in (5.34 metres) long, 6ft 2in (1.88 metres) wide and 2.5 tonnes (2.46 tons) heavy. The extravagance of such an ample car was

■ OPPOSITE *Without a roof the Continental transmuted into the Azure. Pininfarina engineered the superb electric folding roof.*

■ RIGHT *Perhaps the R's handling was still a little barge-like compared with some rivals, but it was far better than previous Bentleys.*

flaunted at its Geneva Motor Show launch, as the show car was painted the brightest shade of red obtainable.

To pull all that bulk, Rolls-Royce engineers stayed with its familiar 6.75-litre V-eight and truck-derived Garrett turbocharging, in this form good for about 385bhp and a huge 553lb ft (750Nm) of torque. Transmitting this tidal wave of power through a GM four-speed automatic gearbox, the R was indecently fast: 0–60mph (0–96kph) in 6.1 seconds and a top speed of 155mph (249kph), or enough to despatch a well-driven Porsche.

Rolls-Royce called the new Continental "the finest sporting coupé in the world", and with some justification: despite its proportions, it handled respectably, rode very comfortably, cosseted the driver and passengers in the utmost luxury and sustained the most unerring ambience of serenity and superiority.

At £160,000 ($269,000) this was also, in 1991, the most expensive British car ever made, yet it sold better than any other model in the Bentley range. Bentley even saw fit to induce yet more from its superlative creation. First came the Continental S, with over 400bhp at its command. Then followed the Azure, the convertible version of the Continental, which was for some time the only car in which to be seen on the Côte d'Azur, justifying setting its owner back a cool £215,000 ($362,000).

The mighty Continental T is the most radical member of the Bentley family. Its wheelbase was shortened, its wheel-arches were flared, and its wheels were massive five-spoke alloys. The interior was laced with milled aluminium. Delightfully, you had to press a big red button to start the engine, which now had no less than 590lb ft (800Nm) of torque to dig into, making it surely the world's most upper-class hot rod.

■ ABOVE *Nothing less than the renaissance of the Bentley marque was how many described the impact of the Continental R, the first specific new Bentley for three decades.*

■ ABOVE RIGHT *Costing a cool £215,000 ($362,000), the Azure was for the seriously wealthy only. The south of France was its natural habitat.*

■ RIGHT *The R had huge pace thanks to its turbocharged 6.75-litre V-eight engine. Naturally, the ride quality was superlative.*

BITTER

■ BITTER

German-born Erich Bitter was a race driver and car-accessories tycoon. He was smitten by two Opel CD prototypes presented in 1969 and 1970 and was so disappointed that Opel did not go into production that he managed to persuade the General Motors-owned company to hand the project over to him. Opel even helped him develop the car into production-ready form.

Since Bitter did not have the resources to set up his own factory, production began in 1971 at coachbuilders Baur of Stuttgart. An Opel Diplomat saloon (sedan) chassis was shortened and its suspension retuned for the lighter car, but otherwise the mechanicals were left untouched, including GM's 5.4-litre V-eight engine.

This was a very handsome car, and definitely in the same league as Italian exotics. It could be ordered in any of 45 different colours, had a luxurious cabin trimmed by Baur and an Opel-sourced dashboard. It was certainly not a cheap car, costing almost as much as a Rolls-Royce, but its quality and dashing looks

persuaded many customers to flock to the hitherto unknown marque. Production got underway at the rate of about one car per week.

The big American-designed V-eight engine provided refined, torquey performance, making it ideally suited to a grand touring role, rather than an overtly sporting one. Handling was sharp but not in the same league as greats like Ferrari and Porsche.

Just as handsome as the CD was Bitter's next car, the SC. This was first shown in 1979 but took another two years to enter production. Again this used Opel parts – the newly launched Senator – and the coupé body was styled by Bitter himself. The 3.0-litre fuel-injected six-cylinder engine was more in keeping with the times than the the old GM V-eight, and the later Bitter-modified 3.9-litre version was even more suitable, having an extra 30bhp at

■ ABOVE *The proud badge of the Bitter CD, neat and effective like the car itself.*

■ RIGHT *The CDs styling was widely admired for its simplicity and good proportions. The elegance factor drew buyers by the dozen. Bitter's cabin used an Opel dashboard but was sumptuously trimmed by specialists Baur of Stuttgart.*

BITTER CD (1971–79)	
Engine	V-eight-cylinder
Capacity	5354cc
Power	230bhp @ 4700rpm
Transmission	3-speed auto
Top speed	129mph (208kph)
No. built	390

■ OPPOSITE *Perhaps even more handsome than the CD was the 1981 SC. Its three-box design was sharp and Italianate, often being compared with the Ferrari 400.*

210bhp. There was even the option of four-wheel drive, but only two cars were so equipped because of the expense.

Attractive cabriolet and long-wheelbase four-door versions were added in 1985, but this course proved far too ambitious: by then the company had overstretched itself and unfortunately production ended the following year; some 450 examples of the SC had been made.

■ BELOW LEFT *With a 6-cylinder fuel-injected engine, the SC was impressively rapid, but its best role was long-distance cruising.*

■ ABOVE *Although it used simple Opel mechanicals, the CD was a real driver's car: fast, assured and a comfortable cruiser.*

Bitter went on to develop other projects but so far these have remained in prototype form. The first was a convertible called the Rallye, based on the Opel Manta, but the impending demise of the Manta led to an evolution called the Type III. In production form, this would have had Opel Senator underpinnings, but sadly plans to market the car were dropped in 1992 amid continuing financial problems. Some years later, Bitter resurfaced with an imposing and elegant new four-door saloon (sedan) car, again based around Opel components, but its production fate remains in the balance.

■ ABOVE *Erich Bitter was the man behind the German-made Bitter CD. He cleverly persuaded Opel to release one of its prototypes for him to modify and manufacture.*

■ BELOW *The Bitter interior cleverly made use of Opel's parts bin in its own setting.*

■ RIGHT *Bitter faded from the scene in 1986, but it continued to exist, promoting new concept cars like the Type III. Isuzu was at one stage going to market this car but sadly that never happened.*

BMW

■ BELOW *With handling comparable to the best Lotus had to offer, the M1 was highly entertaining, yet forgiving, around corners.*

■ BMW M1

The motivation for the BMW M1, still BMW's one and only mid-engined supercar, came from racing and a new set of regulations. In the Group 5 Silhouette formula of 1976, BMW's aging CSL was losing out to Porsche's 935. To regain lost face, BMW needed a mid-engined chassis worthy of its magnificent twin-cam 3.5-litre straight-six engine: 400 examples would have to be built over a two-year period to qualify for the formula.

The M1 was conceived by BMW's Motorsport division. It was to be the first road-car application for BMW's superb M88 twin-cam straight-six engine. In Turbo Group 5 form it would give up to 700bhp, but for the road, BMW deemed

steering. There was a five-speed ZF transaxle to put the enormous power down on the road.

Initially, BMW turned to Lamborghini to sort out the details of the tubular steel chassis, build prototypes and assemble the 400 road cars required for homologation at the rate of two a week. Giugiaro's Ital Design was contracted to shape the body, taking inspiration from Paul Bracq's 1972 BMW Turbo show car. Prototypes were seen being tested

277bhp enough. Only the cast-iron bottom end came off the regular BMW production line; the M88 had a unique 24-valve twin-cam head with chain drive, a pukka forged-steel crank, race-style dry sump and longer connecting rods. It breathed through Kugelfischer-Bosch indirect injection.

The engine sat in-line and well down in the chassis behind the cockpit. Suspension was by unequal-length wishbones and coils, with huge vented disc brakes and rack-and-pinion

■ ABOVE *Thanks to its racing-derived 3.5-litre engine, the M1 was extremely rapid: a top speed of 161mph (259kph) was recorded by one magazine.*

■ RIGHT *BMW's M1 was its only true supercar, conceived as a machine that would be practical and reliable yet racing-car quick.*

■ LEFT *There was no doubt that the M1 was an expensive supercar, but it was also one of the most exclusive ever made.*

■ BELOW *Clever aerodynamics played a large part in the success of the M1's shape. The black ducts are for engine cooling.*

around Sant'Agata in 1977, but by then Lamborghini was in deep financial trouble – and the M1 looked like a possible casualty. Lamborghini's government funding ran out, and delays caused BMW to snatch its M1 project back in April 1978, by which time seven prototypes had been built. It decided to transfer production to Baur, in Stuttgart.

Formally launched late in 1978, the M1 immediately fell foul of new Group 5 regulations that were its *raison d'être*. The revised rules said that 400 cars had to have been already sold to the public before a racing version could be used properly. By the time homologation was completed in 1981, the Group 5 M1 was already out of date, overweight and outclassed by a younger opposition.

If the M1 racer was never much more than a promising also-ran, the road car was always top-drawer material, not only fast (M1s were independently clocked at 161mph, or 259kph) but comfortable, refined, surprisingly frugal and beautifully built.

Handling was impeccable, and no mid-engined upper-echelon supercar rode so well or cruised so quietly. Disparate and convoluted as its cross-Europe design and manufacture had been, the values and quality behind this unfulfilled racer were always pure Munich. It bridged the gap between yesterday's dinosaur heavyweights and today's versatile supercars and is rightly regarded as one of the all-time classic supercars.

BMW M1 (1978–81)	
Engine	6-cylinder
Capacity	3453cc
Power	277bhp @ 6500rpm
Transmission	5-speed manual
Top speed	161mph (259kph)
No. built	450

■ ABOVE *The BMW "kidney" grille looked very purposeful on the aerodynamic nose of the M1. Pop-up headlamps improved airflow in the crucial nose section.*

■ ABOVE *Giugiaro designed the very simple and handsome shape, and it was built half in Italy and half in Germany in a very convoluted production process.*

BMW

■ **BMW 6 SERIES**

BMW has a strong reputation for producing powerful sporting coupés, its tradition stretching back to the earliest days. In the early 1970s, the BMW coupé ideal reached its zenith, the celebrated CSL becoming invincible on the track and accomplished on the road.

■ LEFT *The ultimate 6 Series was the 1983 M635CSi, fitted with a 286bhp M1 engine – good enough for a top speed of 158mph. Today, it is easily the most sought-after 6.*

■ ABOVE *Handsome, well-engineered, powerful and classy – the 6 Series was BMW's coupé for the 1980s.*

■ ABOVE *In typical BMW fashion, the dashboard was designed to curve around the driver. The cockpit was very spacious.*

BMW 6 SERIES (1976–89)	
Engine	6-cylinder
Capacity	2788–3453cc
Power	184–286bhp
Transmission	5-speed
Top speed	122–158mph (196–254kph)
No. built	80,361

By 1975, BMW needed to develop a successor, and the car earmarked to do this was the 630CS/633CSi, launched in March 1976. Compared to the old CS series, the 6 Series was larger, more cosseting and more expensive – a grand tourer, which was extremely good at its job of whisking along the autobahns, but not a true sporting car. The 1979 628CSi, with its even smaller engine, did little to enhance the image.

BMW attempted to remedy a lack of sporting feel by fitting its venerable

3453cc engine into the 6 Series in July 1978, creating the 635CSi. This engine was architecturally the same as that fitted to the M1, though it developed less power (218bhp). A far more sporting feel than the 633s was engendered by uprated dampers, springs and anti-roll bars and ventilated disc brakes.

It was really only a matter of time before BMW bit the bullet and fitted the full-house 24-valve M1 engine to create the M635CSi (M6 in the US). It shared the M1 specification very closely; with

its light-alloy 24-valve head, twin overhead camshafts and central spark plugs, but owing to new induction and twin-pipe exhaust systems and the use of Bosch Motronic II digital engine electronics, it developed 9bhp more than the M1 engine. The new M635CSi was a real road burner.

The more powerful 6 Series BMWs were extremely good cars, notable for their fine handling, luxury, refinement and quality. The successor, the 8 Series, was in many ways less appealing.

■ RIGHT *Later 6 Series models got more power, sophisticated electronics and heightened levels of luxury.*

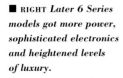

■ FAR RIGHT *While it was refined and rapid, the 6 Series was less sporting than the earlier CS series it replaced. It was really better suited to motorway driving.*

■ BMW Z1

The Z1 was a curiously un-BMW-like product, but enthusiasts everywhere were thankful that the company had the courage to put it into production. BMW was used to making drivers' cars, for sure, but its tendency was always toward the conservative. The Z1 was radical and highly specialized.

The project began life as a development mule for a new type of suspension for the BMW 3 Series. BMW Technik – the company's technical wing, mainly responsible for research and development – designed a body for it that was meant to show BMW was ahead of the game. It was displayed at the 1986 Paris Salon as a pure concept car, but the public response was so overwhelming that BMW boss Eberhard von Kuenheim gave the go-ahead for a production run.

After a series of modifications, the production Z1 was ready in 1988. Its basis was a steel monocoque chassis fitted with a composite thermoplastic body. Immense strength was engineered in by keeping very high sills, which raised a question about the doors; BMW solved this little conundrum by designing doors that dropped away into the sills, operated by electric motors –

■ ABOVE *The Z1 project began life as this development mule for new suspension systems, but the public reaction to its looks persuaded BMW to enter production.*

■ ABOVE *When the electric motors retracted the doors into the sills, getting in was an awkward exercise if the hood (top) was raised.*

great for fine-weather motoring. Aerodynamics were a strong point, and one novelty was a rear silencer (muffler), which also acted as an aerofoil.

The Z-axle rear suspension was the prototype of that for the forthcoming

BMW Z1 (1988–91)	
Engine	6-cylinder
Capacity	2494cc
Power	170bhp @ 5800rpm
Transmission	5-speed
Top speed	140mph (225kph)
No. built	8,093

3 Series, and gave great handling. The chassis could have handled more power than BMW gave it (the standard 325i engine was installed) but there was no questioning the fun factor. Equipment was deliberately sparse but the price tag was distinctly up-market: the Z1 cost the same as a BMW 735i, and was only ever a very limited-production prospect.

■ LEFT *The main party trick was doors that slid down into the high sills, bringing a new dimension to the term open-air motoring.*

BMW

■ BMW M3

In the 1970s and 1980s, BMW was the
most successful Touring Car racing
constructor, a remarkable feat since none
of its cars was a "homologation special"
– they were merely modified versions of
prosaic road cars. That all changed with
the M3, a legendary road car which also
swept the board in racing.

According to BMW's advertising, "M
is the most powerful letter in the world."

■ LEFT *The new-
shape 3 Series was
also made into an
M3 version with even
more power from a
six-cylinder engine,
and it had far fewer
rough edges.*

BMW M3 (1986–91)	
Engine	4-cylinder
Capacity	2302cc
Power	195–220bhp
Transmission	5-speed
Top speed	146–152mph (235–245kph)
No. built	17,969

M stood for Motorsport, a special
division within BMW, which was
responsible for racing and the
development of advanced road-car
projects. The M3 was actually based
on the current BMW 3 Series, but
Motorsport altered almost every
component on the car.

■ ABOVE *The interior of the Sport Evolution
model was covered in leather and race-style
suede and had very special seats. This was the
ultimate M3 model.*

The bodywork became aggressive,
with its flared arches and spoilers, and
four individual bucket seats in the
interior. Under the body, the suspension
and braking was beefed up and the
gearbox had a race-style dog-leg first gear.

Most importantly of all, the M3 got a
very special engine: a large-capacity
four-cylinder unit fitted with a 16-valve
head modelled after the M1. With
200bhp available, it made the M3
outrageously quick. More than this, it
was endlessly entertaining to pilot along
twisty rounds, almost without vices. Very
quickly the M3 became a legend.

Limited-edition Evolution models
were even better, with enhanced
aerodynamics and, in ultimate Sport III
guise, a bigger 238bhp, 2.5-litre engine.
The most expensive M3 of all was the
Cabriolet, individually hand-built by
Motorsport staff.

When the old-shape 3 Series was
retired in favour of the smart new shape
car, there was of course an M3 version,
but it was ruthlessly efficient rather than
exciting. Many enthusiasts remember
the first-generation M3 with greater
affection, particularly its fabulously
controllable handling and raw character.

■ ABOVE *The heart of the M3 was its four-
cylinder engine with a head derived from the
M1. Even in its least powerful incarnation, it
still had 195bhp on tap.*

■ BMW Z3

Not to be left out of the fashionable and burgeoning junior roadster market, BMW launched its Z3 range towards the end of 1995. The plan was certainly ambitious: to engineer a car from scratch and build it in a brand-new factory in Spartanburg, South Carolina, USA. Yet, it definitely paid off: even before the car's official launch in October 1995, posters advertising the new James Bond film, *Golden Eye*, showed exactly what the secret agent's new transport was – a Z3! Within 18 months, over 40,000 had been sold worldwide.

The new BMW roadster handled beautifully and made significant use of existing bottom-of-the-range BMW components, thus keeping the price of

■ LEFT *That BMW could successfully tackle the small sportscar market was proved with the Z3. This is the 1.9-litre model with a 140bhp engine.*

the "poverty" variant down to below £20,000 ($35,000). Where BMW's previous sportscar model (the 1980s Z1) had seemed crisp and forward-looking, many were underwhelmed by the Z3 shape, a not altogether happy mix of current BMW styling cues and half-hearted retro touches, such as the wing vents inspired by the classic 507 of the mid-50s. However, most buyers loved its sassy, overstyled shape.

The Z3 was stronger in many respects than competitors like the MGF and Mazda MX-5 Miata: it had a very solid shell, excellent build quality and great presence. Frugal but uninspired four-cylinder 1.8 and 1.9-litre engines were quickly joined by a powerful 2.8-litre six-cylinder and, in the spectacular M Roadster, the M3's 321bhp engine. This last was a real bargain supercar with beefed-up styling and a special interior.

■ ABOVE *With a 2.8-litre engine, the Z3 became much more of an out-and-out sportscar. Note the wider alloy wheels for extra grip.*

BMW Z3 (1995–)	
Engine	4/6-cylinder
Capacity	1796–3201cc
Power	116–321bhp
Transmission	5-speed manual 4-speed auto
Top speed	115–155mph (185–249kph)
No. built	Still in production

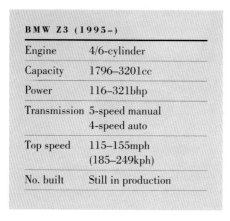

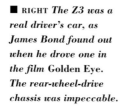

■ ABOVE *The BMW roadster was built at a completely new factory in America, which could hardly keep up with demand.*

■ RIGHT *The Z3 was a real driver's car, as James Bond found out when he drove one in the film Golden Eye. The rear-wheel-drive chassis was impeccable.*

BRISTOL

■ BRISTOL 412 TO BLENHEIM

Bristol enthusiasts wept bitter tears when the 407 – Bristol's first Chrysler V-eight-powered model – hit the road in 1961. Out came the thoroughbred all-alloy straight-six engine – lovingly crafted by Bristol themselves – and in went an iron V-eight, shipped over in a wooden packing case from Canada (to evade import duty) and hitched up to an automatic transmission. To add insult to injury, it even had push-button controls.

It was the only way out for Bristol: the sweet little six, a mere 2.2 litres and 110bhp, was struggling with the weight of the opulent 406, and since Bristol could not afford to fund their own new 3.5-litre straight six, Detroit power was the only way to go.

It was the right decision. Bristol rode out every storm by keeping small, and

■ LEFT *In the early 1970s, Bristol's offering was the 411, a hand-built grand tourer, which essentially dated back to the 1950s.*

selling alloy-bodied, separate-chassised cars to a discreet and discerning few. The shape changed over the years, but the proportions – tall, slim and long – remained consistent right up to the latest Blenheim, still available today.

By 1975, the 411 was the latest incarnation of the Bristol ideal.

Radically different was the curious Zagato-styled 412 of 1975, a convertible coupé with big double roll-over bar. However, it still rode the classic 9ft 6in (2.89 metres) wheelbase chassis – which could be traced back to BMW's pre-war 327 coupé – and still had the 6.6-litre Chrysler V-eight engine.

BRISTOL 412 TO BLENHEIM (1975–)	
Engine	V-eight-cylinder
Capacity	5211–5665cc
Power	Not disclosed
Transmission	3/4-speed automatic
Top speed	120–140mph (193–225kph)
No. built	Not disclosed

■ LEFT *Zagato was responsible for the controversial styling of the 412, launched in 1975. This was a targa-topped convertible four-seater.*

■ OPPOSITE *All Bristols featured this hinging side panel, inspired by aerodynamics. On the other side was a panel for the spare wheel.*

■ BELOW *Many famous celebrities were attracted to the understated character of the Bristol, which was very much a car for the wealthy.*

In 1976, the 412 became a convertible saloon (sedan) with a standard hardtop, while the S2 of 1977 had a smaller 5.9-litre engine. The rapid 140mph (225kph) Beaufighter of 1980 had an American Rotomaster turbocharger, beefed-up gearbox and a restyled front-end, and remained in production until 1992.

The curious 603E and 603S of 1976–82 featured new styling on familiar hardware. They replaced the long-running 411, whose alloy body was basically that of the 406 of 1958. The short-lived E was a 5.2-litre "economy" model, while the S had the usual 5.9-litre engine. Both had cruise control, air-conditioning and the latest Torque-Flite automatic gearbox with long-striding "lock-up" top (a locking torque converter) and self-levelling suspension.

The Brigand and Britannia replaced the 603 in 1982. The Brigand was turbocharged and could sprint to 60mph (96kph) from rest in under six seconds and reach a 150mph (241kph) top speed. The cars ran on alloy wheels and featured new front and rear styling.

The Blenheim of 1993 had yet another new front- and rear-end restyle, but the basic shape was the familiar 603/Britannia body. Bristol claimed that only the roof and doors were retained, but much of the interior looked familiar from previous Bristols, notably the handsome binnacle and round white-on-black instruments.

The Blenheim was fitted with the latest fully managed and injected 5.9-litre Chrysler engine and four-speed automatic gearbox. There was no turbocharger this time, but economy was much better, and certainly the Blenheim made a consummate long-distance express for the wealthy enthusiast who wanted to be a little bit different – owners included Liam Gallagher, lead singer of the UK rock band Oasis, and Virgin business entrepreneur Sir Richard Branson.

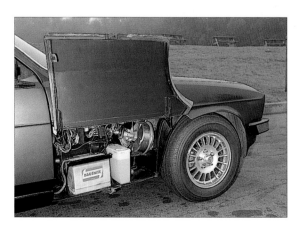

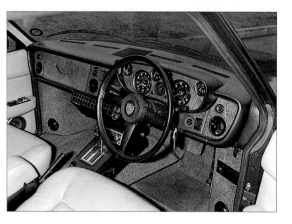

■ LEFT *Traditional British luxury in the cockpit of this Britannia: leather, wood and Wilton carpeting.*

BUGATTI

■ BUGATTI EB110

Following the Second World War, Ettore Bugatti's fabulously engineered, but vastly expensive creations were at odds with the times, and production never really restarted. There were many attempts to revive the name but none was very convincing – until a man called Romano Artioli stepped into the arena. This canny Italian magnate managed to rekindle the Bugatti magic in spectacular fashion, but ultimately the dream proved overambitious and ended in bankruptcy.

The plan was grand: a state-of-the-art factory was built in northern Italy, industry greats were hired (including Paolo Stanzani as technical director and Marcello Gandini as designer – both of them effectively fired later on), and a brand-new V-twelve engine was created from scratch.

The new Bugatti EB110 was to be a superlative mid-engined supercar, the sort of car that Ettore would have been making if he were still alive. The EB110 name was chosen as a composite of Ettore Bugatti's initials and the fact that the car was to be launched on the 110th anniversary of his birth.

The aluminium-bodied Bugatti's styling (created by an Italian architect) was dramatic but controversial: the lines were hardly harmonious and the traditional Bugatti horseshoe grille looked almost farcically small on the car's nose. Inside, meanwhile, the level of finish was superb and equipment levels were generous, but space was severely limited.

Mechanically, the Bugatti was highly advanced. Its centrepiece was a

■ ABOVE *The new EB110 was launched at an incredibly lavish party in Paris. It attracted a huge amount of publicity.*

■ LEFT *The avant-garde new Bugatti factory in Italy was highly regarded.*

■ LEFT *This is the prototype workshop. Clearly visible is one of the amazing V-twelve engines, which were hand-built by Bugatti. Each unit developed at least 553bhp.*

■ ABOVE *Reviving the fabled Bugatti badge was always going to be a hard task. "EB" stands for Ettore Bugatti, the marque's founder.*

V-twelve engine fitted with no less than four turbochargers and 60 valves, developing 553bhp. There was a six-speed gearbox mated to a four-wheel-drive system and suspension, which delivered handling akin to a grown-up Lancia Integrale. Bugatti claimed a top speed of 212mph (341kph) and stated that this was the fastest road car in the world; Jaguar with its XJ220 and McLaren with the F1 might have questioned this, but no one was in any doubt that the Bugatti was an extraordinarily fast and very capable machine.

By the time the EB110 was launched (at a lavish party in Paris in 1991), the supercar sales boom of the 1980s was already well and truly over. The list price was a walloping £285,000 ($486,000) and, if that all seemed a bit pale, Bugatti also developed a lightweight SS model with a 611bhp engine and up to 221mph (356kph) – total cost was an extra £50,000 ($93,000).

In the end, Artioli simply became too ambitious. First he bought up Lotus from General Motors in 1993, then he commissioned Ital Design to build a new four-door super saloon (sedan) called the EB112, but Ital Design stopped work on the project, claiming lack of payment. By 1995, Bugatti was bankrupt and its showcase factory lay tragically deserted. Unfortunately, it is not known exactly how many cars were built; Artioli claimed 154, including the one built for the German racing driver Michael Schumacher.

■ LEFT *Bugatti commissioned a second model, called the EB112, from Ital Design. This would have been an opulent limousine but production was prevented by Bugatti's liquidation.*

■ LEFT *The new Bugatti EB110 was in all respects an amazing car. Strikingly styled, enormously powerful and superb to drive, it fittingly revived the Bugatti name.*

BUGATTI EB110 (1991-95)	
Engine	V-twelve-cylinder
Capacity	3500cc
Power	553–611bhp
Transmission	6-speed
Top speed	212–221mph (341–356kph)
No. built	Not known

CATERHAM

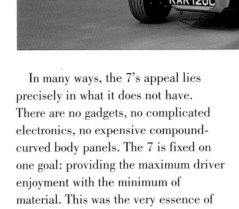

■ CATERHAM 7

The basic design of the Caterham 7 can lay a strong claim to be the oldest still in production. Its origins stretch back to the 1957 Lotus 7, a car that engineering genius Colin Chapman said he "knocked up in a weekend". Lotus made the car for 15 years, while Graham Nearn's Caterham Cars sold them, often when everyone else had given up on it.

When Lotus decided to end production of the 7, Graham Nearn's special relationship with Colin Chapman enabled him to acquire the rights to make the car in 1973. Initially, Caterham Cars struggled to make the plastic-bodied Series 4 Lotus 7. Soon, however, it turned to the simpler and ultimately more purist aluminium-bodied Series 3.

In many ways, the 7's appeal lies precisely in what it does not have. There are no gadgets, no complicated electronics, no expensive compound-curved body panels. The 7 is fixed on one goal: providing the maximum driver enjoyment with the minimum of material. This was the very essence of Colin Chapman's committed crusade for light weight.

In construction, the 7 had a tubular steel chassis clothed in aluminium panels; only the nose cone and wings were made of glassfibre. The rear axle

came from either Ford or Morris, and later Caterham devised its own de Dion rear-end.

For its engines, Caterham initially continued using Lotus's brilliant 126bhp, 1558cc Twin Cam, but eventually stocks ran out and it switched to Ford engines in a variety of states of tune: GT (84bhp), Sprint (110bhp) and Supersprint (135bhp). If you wanted more power you could go for a Cosworth BDA engine with up to 170bhp and, later, a Vauxhall 2.0-litre unit with 175bhp. From 1991, Caterham switched

■ RIGHT *7s were typically very stark affairs, but this cockpit shows that luxury need not be abandoned, with leather trim and a plethora of gauges.*

■ FAR RIGHT *Caterhams were usually powered by Ford-derived engines, but 1991 saw a switch to Rover power, of which this is an example.*

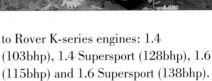

■ LEFT *There is no other car so focused as the Caterham 7. Developed from Colin Chapman's Lotus 7, it embodies speed, passion and sharp senses.*

to Rover K-series engines: 1.4 (103bhp), 1.4 Supersport (128bhp), 1.6 (115bhp) and 1.6 Supersport (138bhp).

The ultimate 7 was, however, the JPE (which stood for Jonathan Palmer Evolution, after the Formula 1 driver who helped develop it). With its 250bhp race-spec engine, lack of windscreen, carbon-fibre wings, extreme light weight and phenomenal braking, this was a very fast car: it did 0–60mph (0–96kph) in under 3.5 seconds and could beat a Ferrari F40 to 100mph (161kph).

■ RIGHT *The sensation of piloting the 7 is unique. A simple journey to the shops feels like driving a lap around a racing circuit.*

■ OPPOSITE *The image of the Super 7 was immortalized in the 1960s TV series The Prisoner, starring Patrick McGoohan. Caterham launched a special edition that encapsulated the spirit of "I am not a number, I am a free man!"*

Caterhams of whatever type offered more fun for your money than any other car. Most were bought in near-complete kit form with some components needing to be installed by the customer, which kept costs down and got round the need to Type Approve (legalize) the design. Most production was exported – Caterham received the Queen's Award for Export in 1993. Even today, over 40 years since the 7 appeared, the Caterham remains the absolute benchmark as far as handling and pure fun for the driver is concerned.

■ LEFT *Caterham promoted several one-make racing series involving 7s. This is action from the fastest class of all, the Vauxhall-powered Class A.*

CATERHAM 7 (1973–)	
Engine	4-cylinder
Capacity	1298–1998cc
Power	72–250bhp
Transmission	4/5/6-speed
Top speed	100–150mph (161–241kph)
No. built	Still in production

■ LEFT *The ultimate road-going 7 was the JPE, which stood for Jonathan Palmer Evolution, for the F1 driver helped develop this 250bhp thundering chariot. It once held the world record for the fastest-accelerating car.*

CATERHAM

■ LEFT *For over 20 years the 7 never changed shape; then Caterham launched the 21, a bold new sportscar with a completely enveloping body.*

■ CATERHAM 21

One guiding principle lay behind Caterham's custody of the 7 legend: you could do anything underneath the car to improve it, but the shape must remain untouched. With the 21, that philosophy was turned upside-down: here was a new model with a chassis based very closely on that of the 7 but with a totally new body. The 21 name indicated the

■ LEFT *This prototype was aluminium-bodied, an option that remained on the price lists after launch. The styling was by Iain Robertson.*

CATERHAM 21 (1996–)	
Engine	4-cylinder
Capacity	1588cc
Power	115–138bhp
Transmission	5/6-speed
Top speed	118–131mph (190–211kph)
No. built	Still in production

way Caterham was thinking: this was its vision of a car for the 21st century.

The plan to create an all-new Caterham began as an intention to make a mid-engined monocoque sportscar, but that would have been too ambitious. Instead, it was decided to create a new enveloping body over a modified 7 chassis. Journalist and designer Iain Robertson was called in to do the styling. For inspiration he turned to the classic racing Lotus XI, and his proposal looked exactly right: curvaceous, taut, recognizably British.

The interior architecture was adventurous and appealing, featuring an elegantly symmetrical design. The narrow cockpit was inherited from the 7, but the wide sills improved elbow room and leg room significantly. A narrow centre console housed switches and minor dials, the speedo and rev counter (tachometer) being sited directly in front of the driver.

Engineering the 21 posed a whole new set of problems for Caterham: never before had it been forced to deal with hinging doors and boot (trunk) lids, curved glass, sophisticated hoods or trimming the boot. It was getting all

these details right that delayed the start of production for two years after the car's first showing in 1994.

The official launch at the October 1994 Birmingham Motor Show was spectacular: no one was expecting the car to be shown in gleamingly

■ RIGHT *In general, production cars had glassfibre bodywork and a painted finish. Demand for the new 21 was high, but production was limited to 200 per year.*

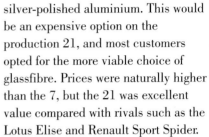

■ ABOVE *On the road, the 21 was every bit as thrilling as the 7, but was far more practical, thanks to a locking boot, weather gear and doors.*

■ ABOVE *The lithe, taut shape drew from past Lotus models for its inspiration, but was undeniably modern as well.*

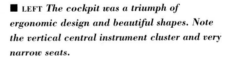

■ LEFT *The cockpit was a triumph of ergonomic design and beautiful shapes. Note the vertical central instrument cluster and very narrow seats.*

silver-polished aluminium. This would be an expensive option on the production 21, and most customers opted for the more viable choice of glassfibre. Prices were naturally higher than the 7, but the 21 was excellent value compared with rivals such as the Lotus Elise and Renault Sport Spider.

The valuable aluminium prototype was loaned to the press for early analysis, and testers were uniformly enthusiastic. This prototype was fitted with a Vauxhall JPE engine and six-speed gearbox – a unique specification, since all production 21s would have Rover K-series 1.6-litre engines or a very special version of the 1.8-litre MGF engine called the VHP (Very High Performance). Thanks to superior aerodynamics, the 293lb (648kg) 21 boasted a much higher top speed and far greater practicality than the 7, while inheriting all of the 7's handling finesse.

With an anticipated production volume of just 200 cars per year, the 21 will always be a rare beast, and its single-minded pursuit of driving pleasure will endear it to future generations of sportscar drivers.

■ ABOVE *The new badge reflected the company's assertion that this was a Caterham for the 21st century.*

■ LEFT *The first car was fitted with an extremely powerful Vauxhall JPE engine and was staggeringly fast. Production cars had Rover engines.*

CHEVROLET

■ LEFT *A convertible body option arrived in 1986 and was immediately very popular – there had not been an open-topped Corvette for over ten years.*

■ CHEVROLET CORVETTE

America's greatest sportscar – and for many years its only sportscar – is the Chevrolet Corvette. The name was born as long ago as 1953 when Detroit launched its plastic-bodied answer to the flood of European imports. A whole dynasty of 'Vettes followed on, up to the Stingray of the 1970s, which was as American as they come.

Then General Motors upped the stakes with a totally new generation Corvette launched in early 1983 as a 1984 model. Here was a thoroughly modern-looking sportscar that was still recognizably a 'Vette. The coupé shape was cleaner both aesthetically and aerodynamically and featured a hatchback and a removable roof panel.

The choice of glassfibre for the body remained, but the chassis was all new and the overhauled suspension used lightweight aluminium and even a plastic transverse spring.

The engine remained the faithful small-block Chevy V-eight, rated at 205bhp. It initially drove through a four-

speed automatic transmission, but soon a four-speed manual was offered with no less than three overdrive ratios. Performance was a strong suit: 0–60mph (0–96kph) in 6.6 seconds was incredibly fast in anyone's book, and the roadholding was excellent.

A he-man clutch, tough steering and heavy brakes justified its reputation as a "muscle car". If there were criticisms to be made, they were minor: an awkward-to-view digital dash, harsh ride, irksome entry and snappy wet-weather handling.

Innovations in coming seasons included, from 1986, a new convertible and, from 1989, a six-speed gearbox and a three-position Selective Ride Control with adjustable shock damping.

■ LEFT *The ZR1 streaked away when the accelerator was depressed, and in addition to its dazzling acceleration was quite capable of reaching a top speed of 180mph (290kph).*

■ ABOVE *All Corvette interiors were luxuriously appointed and extremely well-equipped in the best American traditions.*

■ RIGHT *The Corvette as launched for the 1984 model year was available in one body style: a hatchback coupé with a removable roof panel.*

CHEVROLET CORVETTE (1984–96)	
Engine	V-eight-cylinder
Capacity	5727–5733cc
Power	205–411bhp
Transmission	4/6-speed manual 4-speed auto
Top speed	142–180mph (228–290kph)
No. built	Approx. 320,000

■ RIGHT *The new 1984 Corvette had quite a heritage to live up to: its eponymous brethren stretched all the way back to 1953. No one was in any doubt that the new 'Vette justified its billing.*

While the standard backbone chassis looked as if it came from Lotus, the ZR1 – then the ultimate Corvette of all – did actually owe much of its prowess to the English engineering firm (bought by GM in 1986). The 1990-model-year ZR1 was the new "King of the Hill", boasting a new, technically advanced LT5 375bhp engine that transformed the 'Vette into a crushing supercar: it could do 180mph (290kph) and reach 60mph (96kph) from rest in 4.5 seconds. Small wonder that this was the most expensive car in GM's history, retailing at £35,000 ($59,000). The ZR1's power went even higher in 1993, stretching to 411bhp. Ultimately, the King dropped off the price lists in 1996.

Meanwhile, the standard Corvette range continued, also with more power (305bhp). This generation of Corvettes was replaced by an all-new one in January 1997. The Corvette may never have been a huge seller or a big dollar-earner, but that wasn't the point: it was America's sportscar statement, and a remarkably good one. It's a fitting tribute that, thanks to over 40 years of continuous production, more Corvettes have been made than any other sportscar in the world.

■ LEFT *As America's only sportscar, the Corvette was quick in a straight line and much better around corners than virtually any other American car.*

■ BELOW *The heart of the new ZR1 was its quad-cam 32-valve LT5 V-eight engine, which developed a storming 375bhp.*

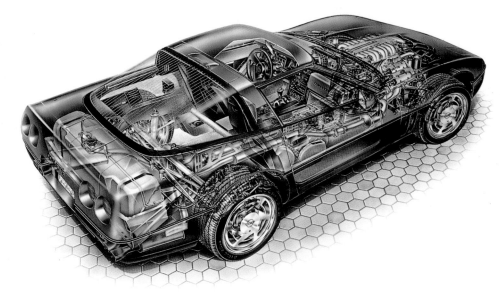

■ LEFT *Technically, the Corvette reiterated all the famous themes: a glassfibre body, powerful V-eight engine and muscle-car running gear. The chassis and suspension were all new, however.*

CHEVROLET

CHEVROLET CAMARO

The unprecedented success of Ford's Mustang sent rivals General Motors into a scurry of activity. However, in the two years it took to bring its answer to production, the great heyday of the "personal coupé" had already passed.

Its answer was the Chevrolet Camaro, and even General Motors could not have been disappointed when it sold 220,000 units in its first year. It was based on the uninspiring Chevrolet Nova body/chassis and mechanical package, but its strong suit was undoubtedly its classic "Coke bottle" styling by Bill Mitchell.

Both six-cylinder and V-eight engines were offered in various states of tune,

■ ABOVE *The fourth-generation Camaro arrived in 1993 as a smooth-looking coupé only; the convertible version did not appear until the following year.*

■ LEFT *The familiar Chevy "small block" V-eight engine powered most Camaros. This is the Z28 version with additional power, although in the 1970s emissions laws strangled power outputs across the board.*

■ ABOVE *One of the best of the "Coke bottle" first-generation Camaros was the Z28 edition, with its uprated engine, transmission, brakes and duck-tail rear spoiler.*

the most extreme being the SS (Super Sport) – of which 96,275 were built – and the RS (Rallye Sport) – 143,592 built. These have since become the most prized of all Camaros. As well as the more common coupé, Chevrolet also offered convertibles.

When it came to replacing the Camaro in 1970, General Motors took its

■ ABOVE *An all-new body shape arrived in 1970 and was essentially "right", lasting a full 11 years in production with no major changes.*

■ LEFT *The Camaro story kicked off in 1966, when General Motors came up with a car to rival the runaway success of the Ford Mustang.*

■ LEFT *The third-generation Camaro kept up the tradition for a very American four-seater coupé. These are IROC-Z and Z28 editions from 1985.*

time and created a bespoke model (dedicated chassis) with monocoque construction instead of a separate frame. While the Mustang became bloated, then emasculated, the Camaro felt balanced in style and leaner, too. While the styling may have been less subtle than the first series (especially from the mid-1970s when the nose was reshaped to satisfy safety laws), the interior may have been cramped and there was no convertible option, it nevertheless struck a chord with the American buying public.

The 1970s Camaro was a big dollar earner for GM, selling almost two million examples. Overall it was nowhere near as powerful as the original series Camaro – even in Z28 form, the most desirable of 1970s Camaros. There was also a Pontiac clone called the Firebird with different engines and alternative front end styling.

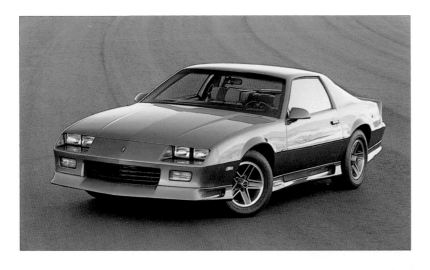

■ FAR LEFT *As the years progressed, the Camaro kept up with the times. This 1991 RS model has a sculpted body, side skirts and modern sports wheels.*

■ LEFT *The Camaro badge always meant something special to American buyers.*

CHEVROLET CAMARO (1970–81)	
Engine	4/6/V-six-/V-eight-cylinder
Capacity	2475–6573cc
Power	90–360bhp
Transmission	3/4-speed auto 4/5-speed manual
Top speed	96–125mph (154–201kph)
No. built	1,811,973

■ RIGHT *The ultimate Camaro in its third generation was the Z28 edition, with a healthy increase in power.*

CITROËN

■ CITROËN CX

For most people the name Citroën conjures up images of cars that are quirky, eccentric, idiosyncratic – in short, weird. More than any other model, the CX is the one which firmly reinforces these beliefs.

However, the CX is also one of the most misunderstood and underrated cars of all time. On the one hand, it is remembered as one of the all-time greats of motoring history; on the other, it has been dismissed as an unreliable, rust-infested, needlessly complex nightmare.

The CX was undoubtedly the last great Citroën, the last car Citroën got to design entirely in-house, before Peugeot bought the company in 1974 and began shaking its rod. Historically, it was the replacement for the brilliant DS, in production since 1955 and in dire need of a modern successor.

What arrived shortly after was more than just modern: it was positively futuristic. Its GS- and SM-inspired shape was not only one of the most aerodynamic ever seen on a motor car, it was also beautiful. Like the DS before it,

■ ABOVE *The cockpit looked like a mix between French art and Star Trek. Note the single-spoke steering wheel, rotating yellow dials and spherical ash-tray.*

■ ABOVE *This is a 1985 GTI Turbo with a 168bhp engine providing near-sportscar levels of performance. The CX was also extremely impressive around corners.*

it bristled with advanced features. The brilliant self-levelling hydropneumatic suspension was there, tied in with the braking and power-steering functions. On all but the earliest CXs, the steering also came with Vari-Power, Citroën's patented weighted power assistance, which altered the weighting of the steering according to your speed.

Europe was impressed enough to award the CX the Car of the Year trophy. Its handling was assured, its ride magical, its cruising ability ultra-relaxed, its character unique. The interior looked as if it had been sculpted by an artist rather than designed for

CITROEN CX (1974–91)	
Engine	4-cylinder
Capacity	1985–2500cc
Power	66–168bhp
Transmission	4/5-speed manual C-Matic semi-auto 3-speed auto
Top speed	91–137mph (146–220kph)
No. built	1,042,300

■ LEFT *The extraordinary shape of the CX, launched in 1974, was unique and way ahead of its time.*

mass consumption, and the instruments, sited in a space-age binnacle, revolved themselves around stationary needles. Compared to the competition, the CX cleaned up – or should have done.

Where Citroën got it so badly wrong was in the build quality. In particular, there was a terminal rust problem every bit as bad as Alfa Romeo's during the 1970s, and it was this, more than anything, which crippled the CX. By the time Citroën had sorted the problem out – which took fully seven years – the CX already had a very bad name, made worse by the public's and the trade's suspicion of the eccentric hydraulic system.

History may well be kinder to the CX. In GTI Turbo form, it was stunningly quick and handled like a hot hatch. In long-wheelbase, luxury Prestige form it was the choice of French presidents. In eight-seater estate (station wagon) form, it was the most capacious European car around. Its replacement, the XM, looked just as individualistic as the CX, but it lost many of the features that made the CX unique.

■ ABOVE *The carrying capacity of the estate (station wagon) was enormous: it was Europe's most capacious car for the whole of its production life. Antique dealers loved them.*

■ RIGHT *Prestige was the name given to the long-wheelbase luxury model that whisked French presidents around Paris.*

■ ABOVE *From the rear the CX looked highly unconventional, with its concave rear window and rear wheels set closer together than the front pair.*

OTHER MAKES

■ CADILLAC
General Motors' premium brand is almost the American Rolls-Royce, with more glitz than any other marque. In the 1970s, it was producing huge, bloated cruisers like the Fleetwood and Eldorado. A significant move toward smaller cars was the 1976 Seville, famous for its 1980 "trunkback" restyle. The 1982 Cimarron (a jazzed-up Chevrolet) was a dead end, as was the Pininfarina-created Allante convertible. Cadillac's main business has always been selling luxury cars to the US establishment, a task which it continues to date, although Seville and recent Opel Calibra-based Catera have been respectable performance saloons (sedans).

■ CHRYSLER
The 1970s was a decade of crisis for America's Number Three car-maker. Ex-Ford man Lee Iacocca reversed the company's fortunes with government help. Chrysler was one of the first to down-size with its 1981 K-series (LeBaron, New Yorker and Laser). The most interesting models

in its line-up were the Laser and LeBaron coupés, plus the TC by Maserati, a high-spec soft-top with a Maserati-tweaked engine, which bombed spectacularly. After flirting with Maserati, Chrysler bought Lamborghini, but this relationship did not last long. Chrysler also invented the "people carrier" (minivan) phenomenon with the 1983 Voyager. Chrysler has pioneered many trends, including "cab-forward" design and the launch of the Viper and Prowler.

■ CLAN
The Clan Motor Company was formed by a group of former-Lotus men in Washington, County Durham. The 1971 Clan Crusader was a quirky little two-seater coupé of glassfibre monocoque construction with a Sunbeam Imp Sport engine. The car passed crash tests and a big factory was set up to produce large numbers of cars, but the economic crisis dragged the firm down in 1973. There was an attempt to revive a modified Clan in Northern Ireland in 1982, and the same operation produced the Alfasud-engined Clan Clover of 1986, but by 1987 it had ended in bankruptcy.

DE LOREAN

■ LEFT *Brushed-steel bodywork, American entrepreneurship, Italian design, Northern Irish construction, British engineering and a French engine – the De Lorean was certainly unique in motoring history.*

■ DE LOREAN

The John Z. De Lorean story is quite an epic. An ex-General Motors high flyer, De Lorean touted his idea for a dramatic but high-volume sportscar around several countries, in the search for financial support. The British government took the bait, offering grants and loans totalling more than £80 million ($134 million) if De Lorean would set up shop in economically disadvantaged Northern Ireland, and he accepted.

The ingredients of the De Lorean

■ BELOW *The use of gullwing doors was chosen for dramatic impact. In practice, the doors caused countless expensive production headaches.*

■ ABOVE *The V-six Peugeot/Renault engine sat in the tail under a large cover. Lotus designers helped sort out the handling challenges of such a layout.*

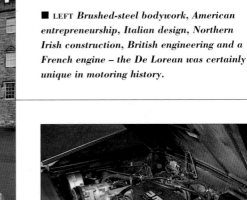

■ ABOVE *After only a brief two-year existence, the De Lorean fluttered out amid financial crisis and scandal.*

DMC-12 should have led to success: a chassis engineered by Lotus, a body styled by Giugiaro and a V-six engine from the Peugeot/Renault factory. Nor, given that it was only for the US market, was there anything wrong with its projected price of £15,000 (US $25,000).

But somehow the reality was different. De Lorean elected to use brushed stainless steel for the bodywork, which looked novel in the showroom but attracted dirt and scratches like chalk in the real world. The gullwing doors were another novelty, but they often leaked and, it was rumoured, could trap the car's occupants in a crash. Furthermore,

DE LOREAN (1980–82)	
Engine	V-six-cylinder
Capacity	2849cc
Power	145bhp @ 5500rpm
Transmission	5-speed
Top speed	130mph (209kph)
No. built	8,583

the quality of the early cars, built by an inexperienced workforce, was such that a second factory had to be opened in Los Angeles to rebuild them. Despite the effort of Lotus, the rear-mounted engine

layout never delivered anything better than indifferent handling. De Lorean announced massive production targets, but only 8,583 cars were built between the car's launch in 1980 and the collapse of the DeLorean Motor Company in 1982.

Thereafter it was controversy all the way: financial irregularities came to light and John De Lorean was arrested, but cleared, on drug-trafficking charges. The De Lorean is now something of a cult car with its own following of devotees.

DE TOMASO

■ DE TOMASO PANTERA

Elvis Presley shot his Pantera when it wouldn't start, and that is undoubtedly how many other owners felt about this enigmatic but slightly dodgy supercar.

Alejandro De Tomaso, an Argentinian tycoon who settled in Italy, built his first car, the Cortina-engined Vallelunga, in 1963. It flopped, and while his second effort, the Mangusta, was fast and beautiful, it quickly got a reputation for evil handling.

With the 1970 Pantera, De Tomaso was determined to get it right – and start making some money, too. He struck a deal with Ford of North America whereby they got his Ghia coachbuilding firm (hence the Ghia badge on today's Escorts and Fiestas) in return for selling his new car – powered by a 5.8-litre Ford V-eight engine – through their dealers in the US. It proved a sharp move as 4000 Panteras were unloaded on unsuspecting Americans before Ford shut the door on imports in 1974, beleaguered by complaints about build quality, rust and overheating.

The Pantera was fast in a straight line, topping 160mph (257kph), and with that mid-mounted engine the handling was copy-book stuff. It was practical, too: smash an engine in a Pantera and there was no need to take out a second mortgage to replace it because it was just a big, dumb Ford V-eight as found in millions of lumbering American saloons (sedans).

The model lasted into the mid-90s, its image progressively cheapened by boy-racerish spoilers and stickers and ever-fatter tyres. De Tomaso, however, had rather lost interest in the car that bore his name in the 1970s when he acquired several new business toys to play with, including Maserati and Innocenti.

■ ABOVE *In GTS form its massive spoiler, fattened wheel arches and prominent decals were so loud they were almost deafening.*

DE TOMASO PANTERA (1970–95)	
Engine	V-eight-cylinder
Capacity	4942–5763cc
Power	247–350bhp
Transmission	5-speed manual, 3-speed automatic
Top speed	150–160mph (241–257kph)
No. built	10,000

■ BELOW *Later Panteras became more rounded in profile, although no more subtle in style. The model stayed in production for an amazing 25 years.*

■ ABOVE *Classic 1970s themes in the interior: lots of chrome-ringed gauges, black-stitched trim and sports-style seats.*

■ LEFT *The relatively obscure Italian De Tomaso name won widespread fame with the Pantera, which was distributed in America by Ford.*

DODGE

■ DODGE VIPER

For decades, America's sportscar tradition hung on one sole car, the Chevrolet Corvette. By the end of the 1980s, however, Chrysler had come through its troubled times and was healthy enough to produce a new American sportscar legend.

When it was first shown at the 1989 Detroit Show, the Dodge Viper RT/10 stunned the crowds. The phrase "AC Cobra for the '90s" was bandied about at the show, and the impression was reinforced by the involvement of Carroll Shelby, the legendary creator of the Cobra, as a consultant. Chrysler

■ ABOVE *Viper was a fitting name for a car that recalled the glory years of the Shelby AC Cobra. Indeed, Carroll Shelby was even involved in the Viper's creation.*

executives displayed it as a concept car, and such was the public reaction that Team Viper was formed to turn dream into production reality, a process that took only 30 months.

The Viper was an amazing machine in all respects. Its plastic bodywork was pure machismo, a bristling contortion of muscular curves and suggestive ducting. There was no roof – except for a tent-like piece of vinyl and side curtains, which were supplied for use in the event of a shower. Just in case you got caught out, the interior was trimmed in waterproof materials. There were no exterior door handles, and the Flash Gordon three-spoke rear wheels were no less than 13-in (33-cm) wide.

The concept car had a truck-derived V-ten engine fitted and, in production form, Lamborghini made some changes, such as switching the block to aluminium rather than iron and giving it a bright-red head. But it remained

■ ABOVE *With its 8-litre V-ten engine, the Dodge Viper was a monster performer. It needed all of its 13-in (33-cm) wide wheels to rein in its 400bhp.*

distinctly low-tech: two valves per cylinder, hydraulic lifters, long pushrods. 400bhp may have been mightily impressive but the truck-like torque curve, peaking at 450lb ft (610Nm), was awe-inspiring. It didn't seem to matter that the engine note was rather subdued.

Acceleration was ballistic: 0–60mph (0–96kph) in 4.5 seconds.

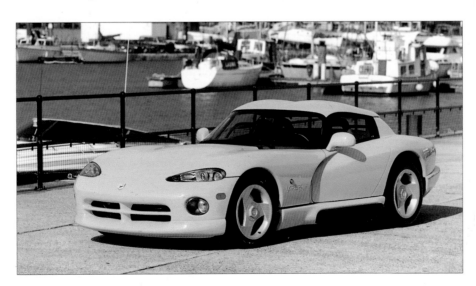

DODGE VIPER (1992–)	
Engine	V-ten-cylinder
Capacity	7990cc
Power	400–455bhp
Transmission	6-speed
Top speed	165–180mph (265–290kph)
No. built	Still in production

■ LEFT *Viper owners usually drove their cars open-topped, but a special "double bubble" hardtop was developed in case you had to go out in rain.*

The Viper was one of the first cars to be fitted with a six-speed gearbox, but that was more to help fuel economy than to encourage stick-shifting: you could exceed 100mph (161kph) in sixth without going over 2000rpm, and still be turning just 3250rpm when you reached 165mph (265kph).

Perhaps the best thing about the Viper was its price: at £30,000 ($50,000) this was a supercar that many could afford, even though its impracticalities made it strictly a fair-weather fun car.

If you wanted more practicality, then Dodge offered just that with the Viper GTS coupé, shown in 1993 but not produced until 1996. This was more than a roof-up roadster, though: just about everything on it was changed. If you opened up the hatchback you had enough room for golf clubs, and you could even power-wind the glass windows: now the Viper had luxury and practicality as well as drop-dead good looks and gargantuan power.

OTHER MAKES

■ DAEWOO
Formed in 1967, Korean-based Daewoo has already become one of the world's great industrial giants. Cars form only a strand of its empire and began as licence-built products of General Motors, such as the Opel Rekord. By the 1980s, it was starting to modify GM's designs for the home market and then began an impressive export operation. The first car engineered by Daewoo was the 1997 Lanos, partly designed by newly acquired operations in Britain and Germany.

■ DAF
For many years the Dutch motor industry was DAF. In 1975, it was bought by Volvo and its existing range of small cars was rebadged Volvo, while a new model in the pipeline emerged as the Volvo 343. DAF's main contribution to the motoring world was its continuously variable transmission by rubber bands. DAF still exists as the factory where the Volvo S40 and Mitsubishi Carisma are made.

■ DAIHATSU
One of Japan's second grade of car-makers, Daihatsu has always specialized in small cars. It had the distinction of being the first Japanese marque to be exported to Europe (in 1965). In the 1980s, it became the leading maker of micro-class cars, and its Mira model was the best-selling car in Japan.

■ DAIMLER
Daimler, one of Britain's pioneering car names, was best known for its limousines (favoured by royalty) and for its sporting saloons (sedans). However this proud company came under Jaguar's control in 1960. Daimler's impressive V-eight engine continued in production until 1969, but by 1964 Daimlers had become essentially badge-engineered Jaguars with fluted grilles and occasionally more luxurious trim, which remains the position today, although Jaguar preserves its identity. The last model unique to Daimler was the darling of mayors across Britain, the DS420 limousine, which survived until 1992.

■ BELOW *The Viper's brawny shape began life as a show car, but public adulation brought it to production. Its burgeoning curves, massive wheels and side-exit exhausts were throwbacks to the muscle-car era.*

FERRARI

■ FERRARI BERLINETTA BOXER

The immortal Boxer was Ferrari's first attempt at a flagship mid-engined model, though its history can be traced back to the 250LM Road Berlinetta, a road version of the 250LM racer, while some see the weird three-seater, centrally steered 365P show car of 1966 as its true spiritual father.

It was not until 1968, with the beautiful P6 show car, that Ferrari's favoured couturier Pininfarina really began to think aloud – and clearly – about the swoopy wedge profile of Maranello's supercar for the 70s, built to challenge the Lamborghini Miura and take over from the front-engined Daytona. Pininfarina's stylists started with a "big Dino" look, then flirted with the radical wedge influence of the 512 Modulo and futuristic 512S Berlinetta. Eventually, they settled on the elegant simplicity of the final production car, announced, prematurely, at Turin in 1971: production did not actually begin until 1973.

Under the big alloy engine cover was a new aluminium 4.4-litre four-cam

■ ABOVE *Ferrari owners are fanatical about their cars, and the Boxer inspired a new kind of loyalty. For many, this was the best car in the world.*

flat-twelve engine, descended from the 1500c 512 Formula 1 car of 1960. Breathing through four triple-choke (throat) Weber carburettors, it was for many the best engine in production, combining searing punch with pin-sharp throttle response and spine-tingling sound effects. Top speed was quoted as 188mph (302kph) – though no independent source confirmed it – 0–60mph (0–96kph) came up in 5.2 seconds.

To save space, the five-speed transaxle was tucked up under the engine, alongside the sump, all hung in an exotic multi-tube frame with a central

FERRARI BERLINETTA BOXER (1973-84)	
Engine	12-cylinder
Capacity	4390–4823cc
Power	340–360bhp
Transmission	5-speed manual
Top speed	175–188mph (282–302kph)
No. built	2.323

■ LEFT *Later cars had a 5-litre twelve-cylinder engine, which was more tractable in everyday use.*

■ OPPOSITE *As Ferrari's first-ever mid-engined flagship, the Berlinetta Boxer was always going to be a classic, and its Pininfarina-styled shape is one of the all-time greats.*

■ LEFT *With radical bodywork modifications, the 512 BB made a fearsome circuit racing machine.*

■ RIGHT *The Boxer's dart-like profile was extremely aerodynamic and unfussy. Note the long black cooling ducts over the mid-mounted engine.*

■ RIGHT *Subtle flowing lines combined with great presence. The rear end was surprisingly compact because the gearbox was mounted underneath the "flat 12" Boxer engine.*

the rear brakes, differently vented engine lid and four tail lights, not six.

The final incarnation of the Boxer was the 512i BB with Bosch K-Jetronic injection, which hacked an alarming 20bhp off the quoted power output but improved tractability and emissions. Production ended in 1984, making way for the controversially styled Testarossa. Ferrari built 2323 Boxers: 387 of the 365 model, 929 of the 512 and 1007 of the 512i.

steel monocoque around the passenger cell. Though the low-slung flat "boxer" configuration had the advantage of a low centre of gravity and better aerodynamics, the 365GT 4BB had a definite rear weight bias, with 56 per cent of its total weight over the rear wheels. At the limit, the handling could be a little ragged, and the Boxer certainly never had the cornering finesse of its arch rival, the Lamborghini Countach. The interior was finished in high-quality leather, and most cars came with air conditioning.

The five-litre 512 BB took over in 1976: its bigger bore engine, now with dry-sump lubrication, produced no extra power but 10 per cent more torque. A 512 could be spotted by its front spoiler, wider rear tyres, side air vents to cool

■ ABOVE *In its day, this was probably the fastest production car in the world. It was also* *fabulously sharp to drive, boasting instant throttle responses and tenacious handling.*

FERRARI

■ FERRARI 308GTB/328GTB

With the authority of a "proper" Ferrari badge – the previous 246 Dino had been marketed as a Fiat – the 308GTB was announced at the Paris show in 1975, supplementing the Bertone-styled four-seater 308GT4. It also marked a return to Pininfarina as Ferrari's favoured stylist with a classically aggressive coupé that displayed little in the way of unnecessary ornament. That it changed so little in 13 years of production says much for its elegant purity. A strict two-seater, the 308GTB reverted to the 92in wheelbase of the V-six Dino, but

■ LEFT *Few cars of the 1970s had as much poise and balance as the GTB around corners. The mid-engined layout and V-eight engine combined to make this one of the best drivers' cars of all time.*

borrowed the tubular-steel chassis and uncompromised double wishbone suspension of the GT4. The large vented and servo-assisted (power) disc brakes made light work of the 1270kg (2800lb)

GTB, but with 3.5 turns lock-to-lock, the rack-and-pinion steering was not startlingly fast.

Mechanically, the car was almost identical to the GT4, producing 255bhp from a dry-sump version of the strident four-cam V-eight with twin distributors, an oil cooler and transistorized ignition. Rational toothed-belt drive for the camshafts hinted at the influence of Fiat, who were paying the bills. The engine was mounted transversely amidships ahead of the rear wheels, with the five-speed transaxle and limited slip diff tucked in behind it. Running a modest 8.8:1 compression ratio, the five-bearing unit took in fuel and air through four Weber carburettors.

■ ABOVE *The circular tail lamps were a real Ferrari/Pininfarina hallmark, distinguishing the already elegant shape.*

■ ABOVE *Ferrari were not averse to making the driving environment luxurious as well as sporty, as the beautifully trimmed leather and electric switchgear show.*

■ RIGHT *As a replacement for the classic Dino, the 308GTB was a brilliant effort. It had all the hallmarks of a classic Ferrari, and yet was the marque's entry-level model.*

■ LEFT *Pininfarina's devastatingly simple, uncluttered bodywork brought the 308GTB instant recognition as one of the design greats.*

■ BELOW *With the name GTS, the targa-topped "spider" version was extremely popular in hotter climates. Not recommended in the snow, though.*

The first cars had glassfibre bodywork, but after 18 months this was abandoned for more traditional steel body construction – adding 250lb (113kg) and the promise of rust problems for future owners. The Americans in particular lapped up the 308, particularly the targa-topped GTS model, which consistently outstripped sales of the closed car by a huge margin.

A significant change was Bosch Digiplex fuel injection (first seen on Ferrari's Mondial), which brought cleaner running but milder performance, as peak power tumbled to just 214bhp for the 1981 GTBi. Within 18 months, the Quattrovalvole (four-valve) model raised power to a healthy 240bhp with an accompanying increase in torque. With subtly bespoiled front and rear to prolong its shelf life, the QV's performance returned to its earlier pre-injection levels.

The final incarnation of this body shape was the 1985 328, bored and stroked to give 3185cc and 270bhp for a top speed of 160mph (257kph). Ferrari claimed that build quality was better and the handling sharper.

Some Ferrari experts tend to think of the 308GTB/GTS as the Ferrari for the common man, which comparatively it is: almost 20,000 were built between 1975 and 1989, of which 1637 came to Britain, making it one of the most successful Ferraris ever in that market. Its exceptional qualities confer it genuine classic status.

■ RIGHT *In ultimate 328 guise, the "baby" Ferrari was even quicker, boasting 270bhp from a 3.2-litre engine.*

■ BELOW *V-eight power for the 308 meant four camshafts, transistorized ignition, a dry sump and 255bhp. Later units gained fuel injection.*

FERRARI 308/328 GTB/GTS (1975–89)	
Engine	V-eight-cylinder
Capacity	2926–3185cc
Power	214–270bhp
Transmission	5-speed manual
Top speed	140–160mph (225–257kph)
No. built	19,555

FERRARI

■ FERRARI TESTAROSSA

There is something magical about the word *Testarossa*, a name that Ferrari has used since the 1950s. All it means is "redhead", and it refers to the colour of the cylinder head on the engine, but the name has acquired a mythical status by association.

The 1984 Testarossa was the successor to the great Berlinetta Boxer, and duplicated much of its specification on the same chassis, but the new car was much more than a rebodied Boxer. The famous 5.0-litre flat-twelve engine was given completely revised cylinder heads with four valves per cylinder (and naturally painted red!), with the result that power rose to 390bhp and flexibility was enhanced. Ferrari also used high-tech nickel-alloy to prevent heat damage to the valves.

■ LEFT *From the rear, the tremendous width was emphasized. It gave the car fantastic presence but made manoeuvring a rather fraught experience.*

■ BELOW LEFT *The 12-cylinder engine's red-painted cylinder head gave the Testarossa its name (Italian for "redhead"), and it was the automotive equivalent of war-paint applied before going into battle.*

■ BELOW RIGHT *Thanks to its side-mounted radiators, the straked cooling side ducts became a distinctive hallmark of the model.*

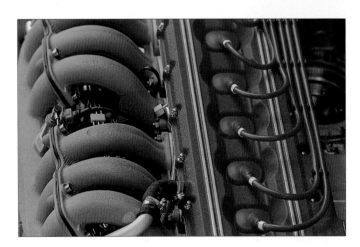

While the Boxer always had front-mounted radiators, the Testarossa switched to rear-mounted cooling, just ahead of the rear wheels. This dictated a new styling trait in the form of extremely wide rear wings punctured by dramatic horizontal strakes, which began in the doors. Pininfarina was responsible for the shape of the body. It was undeniably spectacular from any angle – especially the low, wide rear – but some questioned its audacity after the classically understated Boxer.

To save weight, the bodywork was all aluminium (except the roof and doors) and Pininfarina's wind tunnel confirmed the slipperiness and inherent down-force of the shape. The trade-off of having such a wide body (it was 78in (198cm) across) was that manoeuvring the car proved difficult, and visibility was very poor. This more than anything affected just how fast you could safely pilot the Testarossa.

In other respects Ferrari's new mid-engined top-of-the-range supercar was everything it should be. The engine sounded superb, the cabin was comfortable, the controls were light and – most importantly of all – this was an

■ OPPOSITE *The Testarossa recalled the glory years of Ferrari's Formula 1 effort. The 1984 Testarossa also recalled F1 themes with its mid-engined layout and squat stance.*

■ RIGHT *The final incarnation of the Testarossa series was the F512M of 1994-96. The most notable visible change was the cowled headlamps, but extra power also boosted the top speed to over 200mph (322kph).*

extremely fast car to drive. It could do the 0–60mph (0–96kph) sprint in 5.5 seconds and would keep on going to 180mph (290kph). Responses were always delicate, and the handling was rewarding.

In January 1992, the Testarossa was renamed 512 TR and revised extensively, the aim being to reclaim from Lamborghini's Diablo its title as the fastest car around. The TR name echoed the fact that this was essentially still a Testarossa, and only the new 348-style nose and larger wheels were very different.

Much more happened under the skin: more power (428bhp), lower ride height, better gearbox and improved suspension. The cabin was heavily revised, too. In short, the 512 TR was the best – and fastest – supercar in production.

The final evolution of the redhead was the F512M of 1994. This reflected Ferrari's preferred F prefix, while the M stood for "Modificata". Power went up by another 13bhp, so that its top speed now approached 200mph (322kph) and 0–60mph (0–96kph) came up in under five seconds. Other changes included cowled headlamps, bonnet (hood) ducts, new turbine wheels, restyled interior and classic round tail lights.

FERRARI TESTAROSSA (1984–96)	
Engine	12-cylinder
Capacity	4943cc
Power	390–441bhp
Transmission	5-speed manual
Top speed	180–200mph (290–322kph)
No. built	n/a

■ LEFT *In 1992 the Testarossa was renamed 512 TR after a minor restyle and a boost in power, from 390bhp to 428bhp, making it the fastest car in production.*

■ BELOW *Pininfarina's lines were widely admired – and copied – in the 1980s.*

FERRARI

FERRARI F40

In the 1980s, Ferrari extended the
boundaries of road-car performance with
cars such as the Testarossa and the
limited-production 288 GTO. Even
considering these and other supercars,
nothing came close to matching the F40,
one of the greatest Ferraris of all time.

Enzo Ferrari proposed celebrating 40
years of his marque with a very special
project that would combine race and
road car traits in one machine. The
Ferrari board agreed, and the F40, with
bodywork by Pininfarina, was brought to
production in just 12 months, helped by

the fact that it was based on the platform
of the 1984–87 288 GTO.

The underlying goal during the F40's
development was weight reduction. To
this end, the body made innovative use
of composite materials, which were
claimed to be 20 per cent lighter than
conventional metals. This priority also

meant the interior was utterly devoid of
carpets and door trim. Ferrari certainly
succeeded in its goal, since the F40
weighed in at just 2425lb (1099kg).

For power, Ferrari developed the 288
GTO V-eight to become a 3.0-litre twin-
turbocharged beast. With sequential
ignition and injection, silver/cadmium
conrod bushes and nicasil-coated liners,
the engine was capable of 478bhp –
and up to 200bhp more if you wanted
to go racing.

The performance figures spoke for
themselves: a top speed of 201mph
(323kph), 0–60mph (0–96kph) in 3.9
seconds and 0–124mph (0–200kph) in
12 seconds flat. This was far and away
the quickest machine on the road when
production began in 1988, almost a year
after its debut. It was also the fastest
road car Ferrari had ever built.

In character, the F40 was demanding
to drive but not overly difficult, while it
was hugely tractable yet superbly
balanced in handling terms. The fact

■ ABOVE *The F40
really looked like a
racing car from the
rear, and indeed
many owners used
their F40 in
competition. The
shape of the rear
wing was widely
copied by other
designers.*

FERRARI F40 (1988–92)	
Engine	V-eight-cylinder
Capacity	2936cc
Power	478bhp @ 7000rpm
Transmission	5-speed manual
Top speed	201mph (323kph)
No. built	1,311

■ LEFT *Features such as three-piece wheels,
racing brakes, removable rear bodywork and
soft fuel tanks (cells) hinted at racing origins.*

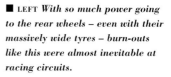

■ OPPOSITE *The inspiration for the F40 was a celebration of the 40th anniversary of Ferrari, and it was undoubtedly the best, and most audacious, car Enzo Ferrari had ever produced.*

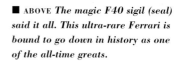

■ ABOVE *The magic F40 sigil (seal) said it all. This ultra-rare Ferrari is bound to go down in history as one of the all-time greats.*

■ LEFT *With so much power going to the rear wheels – even with their massively wide tyres – burn-outs like this were almost inevitable at racing circuits.*

that the cockpit was sparsely trimmed was a positive point, and the sight of raw carbon fibre and exposed tubing was a delight, not a penance. It meant that being in an F40 was an extremely noisy experience but given the sound – as close to a racing engine as you could get – that was also part of what made the F40 experience so unique.

Considering its intended role as a dual-purpose road/race car, the F40 came with numerous competition features such as Group C brakes, three-piece wheels and bag fuel tanks (cells) ahead of the rear wheels.

It was very focused and technically advanced, but not the technological *tour de force* that the Porsche 959 was. Rather it was a car for the dedicated enthusiast, everything being directed towards making it faster and more precise. The fact that many owners successfully took their £163,000 ($275,000) F40 racing proved the point.

■ RIGHT *It may only have had three litres, but the V-eight engine was twin turbo-charged and provided with very special innards. The result was a 478bhp power output in standard road-going tune.*

■ ABOVE *The ultra-lightweight F40 was numbingly fast, and very close to a true racing car in feel and in the demands made on the driver. With a top speed of 201mph (323 kph), it was also the fastest Ferrari yet made.*

FERRARI

■ FERRARI F50

When the time came for Ferrari engineers to build a new flagship in the mid-1990s, the brief was simple and uncompromising: take our 1990 Formula 1 racer (the 641/2) and transform it into a street-legal 200mph (322kph) road car. Enter, in March 1995, the F50, the spiritual successor to the F40 and certainly the most potent road car yet made by Ferrari.

Clothed in a flat-bottomed Pininfarina body that recalled Ferrari's sports racers of the early 70s, it was easily the wildest road car Ferrari had ever built. With such headline-making performance figures, pundits made immediate comparisons with McLaren's stunning F1. It was understandable but in reality these were two very different cars: where the F1's designers pursued refinement and build quality as well as ultimate performance, the F50 – a shade slower than the bigger-engined and lighter McLaren – was more of a raw sportscar created to give its owner Formula 1 sensations on the road.

■ LEFT *Cowled projector headlamps and deep cooling ducts reminiscent of the Ford GT40 dominated the low, wide front of the F50.*

■ LEFT *It may not have had the stripped-out racer feel of the F40, but the F50's very simple cockpit was based on an ethos of comfort and light weight, as evidenced by the leather-covered carbon-fibre seats.*

The F50 neverthless proved a surprisingly easy car to drive with a superb six-speed gearbox, reasonable ride (despite the rock-hard computerized damping and massive 335/30 ZR 18 tyres) and a user-friendly engine. Then there was the small matter of price: at £330,000 ($555,000) the

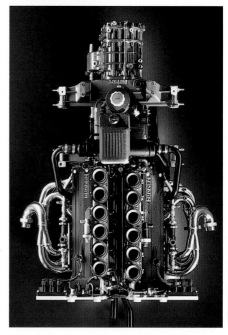

■ ABOVE *The V-twelve engine was essentially a Ferrari Formula 1 unit from 1990. Producing 521bhp, it was the closest a road-car driver could get to the sound and feel of an F1 car.*

■ LEFT *Pininfarina's stylists pulled another design classic. Despite the tight parameters supplied by Ferrari, the shape felt just right.*

■ LEFT *Few people imagined that Ferrari would trump its F40, but it did so with the superlative F50 in 1995. It was more dramatic, faster and more exclusive than the F40.*

■ ABOVE *The liquid-crystal instrument display was inspired by Formula 1 experience. There was even a "black box" flight recorder on board.*

■ LEFT *Everything was derived from racing, including the brakes, titanium uprights, ball joints and inboard pushrod/rocker-arm suspension.*

F50 was hardly cheap but still about half the cost of the British McLaren.

Boasting 521bhp from its Formula 1-derived five-valves-per-cylinder V-twelve engine, the F50 could do 64mph (103kph) in first, 112mph (180kph) in second, 124mph (194kph) in third, 138mph (222kph) in fourth, 160mph (275kph) in fifth and 202mph (325kph) in sixth. The handling was more forgiving than the F40 despite the extra speed, with superb non-assisted steering giving little kick-back but masterly precision.

With the iron crank-cased engine mounted rigidly to the chassis – and the rear wishbones attached to the gearbox – the noise was incredible, both in volume and quality, but nobody was complaining about that. In fact, chain rather than gear drive for the quad overhead camshafts meant less noise than the Formula 1 unit, while producing a smooth

idle and lower peak revs: 8500rpm instead of 14,000. Titanium connecting rods gave the unit high-rev strength.

Like the F1 car it was derived from, the F50 used proper inboard coil springs operated by pushrods and rocker arms, although, to make room for two people's feet, the front-end spring/damper units were transverse

rather than longitudinal. With titanium uprights and magnesium wheels, not to mention all-metal ball joints, it was no wonder the F50 steered with such precision. The F50 was to be much rarer than Ferrari's previous flagship hypercar, the F40: the company decreed that only 349 would be built, compared with 1311 F40s.

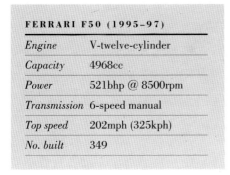

FERRARI F50 (1995-97)	
Engine	V-twelve-cylinder
Capacity	4968cc
Power	521bhp @ 8500rpm
Transmission	6-speed manual
Top speed	202mph (325kph)
No. built	349

■ RIGHT *An extremely neat hardtop could be fitted in poor weather, although the noise with the top on was simply deafening.*

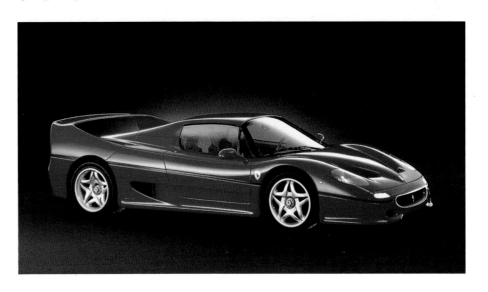

FERRARI

■ ABOVE *Understated simplicity was the theme of the styling, from the mono-colour circular tail lamps to the lack of spoilers.*

■ ABOVE *A typically functional yet elegant and comfortable interior from Ferrari. Note the hallmark metal gear-lever gate.*

■ FERRARI 348/F355

When it came to replacing the noble and long-running 328, Ferrari was forced by tougher crash regulations to expand the size of its new entry-level car, called the 348tb. It also decided to fit the familiar V-eight engine longitudinally rather than transversely as before; the overall length was greater but the engine could now be sited a full 5in (12.7cm) lower down in the chassis.

The lower centre of gravity and stiffer chassis transformed the mid-engined Ferrari's handling from merely superb to deeply impressive. On-the-limit manoeuvres could be accomplished without fear of sudden tail-end break-away, yet it was at all times thrillingly rewarding to drive.

The engine was expanded to 3.4 litres and almost 300bhp, allowing for the expected levels of Ferrari forward thrust. Although the engine pointed front-to-rear, the gearbox was mounted transversely – hence the "t" in the name. Naturally, Pininfarina was called

■ LEFT *With the 348, Ferrari created a genuine masterpiece, especially in dynamic terms. Its low centre of gravity and ultra-rigid chassis produced a handling gem.*

upon to shape the 348 and it did another superb job. Testarossa-style side strakes endowed the otherwise subtle bodywork with a distinctly Ferrari character. A more spacious interior made life much easier, too. As well as the fixed-head tb, there was also a ts model with a removable targa roof and a full Spider

soft-top. In 1994, the 348 was updated to become the F355. At the heart of the newcomer was an expanded quad-cam five-valves-per-cylinder 3.5-litre V-eight. With up to 381bhp on tap, this supremely characterful power-plant delivered even more blistering performance: 183mph (0–294kph) top speed and 0–60mph (0–96kph) in 4.8 seconds. In-gear acceleration was optimized by a six-speed gearbox.

FERRARI 348/F355 (1989–)	
Engine	V-eight-cylinder
Capacity	3405–3495cc
Power	296–381bhp
Transmission	5/6-speed manual
Top speed	171–183mph (275–294kph)
No. built	Still in production

■ LEFT *The full range of 348 models encompassed the tb (coupé), ts (targa) and Spider (full convertible). This series was the most popular Ferrari had yet made.*

■ FERRARI 550 MARANELLO

Maranello is the northern Italian home of Ferrari, and it is fitting that at least one model should bear its name. Ferrari chose it in 1996 for its first new front-engined two-seater since the 365 GTB/4 Daytona, which was launched 28 years previously in 1968.

What could have caused such an about-face following its predecessor, the mid-engined F512M? The answer is that a front-engined car broadened Ferrari's range and made it very much more practical than the old F512M.

In terms of ancestry, the 550 was most closely related to the 456GT, a four-seater Ferrari Grand Tourer launched in 1992. It shared its basic V-twelve engine and suspension layout. Apart from the very special F50, the Maranello slotted in as the company's quickest car, claimed to reach 199mph (320kph) and to do the 0–60mph (0–96kph) sprint in 4.3 seconds.

It was a lot more refined than previous Ferraris, but that was again a reflection of the times. On Ferrari's fabled Fiorano test track, the new 550 proved to be 3.2 seconds a lap quicker

than the model it replaced. Perhaps the 550's greatest strength was that it felt so capable and refined: the world's fastest grand tourer, perhaps.

Some observers felt Pininfarina's styling lacked any real finesse. Good points were the elegant glass house, the subtle hump in the rear wings, the classic circular tail lamps; the real disappointments were the fussy

■ ABOVE *Perhaps this was not one of the great Ferrari shapes, but the 550 found instant acceptance as a very rapid, more user-friendly Ferrari.*

front-end, the un-Ferrari-like shape and unhappy kicked-up tail.

At £145,000 ($244,000) the 550 cost over 50 per cent more than the dynamically more enthralling F355. In truth, the new Ferrari had a different sort of appeal: this was a tool as much for arriving at a destination feeling relaxed as for the sheer experience of driving.

FERRARI 550 MARANELLO (1996–)	
Engine	V-twelve-cylinder
Capacity	5474cc
Power	484bhp @ 7000rpm
Transmission	6-speed manual
Top speed	199mph (320kph)
No. built	Still in production

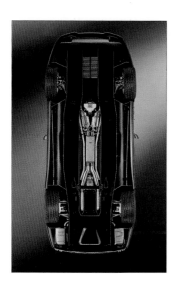

■ FAR LEFT *Where the 550 differed radically from previous range-topping Ferraris was in its front-mounted engine. Note the superbly profiled aerodynamics of the undertray.*

■ LEFT *The 550 lapped Ferrari's Fiorano test track over three seconds faster than the F512M, thanks to a 484bhp V-twelve engine that was capable of powering it to a top speed of nearly 200mph (322 kph).*

FIAT

FIAT X1/9

The Fiat X1/9 is historic for this single fact: it brought mid-engined handling sophistication, previously reserved for exotica like Lamborghini and Ferrari, to a mass audience. Launched to rapturous praise from the world's motoring press in 1972, it was, like its predecessor, the Fiat 850 Spider, destined to sell in large numbers, especially in North America.

Bertone's razor-edged styling incorporated a nifty removable targa roof panel, stored in the front boot (trunk) when not in use. Pop-up headlights were also a novelty for the time.

Initially fitted with a 1290cc four-cylinder 85bhp single overhead-camshaft engine and four-speed gearbox from the Fiat 128 Rallye, the X1/9 was adequately brisk, with a top speed of 110mph (177kph) and a 0–60mph (0–96kph) time of around 13 seconds,

■ ABOVE *Extremely compact, the Fiat X1/9 brought the delights of mid-engine motoring to a wide public. Previously the layout had been the almost exclusive province of expensive exotics.*

FIAT X1/9 (1972–89)	
Engine	4-cylinder
Capacity	1290–1499cc
Power	75–85bhp
Transmission	4/5-speed manual
Top speed	100–110mph (161–177kph)
No. built	180,000

■ LEFT *Pop-up headlamps were a distinctive feature. This is a later-model X1/9 produced by the coachbuilder Bertone (which originally designed the car).*

■ FAR LEFT *Removing the standard targa roof panel produced a virtual convertible - great for sunny days, but practical as well.*

■ LEFT *If you thought, because the engine was in the middle, that you had luggage space in the front, you had to think again, as this picture shows.*

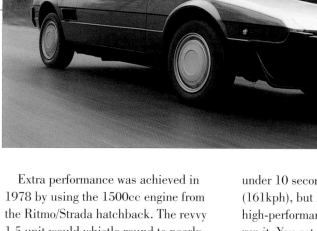

■ RIGHT *Despite its small-capacity engine, the X1/9 was a creditable performer for its day. 100mph (161kph) was available in all versions.*

but this was frankly a waste of its potential grip and razor-sharp handling. Even so, novices and seasoned drivers alike took it to their hearts because it was so easy to drive. The steering was light, precise and full of feel, and the balance of the car was neutral.

Even driven at its limit an X1/9 never snapped, but telegraphed its warnings miles ahead of an impending loss of adhesion. As a bonus, strut suspension gave a relatively comfortable, civilized ride. Fiat boss Agnelli even abandoned his limo so he could drive himself to work every day in an X1/9.

■ RIGHT *Beautifully balanced handling was the main attraction of X1/9 ownership. The chassis was much more communicative than that of almost any other car of its price.*

Extra performance was achieved in 1978 by using the 1500cc engine from the Ritmo/Strada hatchback. The revvy 1.5 unit would whistle round to nearly 7000rpm and turn in 30mpg economy. A good 1500 would touch 110mph (177kph), break 60mph (96kph) in

under 10 seconds and cruise at 100mph (161kph), but by then many ordinary high-performance hatchbacks could out-run it. You got five speeds with the 1500, but big impact bumpers had by then spoiled the once-crisp looks.

In 1982, production was taken over by Bertone, which continued to manufacture and market the car as the Bertone X1/9 until its demise in 1989. Late cars had desirable touches like leather seats, alloy wheels and electric windows. By then the car was notorious for appalling corrosion, and many of the early examples have long since disappeared from the road.

It wasn't until the mid-80s that it had a serious competitor in the shape of Toyota's MR2. There is no doubt that the little Fiat is the father of today's popular mid-engined sportscars. Fiat did not produce its own spiritual successor until the front-wheel-drive Barchetta of 1995.

■ FAR LEFT *A strict two-seater, the X1/9's cabin was cosy rather than spacious. The architecture was distinctly Italian.*

■ LEFT *The X1/9 left production in 1989 with no mid-engined successor. The plain fact was that developments in the front-engined layout had made it a more feasible proposition.*

FIAT

■ FIAT BARCHETTA

Barchetta is an Italian word meaning "little boat", and has come to describe a whole class of open-topped Italian sportscars. Fiat's version was undoubtedly one of the high points of the genre and applied Italian flair to the challenge laid down by the Mazda MX-5.

In style, the Barchetta was both retrospective and modern. The door handles, which popped out of the bodywork at the press of a button, harked back to a classic era, but the purposely curvaceous body accent line and aerodynamic accoutrements

■ LEFT *Barchetta means "little boat" in Italian – a surprisingly fitting description for this diminutive sportscar, which boasted so much design flair.*

■ LEFT *Sportscar drivers felt immediately at home in the cockpit, which was relatively sparsely equipped but suitably angled towards the enthusiast's needs.*

■ ABOVE *On the road the Barchetta was a delight, combining zippy acceleration with tenacious cornering, light steering and a free-revving engine.*

FIAT BARCHETTA (1995–)	
Engine	4-cylinder
Capacity	1747cc
Power	130bhp @ 6300rpm
Transmission	5-speed
Top speed	124mph (200kph)
No. built	Still in production

■ BELOW *The truncated tail with its oblong lamps contrasted with the long nose. The "humped" profile was emphasized by body side accents.*

reminded the casual onlooker that this was a contemporary sportscar.

It may have been based on the floorpan of the humble front-wheel-drive Fiat Punto, but the Barchetta packed a strong punch under its bonnet in the form of a new 1.75-litre fuel-injected 16V twin-cam engine. As the whole car weighed only just over one tonne (ton), performance was enjoyable and the engine would happily spin away up to 7000rpm. That spirited pace was matched by grippy cornering ability and super-sharp steering.

Inside there was a minor feast of detail, from the angled centre console and the smoothly sculpted doors to the intriguing eyeball vents. There might not have been much room for luggage, but this was a sportscar so that was to be expected.

Good value was another Barchetta strong point, and it sold particularly well in Italy. British customers had to make do with left-hand drive but even so were appreciative of the diminutive Fiat sportscar. After all, the Barchetta had all the makings of a genuine classic.

■ RIGHT *Bold slashes in the body sides, bisected door mirrors, a clamshell bonnet and a strongly wedged profile – this could only be Pininfarina's extraordinary design for the Fiat Coupé.*

■ FIAT COUPÉ

Pininfarina was extremely adventurous with its brief to design a new coupé for Fiat, which arrived in 1993. No one could ever mistake the Coupé for anything else, and even if its appeal was not universal, it had all the character you could ever wish for.

From the bold rising slashes in the flanks to the elegantly curved roof, and from the curious "double bubble" headlamp covers to the evocative circular tail lamps, the Coupé made a very strong statement.

Although in feel it seemed like a miniature Ferrari or Maserati, the new Coupé was actually based on the platform of the ageing Fiat Tipo. Considering this basis, Fiat engineers worked miracles to create such a fine-handling sports coupé as this. Limited slip differential kept the front wheels

from spinning when the accelerator was pressed to the floor, while tyre grip remained superb even at very high cornering forces.

At first, there was a choice of two 2.0-litre engines: a 142bhp 16V unit or a 195bhp Turbo. Both were quick but the Turbo was exceptional, having a 0–60mph (0–96kph) time of just over seven seconds. In 1995, the engine range was renewed, starting with the 131bhp Barchetta 1.8 and ending up with a pair of brand-new five-cylinder 2.0 units; the most powerful had a

turbocharger and no less than 220bhp – and was almost indecently quick.

Accommodation was surprisingly spacious for four people, although that meant boot (trunk) space was rather restricted. The adventurous themes of the bodywork were extended into the cabin, such as an effective swage of painted metal running right across the dashboard and doors.

■ BELOW *Few cars in any class handled as well as the Fiat Coupé, which boasted fine grip, sharp responses and entertaining handling for the driver.*

■ RIGHT *With its bold body-coloured finish through the middle of the dash, the Coupé felt very special. The driving position was excellent.*

FIAT COUPÉ (1993–)	
Engine	4/5-cylinder
Capacity	1747–1998cc
Power	131–220bhp
Transmission	5-speed
Top speed	127–155mph (204–249kph)
No. built	Still in production

■ RIGHT *From the rear, the styling was every bit as adventurous as from other angles. The circular rear lights recalled Farina designs for countless Ferraris.*

FORD

■ LEFT *Further modifications were incorporated for rallying homologation on this RS500 edition, including an extra 20bhp and an even bigger whale-tail spoiler.*

■ FORD SIERRA RS COSWORTH

The "Cossie" Sierra has passed into the annals of motoring history as the car that brought rally-style levels of power and grip to a broad public. Its phenomenal performance became a legend, all the more so because it was such exceptional value.

When, in 1986, Cosworth installed its new two-litre twin overhead-camshaft turbo engine into the Sierra bodyshell,

FORD SIERRA RS COSWORTH (1986–92)	
Engine	4-cylinder
Capacity	1993cc
Power	204–224bhp
Transmission	5-speed manual
Top speed	143–149mph (230–240kph)
No. built	26,771

■ ABOVE *Piloting the powerful RS500 was a very special experience, all the more so because a mere 500 examples were built in total.*

■ LEFT *The true "popular" Cosworth was the four-door Sapphire, built from 1988. A modest body kit package and sober clothing belied the car's tremendous ability.*

the inherently fine handling of Ford's rear-wheel-drive hatchback was matched by the power to exploit it. Its 204bhp was generous to say the least and the performance figures proved it: a top speed of 145mph (233kph) and 0–60mph (0–96kph) in 6.2 seconds. What was more, the engine could be easily tuned to stratospheric heights.

Ford's humble sales-rep special could now out-perform some Ferraris, yet it cost only £16,000 ($27,000) – about the same as a BMW 325i or Toyota Supra. The badge on the back – RS Cosworth – came to signify a performance icon.

In truth, the Cosworth may have looked superficially like a body-kitted Sierra but there was little resemblance under the skin. Ford's Special Vehicle Engineering department intended this to be a convincing Group A race and rally car (which it was), and decided to beef up the whole car. There was a close-ratio five-speed gearbox, limited slip differential, power steering, anti-lock braking, thick anti-roll bars, stiff suspension, wide alloy wheels and tyres, and huge disc brakes with four-piston calipers.

The bodywork incoporated no less than 92 modifications, from the widened wheel arches to the dramatic whale-tail spoiler. The aim was to increase

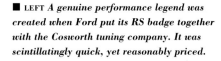

■ LEFT *A genuine performance legend was created when Ford put its RS badge together with the Cosworth tuning company. It was scintillatingly quick, yet reasonably priced.*

downforce, which it did, but aerodynamics suffered, with the Cd falling to 0.34 and criticism coming from certain quarters about stability in cross-winds. Aesthetically, it was hardly subtle either. These drawbacks hardly mattered, however, to the drivers who revelled in the Cosworth's neck-snapping acceleration and finely balanced handling.

Because it was intended as a homologation special for racing, only 6021 Cosworth hatchbacks were made, plus an additonal 500 evolution RS500 models with 224bhp and an even larger rear spoiler. Their successor was the Sapphire Cosworth, a four-door model with much more restrained styling but all the driving ability of the earlier car. Added bonuses included greater practicality and more generous equipment levels.

The theme was extended in 1990 with the 4x4 version, developed to give the Sierra a better chance in rallying. The 4x4 gained an extra 16bhp, thanks to a new 16-valve cylinder head. That meant even more performance as well as sure-

footed handling, which left virtually every other car on the road for dead.

Having been in its lifetime the number one target for thieves and joy-riders in Britain, and hence almost impossible to insure, the "Cossie" has since assumed the mantle of a respected and affordable classic.

■ RIGHT *Able to reach 60mph (96 kph) from rest in a little over six seconds, this Ford, despite its humble origins, could outpace many so-called supercars.*

■ LEFT *Cosworth's 16-valve turbocharged engine produced 204bhp in its original form. Ford lost no opportunities in exploiting the Cosworth connection to the full.*

FORD

■ FORD RS200

In the 1980s, a new breed of supercar hit the streets. Manufacturers wanting to muscle in on the prestigious Group B rally scene were forced by the regulations to build a minimum of 200 cars for homologation purposes, which usually meant having to sell some as road-going cars. Many of these beasts, while brutally effective on forest roads, were hopelessly impractical if you had to drive anywhere on public roads.

Ford's Group B effort, the RS200, was certainly effective, but in road form it was also one of the most practical and comfortable of all, having such luxuries as a fully-trimmed cockpit and even provision for a radio. In racing terms, the RS200 never achieved its full potential because, after just one season (1986), the sport's governing body cancelled the Group B category. It was left to private entrants to pick up honours such as the European Rallycross Championship.

The RS200 was conceived as early as 1983 as a bespoke (dedicated) rally machine. Ghia styled the monocoque bodyshell, which was made of glassfibre

and Kevlar over an aluminium honeycomb floor with steel front- and rear-box sections. It looked a good deal prettier than any other Group B car around. It was short and stubby yet had an undeniable presence, mainly thanks to its large tail spoiler and roof-mounted spoiler/air dam. The windscreen derived from the standard production Ford Sierra.

Cosworth provided the engine, a turbocharged, slightly enlarged BDT development of the BDA unit fitted to the Escort RS1700T. It developed 250bhp in road-going form and could be tuned as high as 450bhp – or even higher – for competition use.

The four-wheel-drive transmission was unusual in that the magnesium-

■ ABOVE *To make the most of the mid-engined layout, there was an unusual four-wheel-drive system developed by FF.*

■ LEFT *The RS200 arrived too late to have much impact on the doomed Group B rally scene, but it was a devastatingly effective rally machine.*

FORD RS200 (1984–86)	
Engine	4-cylinder
Capacity	1803cc
Power	250bhp
Transmission	5-speed
Top speed	140mph (225kph)
No. built	200

■ OPPOSITE *The NSX was designed to compete with Europe's best, such as Porsche and Ferrari. In absolute terms it was easily their equal, perhaps only lacking an indefinable excitement factor.*

■ LEFT *In typical Honda fashion, the NSX's lines were simple and unadorned. This was a devastatingly efficient machine in all respects.*

■ ABOVE *In motion, the 3.2-litre engine had a sound and a performance that denoted engineering purity. Road testers were struck by the sheer ability and range of its dynamics.*

timing and induction, titanium connecting rods, separate coils for each spark plug and an ability to rev to 8300rpm. Its power delivery was smooth, the throttle response was electric, and the noise it emitted ranged from a sweet purr to the scream of a thoroughbred racer. In short, the NSX engine was one of the all-time great power plants.

Its 270bhp was hugely impressive for a 3.0-litre engine. Even though by supercar standards its acceleration was not class-beating, 0–60mph (0–96kph) in 5.8 seconds could hardly be described as sluggish.

In handling terms, the NSX was both forgiving and communicative, aided by superb traction control and accurate steering. This was one of the true masters of the art of cornering.

The NSX was the most expensive car Japan had ever made, but its price still undercut rivals like the Ferrari 348. With almost no faults, it was unquestionably the most mature exponent of the supercar breed.

Later years saw it improve still further, and in 1997 it got the biggest revamp of its life, with a bigger 3.2-litre engine, six-speed gearbox, variable-weight power steering and bigger brakes. It remains one of the most respected cars in the world.

OTHER MAKES

■ HOLDEN
Holden is the Australian outpost of the global General Motors empire. Occasionally it produced or imported European and American GM products (and even badged many models produced by Japanese companies), but more usually it developed cars specially suited to the Australian market. Its main model lines included the Monara, Commodore, Torana and Statesman, which were great cruising machines halfway between European and American idioms.

■ HYUNDAI
The biggest car-maker in Korea has always been Hyundai, and its current size is all the more impressive considering it only began making cars in 1967, producing a version of the Ford Cortina. Its first all-new car was the 1975 Pony designed by Giugiaro. Gradually, its allegiance to Ford switched to Mitsubishi, and it made several licence-built models in Korea. Its position in the West grew yearly stronger with burgeoning exports of conventional but cheap family cars.

■ INNOCENTI
Innocenti began life as the holder of licences to make BMC products in Italy, and it produced the Austin A40, Mini, 1100 and Allegro. In 1976, ownership passed from British Leyland to De Tomaso, which produced over 200,000 Bertone-styled small cars based on the Mini platform. Subsequently, it turned to Daihatsu for its engines. Fiat acquired the marque in the 1980s and kept the name for imported versions of the Fiat Uno, Yugo and Daihatsu Hijet. The marque survived until 1997.

■ ISUZU
In Britain, the Japanese Isuzu name is best known for its four-wheel-drive vehicles, and in America it is remembered for the Gemini (a version of the Opel Kadett world car). Isuzu is basically General Motors' foothold in Japan, but has also made some interesting models. The Bertone-styled 117 coupé of 1968–81 was a design classic, and its 1980s Giugiaro-designed Piazza coupé Impulse was a best-seller. More recently Isuzu has concentrated on licence-built Hondas and sport-utility vehicles.

JAGUAR

■ BELOW *The mid-1970s was an awkward time to launch a luxury sportscar to succeed the immortal E-Type, and the XJS was always more of a grand touring car.*

■ JAGUAR XJS

Jaguar had charmed the world with its glorious E-Type in 1961, but by 1975 this was looking decidedly outdated and needed a successor. That car was the XJS, a car which had all the ingredients in place to make it perhaps the greatest car in the world: a fabulous V-twelve engine, world-beating suspension and all the prestige of the Jaguar badge.

Somehow the XJS lost the magic that made the E-Type so great. The styling rubbed everyone up the wrong way: traditionalists bemoaned its slab flanks, trapezoidal headlamps and black rubber bumpers and asked what had happened

■ ABOVE *The styling attracted some controversy, particularly the treatment of the flying buttress rear pillars. The XJS was accused of a "design-by-committee" birth.*

to Jaguar's traditional grille, its chrome and its walnut veneer dashboard. Sportscar drivers questioned its curious flying buttress styling and cramped interior. The truth is that, unlike the E-Type, which was designed by one talented professional, the XJS was styled by committee and ended up being a compromise.

Jaguar chose to base the XJS on a shortened version of the XJ12 saloon (sedan) platform, so that it kept its drive train, suspension and brakes intact. The standard transmission was a Borg Warner three-speed automatic, and

■ ABOVE *The last XJS models benefited from a major revamp in terms of styling, interior treatment and new 4-litre six-cylinder and 6-litre V-twelve engines.*

■ RIGHT *Front-seat passengers were cosseted in impressive chairs, although those in the rear were severely limited for space.*

■ RIGHT *Every XJS model drove impressively.
Some magazines were tempted to call it the
best grand touring car available by virtue of
its impeccable ride and excellent driving
characteristics.*

■ ABOVE *The fuel-injected V-twelve engine
was a tight fit under the low bonnet-line (hood
line), but the rewards were immeasurable since
this was one of the finest engines produced.*

JAGUAR XJS (1975–96)	
Engine	6/V-twelve-cylinder
Capacity	3590–5994cc
Power	223–333bhp
Transmission	3/4-speed automatic 4/5-speed manual
Top speed	141–158mph (227–254kph)
No. built	112,000

although a manual gearbox was offered
only 352 customers opted for it.
Performance was superb for a grand
touring four-seater, with a top speed of
150mph (241kph) and bustling
acceleration.

The interior was based around the XJ
saloon parts bin but featured a curious
instrument binnacle with inset main
dials and revolving minor gauges on the
dash. There was plenty of space in the

front seats, but the rear pair was really
suitable only for children.

The 5.3-litre V-twelve engine was
given better fuel economy and more
power in 1981 and re-christened XJS HE
(High Efficiency). Now the XJS started
to get some of the chrome and wood that
had been missing. The range was
expanded in 1983 by the addition of a
six-cylinder 3.6-litre XJS and a brand-
new Cabriolet model, which had rigid

targa roof panels and a folding rear
section and was a strict two-seater. This
drop-top model lasted until 1988, when
it was replaced by a new top-of-the-
range full Convertible V-twelve model
with an electric folding roof. A TWR-
developed 333bhp XJR-S version
arrived at the same time.

For 1991, the XJS got a £50 million
($84 million) investment and a new
lease of life. The bodyshell was heavily
reworked, especially at the rear-end,
and the interior was thoroughly
revamped. Another major change was
the adoption of the new AJ6 four-litre
engine. Within three years this was
uprated to AJ16 specification and got an
extra 15bhp, while the venerable old V-
twelve engine expanded to six litres.

The XJS survived until September
1996, making it the longest-lived Jaguar
ever at over 21 years. One measure of its
excellence is that its replacement, the
XK8, was based on the XJS floorpan.

■ LEFT *The
convertible XJS,
which arrived quite
late in the model's
production career,
was an extremely
popular choice
and highly
rewarding to own.*

■ ABOVE *The first XJS models had no wood
and little leather, but later examples redressed
the imbalance.*

JAGUAR

■ JAGUAR XK8

After years of rumours about a true E-Type replacement called the F-Type, Jaguar finally presented its crucial new sportscar, the XK8, at the 1996 Geneva Motor Show.

Officially, this was the replacement for the XJS, but it had so much more appeal that it was really viewed as the spiritual successor to the E-Type. Its svelte lines were created at Jaguar's design head-quarters in Whitley, West Midlands, and it was engineered using the XJS floorpan as its starting-point. The XK8 delivered a distinct blend of style, luxury, craftsmanship and performance in a car that was uniquely British in flavour.

Central to the new design was the all-aluminium AJV-eight engine, the very first V-eight engine ever produced by Jaguar, after an investment of £200 million ($337 million). The 32-valve quad-cam engine delivered power, smoothness and refinement and had such advanced features as variable cam phasing, platinum-tipped spark plugs, split-block cooling and catalysts that began operating only 30 seconds after start-up. The ZF transmission was also new, Jaguar's first five-speed automatic. Other technical advances were electronic variable ratio power-steering, new

■ ABOVE *Jaguar rightly played on the heritage of its E-Type sportscar, for the XK8 was its spiritual successor. Unlike the XJS, it was a genuine sportscar, as well as a comfortable grand tourer.*

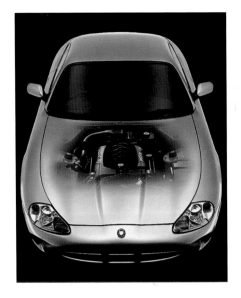

JAGUAR XK8 (1996–)	
Engine	V-eight-cylinder
Capacity	3996cc
Power	290 bhp
Transmission	5-speed auto
Top speed	154mph (248kph)
No. built	Still in production

■ LEFT *Underneath the bonnet of the latest sleek cat lay Jaguar's first-ever V-eight engine, the AJ-V8, which was a technical tour de force.*

■ ABOVE *Rich traditions of leather and wood were kept up, and the game was moved on by the installation of state-of-the-art high-tech electronics.*

■ LEFT *The fabulous XK8 was the successor to the long-running XJS and was a quantum leap beyond it, even though its floorpan was merely an XJS derivation.*

■ LEFT *The design of the XK8 was completed entirely in-house, and revived the glory days of Jaguar's founder William Lyons.*

■ BELOW *The XK8's striking similarity to the Aston Martin DB7 was not lost on many observers. The XK8 was, however, considerably cheaper to buy.*

computer-active double-wishbone front suspension, XJR-derived rear suspension and multiplexed (integrated) electronics.

The result of all this technology was a car which performed superbly. Indeed, it went as fast as the Aston Martin DB7 (a car designed by the same team), and many hailed the far cheaper XK8 as a better car all round. Refined yet explosively fast, smooth yet sporting in character, the XK8 was a brilliant grand tourer and sportscar.

Launched just after the coupé at the New York Motor Show was a convertible with an electric top, which raised in just 20 seconds. Unlike some competitors, the soft top stacked up behind the seats in order not to compromise boot (trunk) space. With the top raised the XK8 felt just as refined as the coupé. The cabin oozed classic-leather ambience and was available in two styles: fashionable art-style "Sport" and full "Classic" treatment with walnut trim and colour-coordinated carpets. All models had air-conditioning, electric seats and cruise control, while audiophiles could specify a Harman Kardon hi-fi.

The XK8 maintained Jaguar's reputation for best-in-class ride and handling. A good example of Jaguar's attention to detail was the fact that each aircraft-spec aluminium front-suspension cross-beam was X-ray inspected prior to installation.

■ LEFT *The addition of a convertible model boosted the XK8's appeal. The soft top could be raised electronically in only 20 seconds.*

■ BELOW *Jaguar's noble sports-roadster heritage stretches back to the SS100 of the 1930s, and the XK8 justifiably took its place alongside the greats.*

JAGUAR

■ JAGUAR XJ220

There are very few production cars that can claim to be have been born out of a spare-time project, but the Jaguar XJ220 is the most famous of all. Jaguar's chief engineer, Jim Randle, dreamt up the idea of creating the ultimate supercar one Christmas and fired up enough enthusiasm with colleagues to start a "Saturday club" to work on the project.

At first not even the Jaguar board knew about the secret tinkering going at its Engineering Department at Whitley in the West Midlands of Britain. When it did find out, the enthusiasm bubbled over, and the new XJ220 was wheeled out at the 1988 Birmingham Motor Show as an official Jaguar concept car. The prototype XJ220 was an immense beast, mainly because it had to be accommodated around TWR racing components and Jaguar's massive V-twelve engine mounted in a central position. Still, Keith Helfet's aluminium bodywork design was a sublime piece of sculpture.

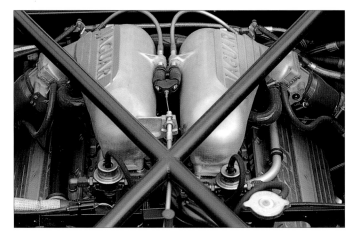

■ LEFT *The V-six engine had twin turbochargers and racing-car-type materials and construction. Its output was a remarkable 500bhp.*

The response at the 1988 show was rapturous, and the affluence of the times persuaded Jaguar to embark on a production run. Because of production practicalities the design was substantially modified. It was decided that the V-twelve engine was too bulky and so a race-derived 3.5-litre V-six engine was installed instead. Its state-of-the-art specification included four camshafts, twin injectors, twin turbochargers, four valves per cylinder and dry sump lubrication, and it was capable of pumping out 500bhp.

JAGUAR XJ220 (1991–94)	
Engine	V-six-cylinder
Capacity	3498cc
Power	500bhp @ 6500rpm
Transmission	5-speed
Top speed	220mph (352kph)
No. built	350

■ LEFT *After it was presented as a prototype in 1988, the public clamour surrounding the fastest Jaguar ever made persuaded the company to enter production with the XJ220.*

■ OPPOSITE *The imposing authority of the XJ220 was confirmed by anyone who drove it. Here was a car which had phenomenal dynamic ability, helped by aircraft-inspired engineering.*

The smaller engine meant that overall length could be trimmed down by a sizeable 10in (25cm), but there was no escaping the massive girth of this sportscar: at 6ft 6in (nearly two metres) wide, this was the broadest British car ever made.

The specification sheet of the XJ220 read like a sportscar-driver's dream. Its bodywork was an aerospace-type bonded-aluminium honeycomb with Group C racing inspired aerodynamics, the five-speed transaxle was mated to a racing AP clutch, there were centre-lock (knock-off) alloy wheels, massive brakes with four- piston calipers and racing-derived wishbone/inboard suspension.

Jaguar's performance claims were equally exciting. Its top speed of 220mph (352kph) and 0–60mph (0–96kph) time of 3.5 seconds made it easily the fastest road car on earth at the time. In-gear acceleration was

■ ABOVE *The best place to enjoy the full performance of the XJ220 – 220mph (352kph) – was undoubtedly a race-track,* *for the immense girth and negligible visibility made it difficult to exploit its potential on real-world roads.*

absolutely brutal. To match that explosive power, the racing suspension made the XJ220 probably the best-handling supercar ever.

A joint Jaguar–TWR venture called JaguarSport set up a brand new production facility in Bloxham, Oxfordshire, to make a strictly limited run of 350 cars, each priced at £403,000 ($678,000). At first, the order book was over-subscribed by speculators but, when it became obvious that the market for supercars had collapsed, legal proceedings ensued as buyers tried to pull out – an ignominious end to an amazing story.

■ RIGHT *The impeccable detailing reflected the XJ220's hand-built nature and extraordinary price.*

■ LEFT *For all its exotic specification, the interior was a thoroughly comfortable place to be. There was room for luxury even at stratospheric speeds.*

■ ABOVE *In high-speed tests the XJ220 proved capable of speeds approaching 220mph (352kph), and of reaching 60mph (96kph) from rest in just 3.5 seconds.*

JEEP

■ JEEP

The great American legend that is the Jeep has its origins in desperate times. In June 1940, the US Quartermaster Corps published requirements for a compact 4x4 quarter-ton truck. It asked potential contractors that a fully functioning prototype should be ready within one month. Of 135 firms polled to do this near-impossible job, only two took up the challenge: Willys–Overland

■ LEFT *Where the legend started: the Second World War Willys Jeep was conceived in double-quick time, and it got on with its job. It inspired a whole dynasty of civilian jeeps.*

aluminium pistons, producing only 49bhp but a massive 105lb ft (142Nm) of torque at just 2000rpm. Drivers had three gears to choose from, plus a two-speed transfer box and switchable freewheel for the front axle.

It was basic in the extreme, but the hastily conceived design was inherently right: no major changes were made despite the arduous tests of war use. Over 600,000 of these machines were churned out until the end of production in 1945, after which the French firm Hotchkiss made Jeeps into the 1960s.

After the war, Willys plugged on with the Jeep in civilian CJ-2A form, with the advertising line, "The sun never sets on

(which asked for an extra 45 days to prepare a car) and a small Detroit engineering firm called Bantam, which got the contract.

Production started at Ford, Willys and Bantam factories. The basic chassis was a box-section twin-rail frame with cross-members, fitted with low-carbon steel bodywork, ultra- simple for ease of manufacture. To enable Jeeps to be stacked on top of each other, the windscreen was removable.

Suspended by leaf springs (and dampers – shocks – only at the rear), the Jeep was powered by Willys's "Go-Devil" 2.2-litre four-cylinder unit with

■ ABOVE *The whole jeep story can be traced through these cars, from the Second World War fighter through the CJ models at the rear, and up to date with the Wrangler editions of the 1980s and 1990s.*

■ RIGHT *This 1990 Wrangler Laredo proves the durability of the Jeep phenomenon. The famous hallmarks of square-cut wings, simple flat surfaces and grille all remain.*

■ LEFT *Modern Jeep Wranglers in their element, crossing the most inhospitable terrain. Jeeps gradually became more lifestyle vehicles than working cars.*

■ BELOW LEFT *A whole new strain of Jeeps was launched with the Cherokee, a multi-purpose 4x4 four-door. This is one of the compact modern versions, dating from 1984.*

■ BELOW RIGHT *Although this is merely a concept exercise called the Jeep Freedom, it shows there is a spiritual connection between the Cherokee and original-type Jeeps.*

the Willys-built Jeep". Farmers loved them, and Jeeps provided cheap, practical transportation in austere times.

The 1946 Station Wagon was America's first steel-bodied estate. The body was recognizably Jeep, but it was on a longer wheelbase, had a six-cylinder engine option and only two-wheel drive. It had non-structural wood applied to its sides and split rear doors. Even more "civvy" was the Brooks

Stevens-styled Jeepster with its bright colour schemes, whitewall tyres, luxurious fittings and detachable hood. The Jeepster name was revived briefly in 1967.

The Jeep CJ evolved slowly, the CJ5 and long-wheelbase CJ6 versions lasting from 1952 into the 1970s, by which time AMC had become the parent company. An important variant was the 1972 CJ5 Renegade, a sporty Jeep with a V-eight

engine, which pointed the way ahead in terms of style development.

Gradually, the range expanded to include the Commando pickup, the four-door Wagoneer and, from 1974, Cherokee sport-utilities. While the CJ soldiered on around the world, in America the Cherokee and larger Cerand Cherokee assumed greater significance, as well as "retro" reworkings of the original idea, sold under the name Wrangler.

JEEP WRANGLER (1986–)	
Engine	4/6-cylinder
Capacity	2464–4235cc
Power	112–184bhp
Transmission	5-speed manual 3/4-speed auto
Top speed	84–108mph (130–174kph)
No. built	Still in production

■ RIGHT *Largest of the jeep family is the Grand Cherokee with its large-capacity V-eight engine and very comfortable interior.*

LAMBORGHINI

■ BELOW *Bertone's stunning original Countach design left every other exotic car for dead. Ultimately, it was the most beautiful Countach of all, completely unadorned by superfluous decoration.*

■ LAMBORGHINI COUNTACH

To top the amazing mid-engined Miura, unquestionably the most exotic car of the 1960s, Lamborghini had to come up with something decisively more dramatic. In that at least the amazing Countach succeeded superbly.

The original bright-yellow Bertone-styled prototype of 1971 was dramatic yet remarkably pure and unadorned compared with the more familiar models of the late 1970s and 80s. Where the Miura had been sensual and muscular, the Countach was futuristic, razor-edged,

■ RIGHT *Banana-shaped leather seats looked more enticing than they really were. Luxury was not squandered in the Countach cabin.*

wedgey, breathing aggression from every pore. Wild as it looked, the Countach was a much better developed car than the flawed Miura, even though it was no easier to live with, owing to the problems with the show-off lift-up doors.

It was a sensation to drive, of course: as well as being more forgiving in its handling – the gearbox was now mounted in-line, ahead of the engine between the seats – it was even faster than the Miura: good for 186mph (299kph), claimed Lamborghini, if you could find a stretch of road long enough. Most road testers managed about 160mph (257kph).

The word *"countach"* is a Piedmontese expletive meaning wow – or something stronger depending on how it was pronounced. The first Countach went to

■ ABOVE *Opening the doors was as dramatic an experience as seeing the car for the first time. This is an LP500 model from 1982.*

■ LEFT *The trapezoidal tail lamps were an unmistakable Countach hallmark, punctuating one of the longest rear decks of any production car.*

LAMBORGHINI COUNTACH (1974–91)	
Engine	V-twelve-cylinder
Capacity	3929–5167cc
Power	375–455bhp
Transmission	5-speed manual
Top speed	186–200mph (299–322kph)
No. built	609

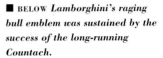

■ RIGHT *Fast, winding roads were the Countach's element, where it was almost indecently fast. Owners were always attracted as much by its brash character as by its raw ability.*

its owner in 1974 amid a blaze of publicity. However, the clean lines of the original became progressively more tasteless as the years went by, especially once the LP500 five-litre model appeared in 1982: its spoilers did nothing for stability, while big ugly wheel-arches housed improbably fat tyres, matched by even bigger NACA ducts to get air into the enlarged engine.

It also became apparent that build quality was merely adequate and the car began to put on as much flab as muscle. Yet its unremittingly powerful character overcame such quibbles and kept the

■ BELOW *Lamborghini's raging bull emblem was sustained by the success of the long-running Countach.*

■ ABOVE *The very last Countach QV models got yet another restyle and a four-valves-per-cylinder head. The model was retired finally in 1991.*

■ LEFT *The powerhouse in the middle of the Countach was a fabulously expressive V-twelve engine, claimed to return 200mph (322kph) performance.*

troubled Lamborghini – long since out of its founder's control – afloat through the dark abyss of the 70s and 80s when lesser models like the Urraco and Jalpa failed to find buyers. Having said that, the Countach never enjoyed the commercial success of Ferrari's much less radical Boxer and Testarossa.

The ultimate QV model – indicating Quattro Valvole (or four valves per cylinder) – bowed out in 1991. By then, its top speed was quoted as 200mph (322kph). In later years, the Countach had become a kind of parody of itself – a car for anybody with too much money and not enough taste – but at least it was recognizable.

■ ABOVE *No one was in any doubt that the Countach was a very quick machine, but in the latter half of its life Lamborghini felt* *obliged to add aerodynamic aids such as giant rear spoilers. In practice they had little effect beyond visual stimulation.*

LAMBORGHINI

■ LAMBORGHINI LM002

When you look at the back catalogue of Lamborghini cars, you will find only high-performance supercars: names like Miura, Countach, Espada, Diablo. There is one name that sticks out in this sleek, knee-high company: what on earth is an LM?

To realize why Lamborghini produced the equivalent of Mad Max, you have to understand why most European farmers are also familiar with the Lamborghini name: its other main business is making agricultural tractors. The LM002 was the perfect, if audacious, synthesis of these two sides of Lamborghini's business – a four-wheel-drive monster with a V-twelve Countach engine!

Its story actually begins with a request to produce a military vehicle for the US, in conjunction with Chrysler. This resulted in the Cheetah of 1977, a massive doorless all-terrain buggy with a mid-mounted Chrysler V-eight engine.

■ ABOVE *Straddling an immense central tunnel, four passengers could be seated in air-conditioned, leather-lined comfort. There was space for four or more on the pick-up rear-bed.*

■ ABOVE *The V-twelve engine from the Countach was stuffed under the bonnet to make a thundering beast in every sense. It had to be mounted rather high up.*

■ ABOVE *Dauntingly large wheels and tyres were specially designed to withstand large, sharp rocks.*

The tail-heavy weight distribution under which this layout suffered led the American government elsewhere (the US-built Hummvee, or Hummer, got the deal in the end).

Lamborghini pressed ahead with its own interpretation of the ultimate off-roader. Its production LM002 was shown for the first time in autumn 1985 with a Lamborghini Countach V-twelve engine up front. Everything about it was bigger and better than any other car.

The LM was immense. At over 16ft (495cm) long, it was about the same

length as a Jaguar XJ, and it was over 6ft 6in (200cm) wide, 73in (185cm) high and weighed nearly 3 tonnes (2.95 tons). It could seat four people inside, two on each side of the largest central tunnel ever seen in a car, and four-to-six more passengers could perch in the pick-up rear. The enormous 345 x 17 tyres were specially made by Pirelli.

That giant Countach engine meant the LM was the fastest off-roader in the world: it could lug the LM up to a top speed of 126mph (201kph), while its 0–60mph (0–96kph) time of 8.5 seconds

■ RIGHT *The audacity which produced the LM002 can only be gawped at. This leviathan was conceived as an all-terrain army vehicle but found favour with anyone with enough money and a desperate need to cross deserts at terminal velocities.*

could embarrass quite a few sportscars. The trade-off was fuel consumption in the region of 7mpg (11.2kpg) – you really needed the 70-gallon (318 litre) fuel tank. Off-road ability was deeply impressive thanks to the all-independent suspension and massive ground clearance.

If you were used to the utility treatment in your off-roader, the LM packed a few surprises. Here was a tough brute with all the fancy trimmings of a limousine: leather upholstery, air-conditioning, lots of electric gadgets, a wood dashboard and deep-pile carpeting.

The LM's natural habitat was the Middle East, where the military and the oil barons lapped it up, and that's just as well because the LM cost even more than the Countach and you really needed your own oil well to run one.

■ LEFT *The world's biggest bonnet (hood) bulges were required to clear the most powerful engine ever fitted to a standard 4x4 vehicle.*

LAMBORGHINI LM002 (1985–93)	
Engine	V-twelve-cylinder
Capacity	5167cc
Power	450bhp @ 6800rpm
Transmission	5-speed, drive to all four wheels
Top speed	126mph (203kph)
No. built	n/a

■ LEFT *On the road the LM002 turned into a GTI, capable of 126mph (203kph) and 0–60mph (0–96kph) in 8.5 seconds. The pay-off was the greediest fuel consumption figures ever recorded for a production car.*

LAMBORGHINI

■ LAMBORGHINI DIABLO

"Diablo" means devil in Spanish, a curious choice for the Italian successor to the legendary Countach. The Diablo was the first fruit of Lamborghini's brief spell under Chrysler's wing, and cost £50 million ($84 million) to develop.

Following the Countach was never going to be easy, but the Diablo succeeded. Above all it looked absolutely startling thanks to the gifted penwork of Marcello Gandini. The dramatic scissor-type doors were retained for the new car and incorporated a deeply swooping waistline. The tail seemed to stretch back for ever, its long centre cut-out full of louvres, its air dams looking purposeful, its profile widening all the way. The nose could hardly have been lower or more stubbed. Construction was of aluminium and composite-plastic body panels over a chassis reinforced with carbonfibre.

Mechanically, the Diablo looked back to the Countach for its inspiration. Its V-twelve engine was a development of the Countach's, expanded, catalyzed and given sequential fuel injection. The result was 492bhp and 428ft

■ ABOVE *Even faster than the Countach it replaced, the Diablo – or "devil" – was a true giant of the supercar world.*

LAMBORGHINI DIABLO (1990–)	
Engine	V-twelve-cylinder
Capacity	5729cc
Power	492–525bhp
Transmission	5-speed
Top speed	186–210mph (299–338kph)
No. built	Still in production

(1404cm) of torque, plus one of the most fulfilling soundtracks of any engine. There was also a new five-speed gearbox geared so that 100mph (161kph) could be reached in second gear.

Lamborghini claimed that the Diablo's top speed of 202mph (325kph) could beat arch-rival Ferrari's F40. It was certainly very quick, as tests of the even more powerful, lightweight limited-edition 525bhp SE30 would show: 0–60mph (0–96kph) in 4.2 seconds was exceptionally rapid. Only its bulk and the heaviness of its steering knocked the edge off this good machine.

■ LEFT *An improbably long tail housed the engine, while the scissor-type doors were a continuation of the theme first seen in the Countach.*

■ ABOVE *The exceptionally neat-looking V-twelve engine developed no less than 492bhp in its original – and least powerful – guise.*

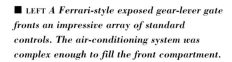

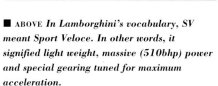

■ ABOVE *In Lamborghini's vocabulary, SV meant Sport Veloce. In other words, it signified light weight, massive (510bhp) power and special gearing tuned for maximum acceleration.*

■ LEFT *A Ferrari-style exposed gear-lever gate fronts an impressive array of standard controls. The air-conditioning system was complex enough to fill the front compartment.*

■ ABOVE *On its way to a 202mph (325 kph) top speed the Diablo would leave behind it a plume of smoke from the quad-exit exhausts – and a terrifying noise.*

Most of the Countach weaknesses – cramped interior, poor visibility, difficult access – were resolved in the Diablo. Luggage space was still at a premium, but the cabin looked and felt classy, boasted a great driving position and featured a control to adjust the suspension settings from the driver's seat. Lamborghini was confident that it could sell 500 cars a year, far more than the Countach had ever achieved.

New for 1991 was the VT (Viscous Transmission) model with full four-wheel drive, although the front wheels only ever got a maximum of 29 per cent of the overall power, and then only after the rear end began to lose traction. Four-wheel drive made the already fine handling even more assured, and the standard adoption of power steering made life behind the wheel much easier, although the penalty was the higher overall weight of the car.

Other variations followed in 1996. The Roadster was just what it said it was: a Diablo with a removable roof, intended to do battle with the similarly configured Ferrari F50. The SV (for Sport Veloce) was the most focused of all the Diablos: a 510bhp engine, lighter weight, lower gearing and even more startling acceleration (although the top speed dropped to "only" 186mph (299kph) owing to the new gearing). There was little doubt that this was the best of the exclusive Diablo family.

■ LEFT *The Roadster version had a hardtop which could be removed completely or pushed back and fixed above the engine bay.*

LANCIA

■ LANCIA GAMMA

When Fiat took control of Lancia and its huge debts in 1969, many pundits guessed that there would be no more true Lancias – technically advanced cars with sporting character. They were wrong. The Pininfarina-styled Gamma saloon (sedan) and coupé announced at Geneva in 1976 boasted all the idiosyncrasies with associated Lancia.

■ LEFT *The 1976 Gamma was Lancia's stab at the executive car market. The big four-door model was always a rare sight, as it seemed to be bought almost exclusively by Italian embassies.*

■ ABOVE *For an interior conceived in the mid-1970s, this was unusually attractive and stylish.*

■ ABOVE *It was perhaps a strange choice to fit a four-cylinder engine in a luxury car, one of the biggest "fours" then in production.*

It was a shame that the Gamma was so underdeveloped because it was a great driving machine, with superb balance and the best power steering around. The saloon was handsome in its own way, but the coupé was a classic of elegant, perfectly proportioned styling.

Series 2 models gained fuel injection, a four-speed auto option and other detail modifications to make the engine more reliable, but it all came too late and in 1984 Gamma production ended. Had the model survived it would probably have been given effective 16-valve technology and there were even turbocharged 180bhp "Federalized" Gammas running as prototypes.

Pininfarina built a Spider version of the coupé in 1978, then a four-door, three-box Scala in 1980, and finally the Olgiata of 1982, a handsome estate (station wagon) version, but sadly all three remained prototypes.

Not the least of these quirks was the adoption of a big 2.5-litre flat-four engine in an executive class more used to six cylinders at the very least. Although the engine was torquey and smooth at high revs, it proved a difficult choice for buyers to accept, not only

because it was rather throbby and unrefined at tick-over but because it rapidly acquired a reputation for serious reliability problems: overheating was common, and the cam belt could strip its teeth if the steering was put on full lock from cold.

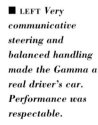

■ LEFT *Very communicative steering and balanced handling made the Gamma a real driver's car. Performance was respectable.*

LANCIA GAMMA (1977–84)	
Engine	4-cylinder
Capacity	2500cc
Power	140bhp
Transmission	5-speed manual 4-speed auto
Top speed	120mph (193kph)
No. built	22,085

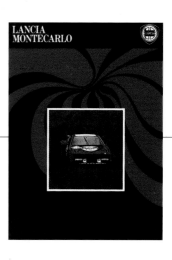

■ LANCIA MONTECARLO

This interesting mid-engined sportscar began life in the Fiat empire as a future sister model for the little X1/9. Indeed, the project was referred to under the name X1/20, but a shuffle of priorities then switched the new model under Lancia's wing.

The Montecarlo was launched at the 1975 Geneva Motor Show in both fixed coupé and targa-topped "Spider" versions. Its clean lines, featuring prominent black bumpers, a forward-thrusting snout and rear flying buttresses, created a stir with fans.

Much of the car was plundered from the parts bin of the Lancia Beta range,

■ ABOVE *The first-series Montecarlo was criticized for its braking performance and wet-weather roadholding, and was actually withdrawn from production for two years.*

■ ABOVE *The Montecarlo brochure celebrated Lancia's racing achievements with its mid-engined sportscar.*

■ LEFT *Pininfarina created the pretty shape of the Montecarlo around mid-engine ideals. Note the rear flying buttresses.*

■ ABOVE *The cockpit was strictly for two passengers, but boasted Italian design flair and a removable targa roof panel.*

LANCIA MONTECARLO (1978–84)	
Engine	4-cylinder
Capacity	1995cc
Power	120bhp
Transmission	5-speed
Top speed	118mph (190kph)
No. built	7595

■ RIGHT *Lancia's Montecarlo was the up-market sister of the Fiat X1/9, larger and more powerful, but no less attractive and very good value.*

including its 2.0-litre engine and many detail items. That kept costs down, and enabled Lancia to sell a car that many likened to a miniature Ferrari for a bargain price.

The story was not all roses, however. The engine was not really powerful enough for a true sportscar, the roadholding was positively dangerous in wet conditions, and severe front-wheel lock-up under braking forced Lancia to suspend production in 1978 pending an 18-month-long return to the proverbial drawing board.

When the Montecarlo reappeared in 1980, Lancia had addressed the problems: the front brake problem was cured by removing the servo assistance and the tail-happy nature was tamed by revised suspension. Also new were the grille, bigger wheels and a six-year anti-corrosion warranty.

In America, the Montecarlo was sold as the Scorpion with a dreadfully underpowered 80bhp 1.8-litre engine. When production ended in 1984 there was no direct replacement, and this was effectively the last real Lancia sportscar.

LANCIA

■ LANCIA DELTA INTEGRALE

In Italian, "*Integrale*" means full, complete, whole, and that fittingly describes the abilities of Lancia's impressive Delta Integrale. Although it was conceived as a car to homologate for rallying, it was quickly recognized as one of the all-time great road cars.

Lancia was a consistently strong rallying contender – one has only to remember the Stratos and 037 – and it had built the mid-engined four-wheel-drive Delta S4 Group 4 car in 1984. However, after such Group B monsters were banned following major crashes and deaths (prompting the nickname "Killer B's"), all attention switched to the milder Group A category for 1987.

Lancia produced the Delta HF 4x4 all-wheel-drive car as a prelude to the full Integrale model, which was launched in October 1987, with its distinctive wide wheel-arches and fat tyres. The Integrale promptly swept the board in rallying events, taking 14

■ LEFT *The magical "HF Integrale" badge came to mean everything that was desirable in performance-car terms.*

■ ABOVE *Across country there was hardly a car that could match the Integrale's pace and roadholding.*

LANCIA DELTA INTEGRALE (1988–94)	
Engine	4-cylinder
Capacity	1995cc
Power	185–215bhp
Transmission	5-speed manual
Top speed	130–137mph (209–220kph)
No. built	Approx 25,000

■ LEFT *It was across rough terrain that the Integrale shone. In World Championship rallies, it was dominant for many years.*

■ RIGHT *In adverse weather conditions, an Integrale was one of the best machines to pilot: safe yet also quick.*

World Championship rallies in 18 months and powering Miki Biasion to two world titles.

Road-car drivers quickly realized what a fabulous machine it was. The sophisticated four-wheel-drive system glued the car to the tarmac, while the 185bhp two-litre turbo engine sprinted the car across country faster than just about anything on the road. This was the fastest, safest point-to-point car in the world – and it was a practical five-door hatchback into the bargain. It felt special inside too: there were Recaro seats, electric front windows and unique instrumentation.

The Integrale just got better with age. In 1989, the old eight-valve cylinder head was upgraded to a new 16-valve head, which pushed power up to 200bhp. The main reason was to homologate the head for rallying, and it took only a few months to sell 5000 cars. The 16V cars won 13 World Championship rallies, and Kankkunen drove one to the 1991 title.

In 1991, a further evolution HF Integrale boasted even more power (210bhp – and later 215bhp – thanks to a larger exhaust), even wider wheel-arch

flares to cover extended front and rear tracks, restyled grille, air intakes, bonnet, wings, bumpers and skirts, and a dramatic new adjustable tailgate spoiler. Officially, this edition was called just HF Integrale (no "Delta" in the name). It took until early 1992 to sell the requisite 5000 copies, and yet again Lancia took the 1992 Championship for Makes, in its last year as an official

works team – not bad for a car that had its roots in the 1970s.

Today the Integrale has a hallowed status among keen drivers. Although it left production in 1994, examples are avidly sought after because there really is nothing like it still in production.

■ BELOW *Cornering at improbable speeds was the Integrale's true forte, and it could show its heels to just about everything else on the road.*

■ ABOVE *Lancia's Delta Integrale did not take long to make a huge impact on the motoring world. Its devastatingly effective brew of all-wheel drive and performance led to it becoming a legend in its own lifetime.*

L E X U S

■ ABOVE *In export markets, the svelte Toyota-built coupé was badged as a Lexus SC. This is a top-of-the-range SC400 model.*

■ RIGHT *Overall the Lexus offered fine value, superlative build quality, attractive styling and crushing ability.*

■ LEXUS SC

In 1989, Toyota set out to beat Europe's finest marques at their own game. It wanted to steal a march on Mercedes-Benz, BMW and Jaguar by producing the world's best luxury saloon (sedan) – even though it had no experience in this market area. It invented a new brand, Lexus, sent its designers to California to discover what customers really wanted, and came up with the LS400 saloon, a car which signally succeeded in providing a genuine alternative to Europe's classic brands.

Lexus did not stop at the LS saloon, which was supremely competent but ultra-conservative in character. In 1991, it added a bit of spice into its new brand with a coupé version, known in the USA as the Lexus SC and in Japan as the

■ LEFT *Highly sophisticated electronics dominated the engine bay of the SC. Several engines were built, from 2.5 litres to 4 litres.*

■ BELOW *Based on the successful Lexus LS400 four-door saloon (sedan), the coupé version added style and a sporting slant. Japanese versions were called Toyota Soarer.*

LEXUS SC (1991–)	
Engine	6-cylinder
Capacity	2491–3969cc
Power	225–280bhp
Transmission	5-speed manual 4-speed automatic
Top speed	146–155mph (235–250kph)
No. built	Still in production

■ BELOW *Satellite navigation was a novelty in 1991. In addition, all the air-conditioning functions were controlled from this LCD screen.*

■ RIGHT *The Toyota Soarer took off not only in Japan but also in America, where it stole sales from the prestige coupés of Mercedes-Benz and BMW.*

■ LEFT *An all-digital dashboard was perhaps a little gimmicky but it fitted the high-tech nature of the Lexus perfectly.*

Toyota Soarer (it was never officially marketed in Europe).

The most striking aspect of the SC was the clean, restrained yet dramatic shape, created in Toyota's California studio. Although it was based on the floorpan of the Lexus saloon, the profile was fresh and boasted many beautiful touches, such as spotlamps shrouded by the subtlest of bulges running the whole length of the bonnet (hood).

In Japan, the catchphrase for the Soarer was "for mind cruising" – which conveyed the new model's primary objective: to transport its occupants over long distances in relaxation and comfort. It also happened to be sizzlingly quick.

The new SC range spanned three engine sizes, from a 225bhp 3.0-litre straight six up to the 4.0-litre V-eight used in the Lexus saloon; not sold in the US, the most powerful member of the family was the 2.5-litre Twin Turbo in-line-six engine, developing 20bhp more than the 4.0-litre V-eight, at 280bhp. The 4.0-litre engine scored 0–60mph (0–96kph) in 6.9 seconds with an automatic gearbox, while the five-speed manual Twin Turbo was nearer six seconds dead.

There was also a choice of three suspension systems. The first was conventional springing. The second was Piezo TEMS, an electronic air-suspension

■ RIGHT *With full active-ride suspension, the Lexus was a forgiving and accomplished cornerer. Its ride was also superior to that of almost any coupé in its class.*

system, which obviated the need for conventional shock absorbers. Controlled by a microchip in the central electronic management computer, it adjusted each wheel's suspension according to the load on it at any given time. Top models got full Active Suspension.

Toyota's engineers went to great lengths to make driving the Soarer an

easy experience. Progressive power steering, which stiffened up as speed increased, limited slip differential and a powerful ABS system eradicated the worries of piloting such a potent machine. Seating was comfortable and the cabin was full of gadgets: satellite navigation, an all-electronic dash with touch-sensitive controls and a television.

LOTUS

■ LOTUS ESPRIT

Colin Chapman, the founder of Lotus, always said that he built the cars he wanted to own, which explained why, as he grew older, his designs matured into ever more sophisticated realms. By the early 1970s, the days of stark Lotus 7s sold in kit form were gone and a new era was dawning.

Chapman was extremely impressed by a mid-engined prototype, which Giorgetto Giugiaro had created for Lotus in 1972. This was the car that, with remarkably little modification, became the new Lotus Esprit, first shown in October 1975.

In construction, the Esprit was classically Lotus, having a steel-backbone chassis, all-independent suspension and a glassfibre body. As launched it had Lotus's brilliant 2.0-litre 16-valve four-cylinder engine mounted amidships. This not only

■ LEFT *Giugiaro's prototype Esprit dates from 1972 and was remarkably similar to the finished production version of the car.*

■ ABOVE *Clean lines, a mid-mounted engine and Lotus's fabled handling prowess made the Esprit a desirable, if flawed, sportscar.*

■ ABOVE *The interior architecture of the Esprit cabin was interesting, the sloping dashboard being a key feature.*

■ LEFT *Lotus boosted the power of its four-cylinder engine by turbocharging it. Up to 264bhp was a remarkable output for a 2.2-litre engine.*

provided convincing performance for its day, but produced probably the best-handling Lotus yet. The five-speed gearbox was taken directly from the Citroën SM.

As it transpired, Giugiaro's clean-cut and simple shape would stand the test of time with honours. The interesting interior architecture was perhaps less

appealing over the longer term but, for its day, the Esprit was a state-of-the-art mid-engined sportscar.

Lotus kept abreast of the opposition's advances with constant developments. An S2 version with an integrated front spoiler appeared in 1978, and the S2.2 with an expanded 2.2-litre engine in 1980, the same year the spectacular

Esprit Turbo was launched. The 2.2-litre Turbo engine developed 210bhp, enough to force a much stiffer chassis with larger wheels and brakes and revised suspension, creating a peerless car in handling terms. The S3 of 1981 incorporated most of the Turbo chassis refinements and added a wraparound front bumper.

■ LEFT *All Esprit models were fast, and no car handled as well as an Esprit. This is a Series 3 model at full chat.*

■ LEFT *The Esprit proved to be a very long-lasting model for the Norfolk company.*

■ ABOVE *In its ultimate guise, the Esprit gained a V-eight engine and a phenomenal power-to-weight ratio.*

In this form the Esprit continued until 1987, when Lotus's in-house designer, Peter Stevens, effected a brilliant restyle of the bodywork, creating smoothed-off and more aerodynamic lines. At the same time, the chassis was stiffened and the gearbox switched to Renault's GTA. The popular Turbo survived in even more powerful guise, boasting up to 264bhp.

There was another restyle in 1993, when the nose and rear wing were reshaped, the interior was improved and power steering standardized. Two new models were launched: the S4S and the Sport 300 with its 302bhp engine (still from just 2.2 litres and four cylinders).

By 1996, the Esprit was 21 years old

and still going strong, but it desperately needed some extra urge to compete with the best from Ferrari. Lotus developed a brand-new V-eight engine for the purpose, twin-turbocharged to produce a

massive 349bhp. Fitted with a six-speed gearbox, the new Esprit V8 was a formidable performer, and looked set to continue to uphold the Lotus tradition for many years yet.

■ LEFT *In 1987, the Esprit got a major redesign by Peter Stevens, rounding off its edges and adding some length.*

■ BELOW *Despite its increasing age, the Esprit remained a competitive and very British sportscar.*

LOTUS ESPRIT (1975–)	
Engine	4/V-eight-cylinder
Capacity	1973–3179cc
Power	160–349bhp
Transmission	5/6-speed
Top speed	130–170mph (209–274kph)
No. built	9,150 (to end of 1996)

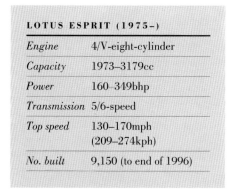

LOTUS

■ LOTUS ELAN

In the 1960s, the Elan name meant just one thing: the best-handling, most fun-to-drive small sportscar you could buy. When Lotus decided, in 1989, to revive the name on its first all-new car in 14 years, it was fully aware of the legacy it had to live up to. Thankfully, in all major areas, it succeeded in creating a worthy successor.

In conception, the new Elan was unlike anything Lotus had tried before, and for one reason: it had front-wheel drive. If traditional Lotus enthusiasts were nervous about this development, they had no need, for the Elan was probably the most competent handling car available. In some eyes it was too efficient, simply gripping the road tighter the more you asked of it and lacking the involvement of other Lotus cars.

Peter Stevens designed the stubby bodywork and ex-Formula 1 driver John Miles developed the interactive suspension. Lotus went to Isuzu in Japan for its engine – a 1.6-litre twin-cam unit in normally aspirated or turbocharged SE forms.

The Elan sold for a very reasonable price, too reasonable as it turned out, as Lotus lost money on each one sold. Yet sales were disappointing, mainly because a worldwide economic recession was beginning to bite and the near-simultaneous release of Mazda's Miata, which offered comparable performance at half the cost. Amid financial problems, Lotus was forced to abandon production after just two years.

A saviour appeared in the form of Bugatti, which bought Lotus from its parent company General Motors and in 1994, using existing components, embarked on a limited run of 800 additional S2 Elans. These featured some 100 changes, including better suspension, larger wheels, new seats and a better hood. Later, the Elan project was revived by Kia in Korea.

ABOVE *All black and red: the cockpit was completely geared towards making the driving experience as visceral as possible.*

LOTUS ELAN (1989–94)	
Engine	4-cylinder
Capacity	1588cc
Power	130–165bhp
Transmission	5-speed
Top speed	122–137mph (196–220kph)
No. built	4,655

■ LEFT *Peter Stevens created another masterpiece of design, no mean feat considering the very short wheelbase he had to work with.*

■ ABOVE *The stubby two-seater had an effective folding top to make it a practical year-round car.*

■ RIGHT *The first new Lotus for a decade was always going to be greeted with intense interest, and the Elise marked a true revolution in sportscar design with its extruded-aluminium chassis.*

■ LOTUS ELISE

Light weight was always Colin Chapman's very first priority when designing a new Lotus. After his death in 1982, Lotus engineers adhered to this principle, and in the Elise, which epitomised it, they produced a spiritual successor to the immortal Lotus 7.

The heart of the Elise, and the reason why it was so light, was its perfectly functional chassis. Breaking with Lotus tradition, it was a monocoque design formed from pieces of lightweight aluminium, literally stretched into shape and glued together. Even the brakes were aluminium composite. This was the secret of its lightness.

The suspension was so good it needed no anti-roll bars, and testers were unanimous in their praise: this was simply the finest handling car ever made.

While the 1989 Elan was front-engined and front-wheel drive, the Elise was mid-engined and rear-wheel drive, and all the more enjoyable for this change. The chosen engine was Rover's all-aluminium 1.8-litre K-series (as fitted to the MGF), complete with its gearbox. This provided all the performance it needed: after all the Elise was only about half the weight of a small family hatchback.

The best thing about it, though, was its price: at under £20,000 ($33,000) in the UK it was a bargain.

LOTUS ELISE (1996–)	
Engine	4-cylinder
Capacity	1795cc
Power	120bhp @ 5500rpm
Transmission	5-speed
Top speed	124mph (200kph)
No. built	Still in production

■ ABOVE *Leaving the aluminium chassis exposed in the cockpit was an inspired move, utterly in keeping with its role as a super-lightweight, no-frills sportscar.*

■ ABOVE *Thanks to extreme light weight, the Elise was a good performer despite its mild 120bhp engine: 0-60mph (0–96 kph) in 5.5 seconds was extraordinarily quick.*

OTHER MAKES

■ LAND-ROVER

After the Second World War, Britain needed a jeep-style all-rounder and the Willys Jeep was used as a template to create the Land-Rover in 1948. It quickly became an international legend, very tough and unassailable off-road. The same basic design remains in production today as the Defender, although Land-Rover branched out in 1970 with the sophisticated Range Rover, in the 1980s with the Discovery all-rounder, and in the 1990s with the smaller Freelander series.

■ LIGIER

French millionaire racing driver and ex-rugby international Guy Ligier decided to build his own sportscar in 1970. The JS designation was in memory of his friend, Jo Schlesser, killed racing in 1969. A pressed-steel platform was fitted with a glassfibre coupé body. As presented at the 1970 Paris Salon, it had a mid-mounted Ford Capri engine, but production cars had Citroën SM V-six engines. Ligier went on to make very successful Formula 1 racing cars and a range of top-selling microcars.

■ LINCOLN

Ford of America's premium brand is Lincoln, purveyors of limousines and the darling of American presidents. Its mainstay, the Continental, was by the 1970s obscenely bloated. Long after every other American marque had down-sized, Lincoln continued to offer "full-size" cars. By 1977, even Lincoln was offering an alternative with the luxury, compact Versailles, which did not do well. More successful were its big coupés such as the Mark VII and LSC, but overall Lincoln never matched the success of its main GM rival Cadillac.

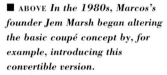

MARCOS

■ MARCOS

The name Marcos was a composite of two illustrious characters in the world of specialist motoring, Jem Marsh and Frank Costin. The first model they created was an all-wooden sportscar, which was brilliant on the track (Jackie Stewart started off in one) but was so hideous that it acquired the nickname "ugly duckling".

Out of this unusual birth came the definitive Marcos in 1963, whose basic shape remains in production today. The

■ ABOVE *It is an impressive fact that Marcos began producing this GT car in 1964, and it continues to be a popular new sportscar in its fourth decade.*

■ ABOVE *In the 1980s, Marcos's founder Jem Marsh began altering the basic coupé concept by, for example, introducing this convertible version.*

■ ABOVE *Enthusiasts respect the Marcos badge as one of the great British sportscar companies, with an impressive competition record and successful road-car range.*

■ ABOVE *Aerodynamic and lightweight, all Marcos models were fast and furious, especially with the modifed Rover V-eight engines the company fitted from the mid-1980s.*

Adams brothers, Dennis and Peter, designed the new Marcos and, at its debut at the 1964 Racing Car Show, it stole the honours. A futuristic glassfibre body sat on the familiar Marcos wooden chassis.

The original intention had been to create an "all-new" car with its own tailor-made suspension, but financial constraints led to Triumph wishbones being used on the front, although a novel de Dion rear end with Triumph arms was

fitted. Even this, however, was later changed to a Ford live-axle set-up. Marcos cars used Ford, Volvo and Triumph engines.

Marcos's "pot-boiler" in the 1960s was the Mini-Marcos, a quite ugly little buzz-box whose main distinction lay in its being the only British car to finish the 1966 Le Mans 24-Hour Race. Powered by a Mini engine, it was cheap but crude and was still available new as late as 1994.

MARCOS GT (1964–)	
Engine	4/6/V-eight-cylinder
Capacity	1498–4999cc
Power	82–352bhp
Transmission	4/5-speed manual
Top speed	110–171mph (177–275kph)
No. built	Approx. 1,500 to date

■ RIGHT *There was no other car with a shape like that of the Marcos, which was at once muscular, individual and futuristic.*

■ ABOVE *Despite its extremely low profile, there was enough room to make the driver feel very comfortable. The seats were fixed and the pedals could move to fit the driver.*

Marcos underwent a temporary demise as a producer of cars in 1971. Marsh continued to provide servicing and parts for Marcos cars for ten more years, and then boldly relaunched the two-seater in 1981 with a variety of Ford engines. In a world starved of sportscars, the Marcos met with immediate success, especially when Marsh installed a Rover V-eight engine to create the Mantula in 1983. Even more attractive was the drop-top Spyder model of 1985. All Marcos models shared the same basic shape as the classic Adams-penned

1800 of 1963, though the profile evolved with wider wheel arches, spoilers and fatter wheels and tyres.

In 1992, a new chapter was written with the arrival of the fully built Mantara, a totally new car with different front suspension and a more radical interpretation of the classic body shape. The Mantara had the option of a Rover 4.5-litre engine, giving a top speed of 160mph (257kph) and a 0–60mph (0–96kph) time under five seconds.

Even more spectacular was the 1994 LM series, the letters of its name hinting

at Marcos's re-entry into the Le Mans racing arena. Two versions were offered, the LM500 with a 4.0-litre V-eight engine and the LM600 with a 5.0-litre engine and 320bhp, enough to reach a cool 169mph (272kph).

In 1996, Marcos turned to Ford of America for the Mantis which had a quoted top speed of over 170mph (274kph) and a 0–60mph (0–96kph) time of 4.1 seconds. Ford's quad-cam V-eight engine, with its 352bhp of power, was described as "adequate for a car that weighs 1050kg (2316lb)"!

■ ABOVE *As the years progressed, Marcos cars developed wild arches and aerodynamic aids. This is a 1993 Mantara.*

■ RIGHT *In 1996, Marcos switched from Rover to a Ford V-eight engine in its Mantis. With a top speed of 171mph (275kph), this was now a true supercar.*

MASERATI

■ MASERATI BITURBO

By the 1980s, the once-great name of Maserati was fading fast. Citroën had taken an interest in 1968 but sold out to De Tomaso in 1975, after which Maserati's model development stagnated and production dwindled. When a bold new model was launched in 1981, the intention was to boost Maserati production. The Biturbo certainly did that, but at the cost of permanently denting Maserati's reputation.

While the car had its faults, the main problem was that it didn't look or feel like a real Maserati. In style it was a dead-ringer for the BMW 3 Series; but for its trident grille it looked utterly anonymous.

If the Biturbo had one strength, it was the performance delivered from the twin-turbocharged multivalve V-six engine. Producing 180bhp initially, it was a very quick car if one had the patience to wait for the turbo-lag to disappear after the throttle was floored. The original 2.0-litre engine (really confected to exploit Italian tax rules) was expanded to 2.5 litres in 1983, and up to 2.8 litres in 1987, by which time power output had reached 224bhp.

Its price and badge made a quick killing for owners De Tomaso. In America especially, the Biturbo sold in very large numbers in the booming 80s. This was a quick route into sharp-suited Italian haute couture, especially in ostentatious open-top Spyder form.

Its oft-quoted shortcomings included evil handling, especially in the wet, cramped rear-seat accommodation and an interior of dubious taste, crowned as it was by a huge clock and acres of lush wood. Owners also found themselves stranded by unreliable engines and

■ ABOVE *The appeal of the Biturbo range was extended with the launch of a 425 four-door-saloon (sedan) version in 1983.*

■ LEFT *The maze of plumbing betrays the technology that gave the Biturbo its name: two turbochargers. They boosted out 180bhp but suffered from turbo lag.*

MASERATI BITURBO (1981–91)	
Engine	V-six cylinder
Capacity	1996–2790cc
Power	180–241bhp
Transmission	5-speed manual
Top speed	132–143mph (212–240kph)
No. built	Approx. 40,000

■ OPPOSITE *The world was plainly ready for a compact sports saloon with a Maserati badge, as the popularity of the Biturbo proved throughout the 1980s.*

■ BELOW *Later Biturbo models were badged 222, 224 (illustrated here) and 228. These were even more powerful than the early cars.*

■ ABOVE *Perhaps the most desirable of the Biturbo models was the fully convertible Spyder. It offered the same huge performance, open-topped fun and seating for four adults.*

distinctly cheesed off all round by rather poor craftsmanship.

Perhaps the redeeming feature of the Biturbo was that it put Maserati back on the map. It sold well enough to re-establish a fading name, and it did give rise to a bewildering profusion of follow-up models. These included a four-door version variously called the 420/425/430, a Spyder convertible, and the second-generation 2.22 and 2.24 (which lost the Biturbo label). Vastly superior were the stunningly fast Karif, Shamal and Ghibli of the 1990s, whose heritage was clearly traceable back to the first Biturbo but otherwise had almost nothing in common with it.

When Ferrari assumed overall control of Maserati in 1997, quality took a quantum leap in the right direction and the bad old days were forgotten. The Biturbo can be seen as the model that delivered Maserati safely into its new owner's hands.

■ ABOVE *Sumptuous leather and rich wood was a Maserati hallmark, and made the cabin feel very special. The dash was dominated by Maserati's trademark oval clock.*

■ RIGHT *The smart Italian clothing stood the Biturbo in good stead for many years, although some Maserati aficionados bemoaned a certain flash-in-the-pan flavour.*

MAZDA

■ MAZDA RX-7

Mazda will go down in history as the staunch defender of Wankel's rotary engine, and as the company which finally sorted its problems out. Long after pioneer NSU had bitten the dust, Mazda pursued the rotary ideal with a whole string of models, including saloons (sedans), coupés and sportscars.

Mazda had the courage to realize the inherent strengths of the rotary engine. The design was very compact and lightweight, it could run to extremely

■ ABOVE *The heart of the RX-7 was its rotary engine. Long after other manufacturers had abandoned it as a poor idea, Mazda proved it was possible to make it a success.*

■ BELOW *The second-generation RX-7 was softer, more practical, less characterful and more comfortable, but still had rotary power.*

■ ABOVE *Mazda's RX-7 sportscar was highly respected in enthusiast circles. Its smart shape, speed, technology and character were sharply focused.*

■ LEFT *Although the raw performance of the first-generation RX7 may not have been high-ranking, its cornering ability certainly was.*

high revs and was smoother than any other four-stroke engine. Its biggest fault was a propensity for drinking fuel.

The other original major concern was reliability. The engine depended on the integrity of the tips of the rotating triangle, which span around inside the combustion chamber. These tended to wear quickly and cause running difficulties. Modern technology finally addressed this problem (Mazda certainly had it cured during the life cycle of its RX-7) but by then the make's poor reputation was firmly established.

■ LEFT *Advanced materials and technology made the third-generation RX-7 an extremely rapid and enjoyable car.*

In later years, Mazda reserved the rotary engine for its range-topping coupés and sportscars. The RX-7 was an undoubted classic. For its day (it was launched in 1978), it was a unique blend of style and talent.

The centre of the magical RX-7 equation was the engine. Charismatic, sweet-running and powerful, there was nothing else like it. It may not have been overly fast, with a top speed of 120mph (193kph) and 0–60mph (0–96kph) in 8.6 seconds, but it was entertaining – except for a tendency to back-fire. When taken around bends there was little to fault the RX-7's

■ ABOVE *Japan had learned from Europe's best, and the latest RX-7's interior oozed class and purpose.*

■ BELOW *In 1992, the RX-7 evolved into a real supercar, with high performance now top of the agenda. 237bhp was very healthy for a car of its price.*

enthusiasm, and in character it was pure sportscar. If you wanted more performance you could take your RX-7 to a specialist like TWR, which offered a potent turbocharged conversion – and many customers did.

The RX-7's shark-nose coupé style was distinctive and, with the pop-up headlamps down, extremely clean.

■ ABOVE *The more cosseting interior of the 1986-92 RX-7 reflected its move up-market.*

Although it had a pair of rear seats, they were so small that this was essentially a two-seater. The first cars were quite starkly equipped, but gradually refinements like electric windows and a spoiler were introduced.

The second-generation RX-7 of 1986 was larger, heavier and softer, far less of a sportscar and more of a boulevard cruiser (especially in soft-top form, a body style never offered on the first RX-7). By 1992, the third-generation RX-7 had catapulted Mazda back into the sportscar league with a twin-turbo engine, an advanced and extremely attractive body structure and bristling performance.

Neither really duplicated the original purity of the first RX-7, which ranks as one of the most successful sportscars ever, with almost half a million of the first generation sold.

MAZDA RX-7 (1978–86)	
Engine	Twin-rotor Wankel
Capacity	2 × 573cc
Power	105–135bhp
Transmission	5-speed manual 3-speed auto
Top speed	113–125mph (182–201kph)
No. built	474,565

MAZDA

■ MAZDA MX-5

In the 1980s, sportscars went completely out of fashion, not just passé but completely dead. All the great open sportscars were stamped on: MG, Triumph TR, Fiat Spider; only the Alfa Spider could be said to have kept the spark alight, and then only just. Against this background, Mazda made a courageous decision: it would single-handedly engineer the rebirth of the sportscar.

That 1989 decision was bold but it paid off handsomely. Other manufacturers may have decided that sportscars were no longer profitable, but the consumer had different ideas. The

■ ABOVE *Simple in style, the MX-5 exploited the rear-wheel-drive two-seater-roadster style abandoned by virtually every other major manufacturer.*

■ LEFT *The 1.8-litre engine was modest, perhaps, but just right for a car that was designed as an accessible small sportscar.*

■ LEFT *At speed the MX-5 impressed all who drove it. It was snappy, sharp around corners, responsive, yet refined.*

■ ABOVE *There were no frills in the instrument layout and choice of materials. The inspiration came from classic sportscars such as the MGB.*

world still wanted to drive sportscars, and Mazda got the confection absolutely right in its MX-5.

Here was a cheap two-seater open-topped car with a front-mounted engine and rear-wheel drive. To many onlookers this sounded rather like an MGB, an impression reinforced by the compact, curvaceous shape. Where the MX-5 excelled – and dispelled any criticism of plagiarism – was in its handling. Unlike the antiquated manners of the MGB, the

MX-5 was superbly modern: just the right degree of handling aplomb was engineered in for safety and fun.

This was a classic design in which everything was somehow right, from the evocative rear lights and front pop-ups to the simplicity of the specification and the enjoyment factor. Underneath it was brilliantly engineered, with engine, gearbox and final drive carried on a separate subframe, and double-wishbone suspension for crisp handling.

The interior was kept sparse in the best sporting traditions: little in the way of electronic gizmos and a great sense of quality and simplicity. The only criticisms were over-light power-steering and a lack of performance from the 1.6-litre engine.

In Japan, the car was launched as the Eunos Roadster, in Europe it was the Mazda MX-5 and in America it was the Miata. In each market, the model became a legend. Thanks to its very

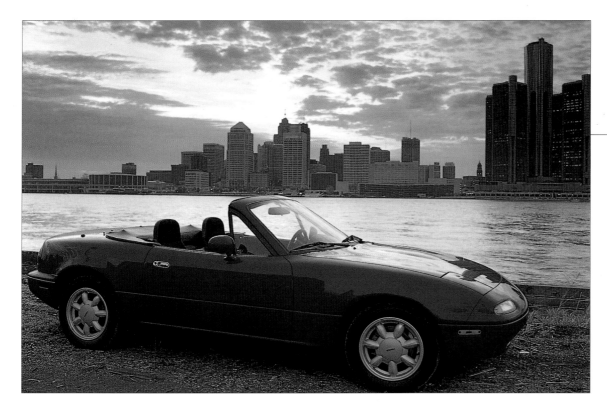

■ LEFT *The world welcomed the Mazda MX-5 with open arms. Here was a car designed for pure enjoyment to a fabulous classic formula.*

reasonable price, it was accessible to many drivers and it sold in vast numbers. Admittedly, it had little competition, but there is no denying its essential brilliance. In any case, in many markets the MX-5 sold best in its later years when there was plenty of competition from the likes of the MGF, Fiat Barchetta and BMW Z3. The plain fact was that the little Mazda paved the way for everyone else: it really brought about the renaissance of the sportscar.

Very little changed during its career. The addition of safety features such as side-impact bars and airbags increased its weight, so the MX-5 got a 1.8-litre fuel-injected engine in 1993; a 1.6-litre model was kept going as a bargain entry-level model.

It took until 1997 for a replacement for the MX-5 to arrive, and it precisely duplicated the format of this ultra-successful car. By then the MX-5 had become the world's favourite sportscar, with a production tally over 400,000.

■ ABOVE *Two comfortable seats, an open roof and an open road – one very simple formula for success.*

■ LEFT *A big splash is the only way to describe the MX-5's impact. Within a few years, numerous manufacturers had launched their own junior sportscars on the back of the MX-5's success.*

MAZDA MX-5 (1989–97)	
Engine	4-cylinder
Capacity	1597–1840cc
Power	90–131bhp
Transmission	5-speed manual 4-speed auto
Top speed	108–122mph (174–196kph)
No. built	Over 400,000

■ BELOW *The McLaren F1 laid the strongest claim to be the world's ultimate car. Its provenance from a World Championship Formula 1 team was decisive.*

McLaren

■ McLAREN F1

It's not every designer or engineer who has the chance to build the ultimate car, with absolutely no expense spared. Perhaps Bugatti did it with the extravagant Royale in the 1930s, but few in the industry could argue that Gordon Murray's McLaren F1 was anything but the ultimate road-going car.

A former chief Formula 1 designer at Brabham, then at Woking-based McLaren, Murray had a burning but unfulfilled passion to build a machine that qualified as the fastest, most involving road car yet made – and, of

■ ABOVE *The purchase of an F1 was reserved for the privileged few, since its price (£635,000 ($1,070,000)) was vastly higher than that of any other car ever made.*

■ ABOVE *Surrounding the specially designed BMW V-twelve 6.0-litre engine was a hand-finished film of pure gold, chosen for its heat-dissipating qualities.*

course, the most expensive. Yet it would also have to be a car you could happily drive into town.

Ideas at McLaren began crystallizing during 1988, and in March 1989 Murray announced his plans to the public. Murray was in charge of design and development, while Lotus stylist Peter Stevens would pen the car's shape, and BMW's Motorsport division had agreed to design an all-new V-twelve engine from scratch. Everything revolved around Murray's ideal precepts, such as the innovative three-seater cabin with

MCLAREN F1 (1993–97)	
Engine	V-twelve-cylinder
Capacity	6064cc
Power	609-627bhp @ 7400rpm
Transmission	6-speed
Top speed	231mph (372kph)
No. built	100

■ LEFT *The stunningly simple yet aggressive shape was designed by Peter Stevens. The bodywork was realized in exotic carbonfibre.*

■ LEFT *In dynamic terms the F1 had no peers: it was faster, more responsive, more refined and more rewarding in every way than any other car in the world.*

■ ABOVE *Project creator Gordon Murray insisted that there should be three seats, the central one occupied by the driver. The "arrowhead" formation proved practical.*

the driver sitting in the middle ahead of the two passengers.

Another crucial factor was the target weight: an unbelievable 2205lb (1000kg) (Ferrari's F40 weighed 2720lb (1235kg) and Jaguar's XJ220 weighed 3240lb (1470kg)). Every detail was under scrutiny to see if it could be made lighter.

With no less than 627bhp on tap from the 6064cc BMW V-twelve engine, the truly explosive performance which Murray had been aiming for became a reality. Ex-Formula 1 driver Jonathan Palmer flew to the Nardo test track in Italy in August 1993 and, in the searing heat, he drove the F1 at an incredible 231mph (372kph). Tests betrayed more amazing figures: 0–60mph (0–96kph) in 3.2 seconds, 0–100mph (0–161kph) in 6.3 seconds and 30–70mph

■ ABOVE *Every component on the F1 was designed especially for its role, from the wheels and tyres to the hi-fi system. Everything was engineered down to a weight.*

(48–113kph) in just over 2 seconds. Such incredible performance made the F1 almost invincible on the track: an F1 GTR came first in virtually every GT Endurance race it entered, and the F1 was triumphant at Le Mans in 1995.

Then there was the cost: no less than £635,000 ($1,070,000), reflecting the huge development budget, ultra-high

technology and the fact that, initially, each one took 6,000 man-hours to build. Then there were all the little touches that made the F1 so special, like the gold-insulated engine bay, the unbelievably complex sound system, total leeway for individual colour choice and tailored luggage. If you had car problems, McLaren would jet out a mechanic on the next available flight.

The first customer car was finished on Christmas Eve 1993, and the last one of a total of exactly 100 cars – far short of the initial target of 300 – was completed in 1997. There could hardly be a more exclusive car than this.

■ ABOVE *The high-tech gauges said it all: with a dial going up to 240mph (386kph) .*

■ RIGHT *The F1 LM was a limited-edition model painted in the racer and race-car constructor Bruce McLaren's racing orange and fitted with a rear spoiler, special wheels and modified bodywork.*

MERCEDES

■ BELOW *While other roadsters in the 1970s became bloated or disappeared altogether, Mercedes-Benz produced the superbly strong SL series.*

■ MERCEDES-BENZ SL

SL has traditionally denoted Mercedes-Benz's sporting models, and the two letters were always taken to mean Sport and Leicht (lightweight). The first SL was the 1954 300SL Gullwing coupé, and the most popular were the "pagoda roof" models produced between 1963 and 1971.

When it came to replacing these classic SLs, Mercedes-Benz took an important step into its own future in 1972. Gone were the stacked headlamps of all

MERCEDES-BENZ SL (1989–)	
Engine	6/V-eight-/V-twelve-cylinder
Capacity	2799–5987cc
Power	190–389bhp
Transmission	5-speed manual 4/5-speed auto
Top speed	138–155mph (222–249kph)
No. built	Still in production

■ LEFT *In one of its ultimate W107 series guises, the 500SL seen here, the drop-top Merc had a fabulous 241bhp 5.0-litre V-eight engine*

previous Mercedes models, replaced by strong horizontal rectangular units (US models received a pair of round lamps) and wrap-around indicators, anticipating future themes on its saloons (sedans).

Viewed objectively, the so-called

W107 SL was an absolute classic, which lasted in production for almost 20 years. It was quite a different car, expanded in every way over the "pagoda roof" SL and considerably improved in safety matters.

The new SL was initially powered by

Mercedes-Benz's 3.5-litre V-eight, or its even more powerful 4.5-litre V-eight. Modernized suspension featured a semi-trailing-arm rear-end, and there was standard power-steering, and a popular optional automatic gearbox. From 1974, the entry-level 280SL was launched in Continental Europe (but not in the UK or the US), sporting the twin-cam six-cylinder engine from the 280E.

The SL Series was revamped in 1980 as a new range of engines slotted in. The full list during the 1980s was: 280SL, 300SL, 380SL, 420SL, 500SL and 560SL. A second SL sub-species was the longer-wheelbase fixed-head SLC series produced from 1972, which were proper four-seaters and probably the best grand tourers made in the 1970s.

■ RIGHT *With a lengthened wheelbase and a fixed roof, the SL transformed into the Grand Touring SLC four-seater, a strong contender in its day for the accolade of best car in the world.*

By the late 1980s, the SL had lost its sporting edge, and Mercedes-Benz aimed to address that problem with a brand-new SL series in 1989. The result was one of the best cars Mercedes-Benz ever produced. It looked wonderfully balanced, drove like a sportscar or a tourer, depending on your mood, and had all the qualities one would expect of a top-flight model from Stuttgart.

It was launched with a choice of two engines: the 300SL six-cylinder (offered in 190bhp standard and 231bhp twin-cam forms), and the deeply impressive 500SL V-eight. Naturally, there was a power-operated soft-top and a wind deflector to keep your hair style in order, and one extraordinary novelty was a hidden roll-over bar, which popped up when the car reached a certain angle,

■ ABOVE *The SL heritage stretches right back, through these five generations, to the celebrated 300SL of the 1950s.*

■ LEFT *In addition to a very effective electric folding roof, an important safety measure was a roll-over bar, which automatically popped up in case of an accident.*

■ BELOW *With an optional hardtop fitted, the SL became an attractive and snug coupé.*

telling an on-board computer that a serious accident was imminent. Another interesting option on the V-eight was its speed-sensitive suspension.

Mercedes-Benz's most expensive car arrived in 1992 in the V-twelve-powered 600SL. With its 48-valve 389bhp engine and automatic damping it was crushingly quick, yet still superbly refined. The ultimate version was the six-litre V-eight AMG-tweaked SL60 with body kit, 381bhp and huge 18in (45.7cm) wheels.

■ ABOVE LEFT *When it came to replacing the SL in 1989, Mercedes produced its best incarnation yet. Low-slung and elegant, it epitomized the luxury roadster form.*

■ RIGHT *Mercedes interiors are nearly always sober affairs, with solidity and logic given higher priority than design flair.*

MERCEDES

■ MERCEDES-BENZ SLK

In the parlance of Mercedes-Benz, "K" signals *"Kompakt"*, and indeed the SLK was a smaller breed of bargain-priced Mercedes SL sportscar, and the first junior Mercedes sportscar since the 190SL of the late 1950s. It was a perfect foil to the new Porsche Boxster and BMW Z3 roadster, selling to a new kind of customer for Mercedes: a telling statistic is that over half of those who ordered an SLK had never had a Mercedes before.

■ ABOVE *A brilliantly effective solid roof folded at the touch of a button under the boot (trunk) lid. The lid would then open the opposite way to permit luggage storage.*

■ BELOW *In its most sporting guise, the 230 Kompressor pictured here, the SLK was a very rapid sportscar, up to 143mph (230kph) being possible.*

■ ABOVE *Mercedes-Benz could hardly have produced a more desirable junior sportscar than the SLK, its first attempt at this growing market. With the top raised, it looked and felt like a proper coupé.*

To cut costs, the engine and driveline components were shared with the C Class saloons (sedans), the brakes came from the E Class, and seats were bought in from Recaro. The headlights were unique but moulded in plastic. Expensive magnesium structural components were used, but they saved space and enhanced safety.

The car's party trick was an exotic electric roof. In 25 seconds, the SLK's solid Vario roof arched into the air, folded itself in two and carefully stowed itself away in the boot (trunk) before a metal cover snapped shut. The sequence even wound the windows down for you. It worked just as well in reverse, transforming the SLK back into a draught-free coupé, and you didn't even have to clip the roof on to the windscreen edge. Mercedes promised that the electric motors and hydraulic rams were good for at least 20,000 repeat performances.

Inside, the car's cabin was highly styled with embracing bucket seats, and carbonfibre-look cladding on the dashboard and white back-lit dials sunk into chrome-edged portholes.

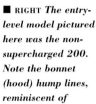

■ RIGHT *The entry-level model pictured here was the non-supercharged 200. Note the bonnet (hood) hump lines, reminiscent of the classic SL of the 1950s.*

This was a rear-drive car but, with anti-lock brakes and traction control, only the reckless could provoke the back of the SLK out of line. Its ride and roadholding balance were superbly fluid, and, as with all Mercedes automatics, you could flick the shift down for a faster getaway or change-down for a corner. With the 193bhp supercharged four-cylinder engine, the car's top speed was more than 140mph (225kph), with 0–60mph (0–96kph) in 7 seconds, while there was a cheaper non-supercharged model, too.

The SLK proved amazingly popular, with orders backed up until the end of the century: it seemed that Mercedes's biggest problem with the SLK was building enough of them.

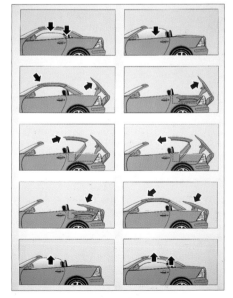

■ ABOVE *Detail of the ingenious electric hood (top) operation.*

■ ABOVE LEFT *The word Kompressor on the cylinder-head cover indicates the presence of a supercharger in the 2.3-litre engine, good enough for 193bhp.*

■ ABOVE RIGHT *Especially classy was the interior treatment, with carbonfibre-style overlay, white dials apparently hewn out of the dash and a classic Mercedes steering wheel.*

MERCEDES-BENZ SLK (1996–)	
Engine	4-cylinder
Capacity	1998–2295cc
Power	136–193bhp
Transmission	5-speed manual or auto
Top speed	126–143mph (203–230kph)
No. built	Still in production

MG

■ MG RV8

MG is without doubt one of the great sportscar names. Sadly, however, that name was squandered by British Leyland, its parent company in the 1970s, and its once-great sportscar line was left to wither on the vine until the compromised, outdated MGB shuddered out of existence in 1980.

Although the MG badge survived on performance versions of some Austin cars, this seemed to be the end for the MG sportscar. MG enthusiasts never forgot the "B", however, and a huge industry quickly grew up around

■ LEFT *Thirty years after the MGB's birth, Rover revived its seminal sportscar and gave it a thorough revamp and a V-eight engine to create the MG RV8.*

■ BELOW *The gadget-laden RV8 interior, rife with gauges, was a much more cosseting location than the stark old MGB.*

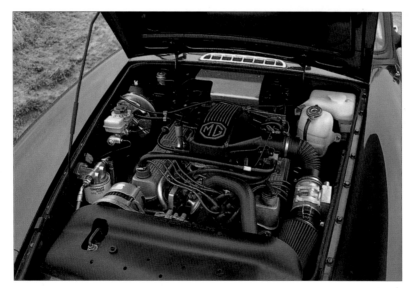

■ LEFT *No MGB-manufactured roadster had ever had a V-eight engine. The 1990s version was engineered to accept Rover's 3.9-litre Range Rover unit which developed 190bhp.*

■ ABOVE *After more than a decade in a wilderness devoid of sports models, the MG badge was revived to the cheers of enthusiasts.*

restoring this enduring classic. Even Austin-Rover got involved in 1989 when its Heritage division went into production with brand-new replacement MGB bodyshells.

The Rover Group realized that the MG badge still had tremendous potential, and it set about a relaunch of the brand. Its main aim was to produce an all-new mid-engined car (which became the MGF), but almost as an appetizer it decided to produce a radically updated MGB for the 30th

anniversary of its birth. Not only would it look different, it would have an engine that the drop-top "B" had never had – the venerable Rover V-eight – and would come with the name MG RV8.

The idea came about because its Heritage division had the capacity to make a respectable number of bodyshells (about 15 per week). Although the new design was much modified, many of the original pressings were unaltered, so it made sense logistically to do this.

■ BELOW *Always exclusive, the MG RV8 found many homes in export markets such as Japan.*

■ RIGHT *Typically British in every way, the interior reeked of walnut capping, rich leather and chrome detailing.*

Rover stylists set about beefing up the old "B". The bonnet (hood), boot lid (trunk) and doors were kept the same but the rest of the bodywork was retouched, notably having wider wheel-arches, new bumpers, faired-in headlamps and skirts. Its more purposeful look was boosted by very smart spoked alloy wheels and wide tyres.

The basics of the mechanical package remained rather antique, including a live rear axle suspended on leaf springs. Rover's team tried to improve handling by widening the track and fitting Koni dampers, but there was no escaping the age of the design.

The best news was the installation of Rover's aluminium 3.9-litre V-eight engine, not only decently powerful but boasting a huge spread of torque. A claimed 0–60mph (0–96kph) figure of six seconds was backed up by a top speed of 135mph (217kph).

The interior was classically British: walnut veneer for the dashboard and door cappings, chromed door handles, lots of leather trim and a plethora of small gauges. The lack of such modern-day gadgets as electric windows and mirrors and power-steering merely

seemed to add to the olde worlde aura.

Its launch price of just over £25,000 ($42,000) looked good, and immediately there was a long queue of customers. Admittedly, since the RV8 was hardly at the cutting edge of sportscar technology, the main appeal was nostalgia and the fact that production would be very limited, but the RV8 was always in demand right up until its demise in 1996.

MG RV8 (1992–96)	
Engine	V-eight-cylinder
Capacity	3946cc
Power	190bhp @ 4750rpm-
Transmission	5-speed
Top speed	135mph (217kph)
No. built	n/a

■ BELOW *It may have shown its age in action, but there was no denying that the RV8 had strong performance and great presence.*

M G

■ MGF

Those who thought that the MG sportscar was dead eventually got the news they had been hoping for: the MG RV8 retro sportscar would be a precursor to an all-new, thoroughly modern MG. This would be a car as the MGB would have evolved, not a throwback to an antique age. For sure, all the qualities which made an MG special would be carefully dialled into the design equation, but this was meant to be a cutting-edge, affordable sportscar for the 1990s.

When it was launched at the 1995 Geneva Motor Show, the new MGF did not disappoint the crowds. Parent company Rover decided to opt for a centrally mounted engine because it gave the best handling potential, and in

that respect the MGF was triumphant. Every tester returned with stories of tenacious grip, fluid cornering and an impressively stiff bodyshell.

The shape was tailored to appeal. Unambiguously modern, it took the theme of the MG grille and extrapolated a smooth, purposeful profile. Some thought it perhaps too anodyne, too close to the Japanese school of design, but no one questioned its effectiveness.

Inside, the traditional MG cues were

more abundant but still not over-embellished. Even the moulded MG badges were restrained. The general feel was very classy, with white dials, leather steering wheel and attractive trim.

For its power, the MGF drew on the acclaimed K-series engine in 1.8-litre form. Two versions were offered: the 120bhp 1.8i and the powerful 145bhp 1.8i VVC, which could reach 60mph (96kph) from rest in just seven seconds thanks to its Variable Valve Control

■ LEFT *In 1997, a heavily modified MGF called the EXF was driven at the Bonneville salt flats in America to a top speed of 217mph (349kph) – the fastest MG ever.*

■ ABOVE *With the VVC engine, the MGF was capable of 0–60mph (0–96kph) in seven seconds and a top speed of 130mph (209kph).*

MGF (1995–)	
Engine	4-cylinder
Capacity	1795cc
Power	120–145bhp
Transmission	5-speed manual
Top speed	120–130mph (193–209kph)
No. built	Still in production

■ LEFT *Sportscar enthusiasts around the world applauded the official rebirth of the MG sportscar when the MGF was launched.*

■ OPPOSITE *In 1.8i VVC form, the MGF was equipped with special five-spoke alloy wheels, power-steering, ABS and – most importantly – a more powerful 145bhp engine. An optional hardtop was available.*

■ BELOW *The cockpit of the MGF was very sporting (white gauges, sports steering wheel, attractive upholstery) and was applauded for not overdoing the number of MG badges.*

engine mapping. The VVC also added standard power-steering, anti-lock brakes and unique alloy wheels.

A waiting-list immediately sprang up for the MG in Europe and Japan, with most buyers wanting the VVC version. The average age of an MGF buyer was over 50, but this came down as the model grew in acceptance.

■ ABOVE *The MGF may have looked back to the MGB for its grille, but there the similarity ended. The mid-engined layout was thoroughly modern and delivered one of the best driving experiences around.*

OTHER MAKES

■ MATRA
With a background in aerospace and weapons, Marcel Chassagny's Mécanique Aviation Traction (or Matra) also became a car-maker when, in 1964, it took over René Bonnet's sportscar operation. The bizarre 530 followed the Djet in 1967 and, in 1970, Chrysler-Simca took the firm over. The 1973 three-seats-abreast Bagheera used a Simca engine. After the post-Peugeot take-over, another name change in 1979 to Talbot-Matra coincided with the launch of the Murena coupé and Rancho estate. Renault acquired Matra in the 1980s and inherited an MPV (minivan) prototype that Matra had developed (the Espace, which Matra manufactured).

■ MERCURY
Mercury was born in 1939 as a species of Ford that slotted in below Lincoln. Its 1970s offerings mirrored Ford's, the highlights being the Cougar and Marquis coupés and the Capri (initially a German Ford import, later a clone of the Mustang II). In the 1980s, Mercury's success was bolstered by solid mid-range virtues and the occasional character car like the Capri convertible.

■ MINI
Alec Issigonis's masterstroke Mini started off life in 1959 with Austin and Morris badging. After ten years in production, the Mini was launched as a marque in its own right under British Leyland. The legendary Mini-Cooper was launched in 1961 and production ended in 1971. Mini became Britain's best-selling marque in the 1970s (over five million made). Packaging included larger wheels in 1984, a Cooper relaunch in 1990, 1275cc engine only from 1992 and fuel injection from 1996. The Mini brand was relaunched in 1996 as a prelude to an all-new, 21st-century Mini.

■ MITSUBISHI
Japan's Number Three marque has always been very conservative and sold better in the domestic market than abroad (where it was called Colt for many years). The most interesting Mitsubishis were the 1970–6 Galant GTO coupé (a Japanese Mustang), the 1976–85 Sapporo, the 1982–90 Starion and the Car of the Year award-winning 1994 FTO coupé. Mitsubishi also pioneered direct petrol injection technology and established a European co-venture with Volvo in Holland.

■ MORGAN
Morgan is a unique company. It alone continues to make a car that looks and behaves exactly the same as it did 50 years ago: separate chassis, sliding pillar suspension, ash frame and hand-made bodywork. H.F.S. Morgan started production of three-wheelers in 1910 at Malvern, England, and this was continued by his son Peter and grandson Charles. Four-wheelers were made from 1936. The best Morgan was the Rover V-eight-engined Plus 8, made from 1968. Morgan has always thrived: there is a long waiting-list for all of the 450 cars it can produce per year – still in the factory where the cars have been made for over 75 years.

■ MORRIS
In 1912, William Morris (later Lord Nuffield), started building cars in Cowley, Oxford, and Morris Motors became one of the Britain's biggest companies. It grew up to become the Nuffield empire, incorporating names such as MG, Riley and Wolseley. In 1952, the group united with Austin to form the British Motor Corporation, then Europe's biggest car concern. By the 1970s, Morris was earmarked as the conventionally engineered badge. The last Morris was the lack-lustre Ital, which died in 1984.

NISSAN

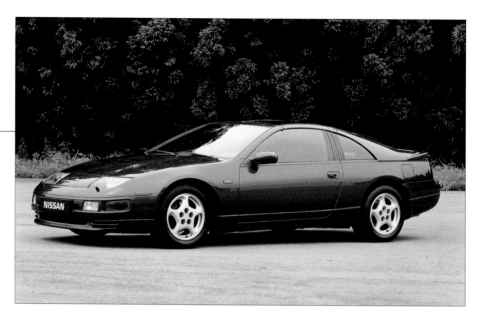

■ NISSAN 300ZX

Nissan's Z series sportscars date back to the classic Goertz-styled 240Z coupé, one of the world's most successful sportscars. By the 1980s, however, the original ideals of light weight, sharp styling and quick responses had been lost in the bloated, suburban ZX of 1984–9, which was obviously meant for posing rather than driving.

That whole dead end was smashed through with the stunning new 300ZX of 1990. *Autocar* magazine called it "Japan's first-ever supercar" after it recorded a top speed of 155mph (250kph) and a 0–60mph (0–96kph) time of just 5.6 seconds. That was

■ ABOVE *The cabin could have been mistaken for that of a prestige European sportscar. The two-plus-two seating arrangement was, however, rather cramped.*

courtesy of a 300bhp twin-turbocharged three-litre engine with variable-valve timing sited up front and driving the rear wheels.

Even more impressive was the suspension, a complex multi-link set-up with HICAS four-wheel steering which automatically adapted itself to the driver's style. This enhanced turn-in, improved grip and stability and helped provide magnificently neutral cornering, although caution was required in very wet weather.

The interior looked and felt better than most Japanese cars, although it was rather cramped. Lift the T-bar roof off, however, and you had a feeling of open-air motoring.

Like the styling, the character of the 300ZX was up front, and customers appreciated its fine value for money and

■ ABOVE *Japan's first supercar was an accurate assessment of Nissan's bold new 300ZX of 1989.*

rewarding attributes. In America a convertible version won even more friends, but in Britain the 300ZX was suddenly dropped in 1994 after falling foul of emissions legislation. Elsewhere it continued for another two years.

NISSAN 300ZX (1989–1996)	
Engine	V-six-cylinder
Capacity	2560cc
Power	300bhp @ 6400rpm
Transmission	5-speed manual 4-speed auto
Top speed	155mph (250kph)
No. built	Not known

■ FAR LEFT *An attractive full convertible 300ZX was sold in certain markets such as the USA. This model was selected as the PPG circuit Pace Car in America.*

■ LEFT *The twin-turbocharged 3.0 litre V-six engine developed 300bhp. This was a very sophisticated unit boasting variable valve timing.*

■ RIGHT *The normal Skyline was a saloon (sedan) car from the middle of Nissan's range, but the GT-R with its spoilers and skirts was a technological firecracker of a fast car.*

■ NISSAN SKYLINE GT-R

Skyline is a badge which Nissan has used since 1955, more recently denoting its more sporty upper-medium saloon (sedan) range. Everything changed in the 1989 eighth-generation Skyline, however, for a brand-new model joined the line-up: the legendary GT-R.

With its deep front air dam, wide wheel-arches and tall rear spoiler, this two-door saloon (sedan) looked as if it would go fast. The 2.6-litre twin turbo six-cylinder engine made sure that it did, all 280bhp of it ensuring sizzling performance, such as 0–60mph (0–96kph) in five seconds and a top speed of 153mph (246kph).

That was just the start of the GT-R's wizardry. It also boasted four-wheel drive with sensors on each wheel to control the split of torque front-to-rear, plus active suspension and four-wheel steering, which adjusted the angle of the

NISSAN SKYLINE GT-R (1989–)	
Engine	6-cylinder
Capacity	2569cc
Power	280bhp @ 6800rpm
Transmission	5-speed manual
Top speed	153mph (246kph)
No. built	Still in production

rear wheels according to the pressure being exerted on them. The result was that the GT-R pulled through corners amazingly quickly and safely while the excitement of piloting it was undiminished. It's little wonder that a GT-R recorded the fastest time ever for any road-going car around the legendary Nürburgring circuit in Germany.

In 1994, the next generation GT-R arrived, looking smoother and more rounded but with no loss of character. Initially sold only in Japan and Australia, it became a UK market debutante in 1997 with a price tag of £50,000 ($84,000).

■ LEFT *If 280bhp was too little for you, the GT-R provided the ideal basis for extreme tuning for road and track. Power outputs were known to go as high as 1200bhp.*

■ LEFT *A GT-R famously recorded the fastest time ever for a production car around the Nürburgring in Germany: it was the only such car to go round in under eight minutes.*

OTHER MAKES

■ OLDSMOBILE

Born in 1897, Oldsmobile is America's oldest name-plate and part of the General Motors combine. By 1975 it was a middle-class luxury leader with a conservative slant, although models like the Starfire coupé and front-wheel-drive Toronado were more adventurous. Gradually, most of Oldsmobile's own model range declined into badge engineering, but unique cars such as the Cutlass and Aurora kept the flame burning.

■ OPEL

Opel has been General Motors' German wing since 1929. It relied on volume sales of medium-class cars like the Olympia, Rekord and Kapitän before moving into the small car arena with the 1962 Kadett. In the 1970s, Opel's strength lay in producing good-looking cars such as the Manta, GT and Commodore, while the 1973 Kadett was a true world car. British Vauxhall and German Opel products converged so that, by the 1980s, the differences were in the grilles and wheel-trims only.

PANTHER

■ PANTHER

Panther is one of the most unusual companies in motoring history. In the 1970s, it became one of the most spectacularly successful British specialist manufacturers with a startlingly wide range of products.

Founded by Robert Jankel in 1972, Panther Westwinds started life with pastiches of bygone classics. The J72 was the first, a copy of the pre-war SS100 using Jaguar engines. The hand-built J72 sold to the rich and famous, including the film star Liz Taylor, for it certainly wasn't cheap, retailing at almost twice the price of an E-Type Jaguar.

Its next car was the 1974 De Ville, a creation of unrestrained opulence, with vaguely Bugatti Royale lines and superb craftsmanship. Mechanically, the De Ville was all Jaguar XJ12, including its suspension. In 1976, came the two-door De Ville Convertible, famous for being the most expensive car on British price lists – and the motorcar star of the film *101 Dalmatians*.

The concept behind Panther's 1975 Rio was quite sound: to create a small, economical car with the finish and luxury of a Rolls-Royce. In the troubled fuel crisis days of 1975, it looked

■ ABOVE *This is the interior of the J72, a feast of walnut and leather in the best neo-classic traditions.*

■ ABOVE *Panther Westwinds made its living producing hand-built pastiches of a bygone era of motoring. The Kallista vaguely recalled the 1930s.*

■ ABOVE *Acres of chrome dazzled for effect on the nose of the De Ville. The hand-crafted coachbuilder's art was fostered at Panther.*

promising but suffered from comparisons with the car on which it was based, the Triumph Dolomite, which cost a third of the price. In commercial terms, the Rio was a complete flop and perhaps deserved a better fate.

Not so the Lima, Panther's "car for the masses", which sold very well. The recipe was simple: a 1930s-style two-seater open glassfibre body on a strengthened Vauxhall Magnum floorpan, including the Magnum's engine, gearbox, suspension, steering and brakes.

Its successor was the 1982 Kallista. This used all-Ford components, including Cortina double-wishbone front suspension and a Capri live rear axle, and the revised bodywork was aluminium. It was not particularly quick, but was more roomy, more refined and better-handling than the Lima. It sold very healthily.

Apart from the incredible six-wheeled

■ LEFT *Panther's most extravagant car was the De Ville, a huge Bugatti-inspired device using Jaguar parts. In the film 101 Dalmatians it was the ideal choice for Cruella de Ville.*

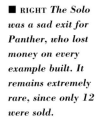

mid-engined Panther 6, Panther's last model was the 1990 Solo, a monocoque aluminium-and-carbon-fibre 2+2 supercar fitted with Ford's Sierra Cosworth 2.0-litre turbo engine and Ferguson four-wheel drive, making it the world's first mid-engined four-wheel-drive production car. Some described it as the best-handling road car of all time, but its disappointing performance, harsh ride and questionable build quality were unforgivable in a £40,000 ($67,000) sportscar. Even at that price, it was uneconomic to make. After one of the shortest production runs ever, the Solo was axed with just 12 cars sold.

In 1987 Panther had been acquired by the Korean firm SsangYong, which wound production down and used Panther expertise to design new SsangYong products. In retrospect, Panthers are often regarded as vulgar and unseemly jewellery, but they were all hand-built to the highest quality.

■ ABOVE LEFT *Most road testers were agreed that the Solo was an exquisite car to drive: very fast and extremely good around corners.*

■ ABOVE *The small Kallista was Panther's car for the common man, and easily its best-selling model. It used Ford engines.*

■ LEFT *Mid-engined finesse from the 1990 Solo, a striking coupé with such advanced features as four-wheel drive, aluminium and carbonfibre bodywork and Cosworth turbo power.*

■ RIGHT *The Solo was a sad exit for Panther, who lost money on every example built. It remains extremely rare, since only 12 were sold.*

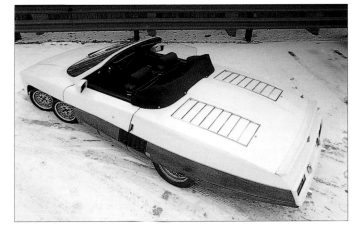

■ LEFT *Six wheels on my wagon. Only Panther could have come up with such an outlandish creation. Its mid-mounted turbocharged Cadillac V-eight was claimed to push this leviathan to 200mph (322kph).*

PANTHER LIMA (1976–82)	
Engine	4-cylinder
Capacity	2279cc
Power	108bhp @ 5000rpm
Transmission	4-speed manual 3-speed auto
Top speed	105mph (169kph)
No. built	918

PEUGEOT

■ PEUGEOT 205GTI

The Volkswagen Golf may have started the hot-hatch craze in the 1970s, but it was Peugeot that made the best of the breed in the 80s. Its 205GTI became a performance car legend, for it stood head-and-shoulders above the competition, right up until its death.

It started from a wonderful basis: the Pininfarina-designed 205 was a very competent little hatchback. Its combination of a pleasing shape, supple ride and outstanding handling made it one of the most popular cars of its time – and it was still in production after 14 years. However, it cried out to have more power, and so the GTI was born in 1984.

■ RIGHT *No one who drove a 205GTI could fail to be impressed by its agility around corners.*

■ BELOW *The 205GTI sired the very special Turbo 16 mid-engined road/rally car. It arrived shortly before the Group B rally class was axed.*

Crisp, agile and offering more grip around corners than anyone had a right to expect from a car costing so little, the 205GTI was an instant hit.

Perhaps the power output of the first 1.6-litre engine was too low: 105bhp was less than rivals such as the Opel Astra GT/E and VW Golf GTI. Peugeot offered a Sport kit to boost power by 20bhp, but plainly the standard GTI needed to keep pace, and within two years Peugeot had upped the output of the 1.6-litre engine to 115bhp, and at the same time an even more powerful 130bhp 1.9-litre model was added. This larger engined version with its bigger alloy wheels proved to be the definitive GTI.

Inside, rally-style seats hugged the passengers and a tasteful arrangement of black, red and grey upholstery was standard. Instrumentation was complete and equipment generous. There wasn't much to criticize. The hard suspension gave an uncomfortable ride but this improved with successive tweaks. Build quality was a consistent problem, too, but probably the worst foible was on-the-limit handling. Although it took a lot to get a 205GTI out of shape around corners, when you did (by lifting off the throttle in mid-corner for instance), it was all rather a handful.

Another GTI variant was the 1986 CTI, the convertible version, which was partly built by Pininfarina. Most were made with 1.6-litre 115bhp engines, but eventually Peugeot succumbed and fitted the 130bhp 1.9 unit for another cracking car.

■ OPPOSITE *Compact, nimble, very grippy and entertainingly fast, the Peugeot 205GTI redefined the parameters of the hot hatch in the 1980s.*

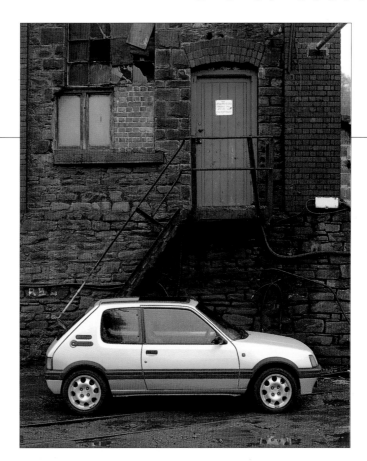

■ LEFT *With the arrival of the 1.9-litre 205GTI (identifiable by its larger alloy wheels and 1.9 badging), power rose to 130bhp and the 205GTI stepped up another rung in the performance league.*

When the 205GTI retired in 1994, there was no direct successor. The 306 was a much larger car, which, initially at least, had none of the GTI's performance and agility. Eventually, hot versions of the 306 and smaller 106 came along to fill the gap: the 306 S16 and GTi-6 were stormingly powerful hot hatches in the best traditions, while the 106GTI was possibly the most entertaining performance hatchback being made when it arrived in 1997.

By this stage, however, the heyday of the GTI had already passed. And in the 1980s, when it really was all the rage, the little Peugeot 205GTI was undoubtedly king of the breed.

■ LEFT *Like the hatchback, Pininfarina designed the attractive CTI convertible, but here it also helped to manufacture it.*

■ BELOW *Top down, the CTI could be happily described as a 1980s equivalent of a sports roadster.*

PEUGEOT 205GTI (1984–94)	
Engine	4-cylinder
Capacity	1580–1905cc
Power	105–130bhp
Transmission	5-speed manual
Top speed	115–123mph (185–198kph)
No. built	Over 4 million 205s

■ RIGHT *Simple yet stylish, the GTI's interior was a feast of sporty details. The red/black/grey colour scheme was effective.*

PLYMOUTH

■ PLYMOUTH PROWLER

Having paved the way with the extraordinary Viper, Chrysler's management (headed by Bob Lutz) felt bullish enough to take its dream-car-to-production route one step further. The Plymouth Prowler was a rare example of a genuine show car reaching the public.

It all started with Tom Gale, the head of Chrysler's design team, who had always harboured a passion for hot rods.

■ LEFT *This is the sort of car you'd want to step aside for if you saw it bearing down on you.*

the Prowler on the market. Its rod style was neat, melding classic themes such as separate fenders, jut-forward chin and a lack of spurious adornments with modern materials and a technological spin around the edges. Underpinning it all were massive 20in (50cm) rear wheels and fat 295-section rubber, alongside which the still-large 17in (43cm) front wheels looked dwarfed. There was no room for two spare wheels, so the rear ones had a run-flat capability. The sophisticated suspension was elegantly exposed to view. Cockpit space was generous, although the boot (trunk) was completely taken up by the folding roof when it was down.

He penned a modern interpretation of the classic "bucket-rod" theme and put it on Chrysler's stand at the 1993 Detroit Auto Show. The reaction to it was so positive that Chrysler's board ordered a feasibility study and gave it the green light for production with a budget of $75 million – peanuts in Detroit terms.

Chrysler's theory was that hot rods were ingrained in the American subconscious and lots of people actually wanted to own one but never had the time or inclination to build their own. Step in the Plymouth Prowler, ready-made in Detroit for such an audience.

There was nothing else remotely like

■ ABOVE *Chrysler's Plymouth division went out on a limb to produce its Prowler, born of designer Tom Gale's passion for hot rods.*

■ RIGHT *The cabin was a mix of modern and classic hot-rod themes. Note the bold scalloped instruments.*

■ LEFT *The styling themes were all pure American hot rod, with a dash of modern spice to give it a marketing shine. Only 3,000 were to be made in the first year.*

■ ABOVE *Hot-rod fans might have been disappointed by the fitment of a V-six engine rather than a V-eight, but in truth it was quick enough for most tastes.*

In construction the Prowler was formed of steel and aluminium panels over a steel frame. Despite its radical looks, it complied with US safety laws, which necessitated such features as big front and rear bumpers and a high-level stop light.

Hot-rod fans were mildly miffed when, instead of a true blue American V-eight engine, Chrysler decided to fit its Vision 3.5-litre V-six instead. Still, with its 218bhp it was more than fast enough to satisfy most tastes: since it weighed only 1315kg (2900lb), 0–60mph (0–96kph) came in an impressive 7.7 seconds, and top speed – limited by poor aerodynamics – was 125mph (200kph).

Chrysler showed the series-form Prowler at the 1996 Detroit show, and production was due to begin for the 1998 model year. All 3000 of the first year's production were to be painted the same colour – purple! If nothing else, the Prowler raised dowdy Plymouth's profile. By tapping into a national passion for hot-rodding, Plymouth had cleverly earned itself a whole set of values that no amount of advertising could ever have created.

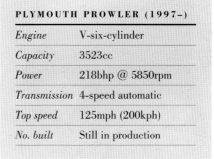

PLYMOUTH PROWLER (1997–)	
Engine	V-six-cylinder
Capacity	3523cc
Power	218bhp @ 5850rpm
Transmission	4-speed automatic
Top speed	125mph (200kph)
No. built	Still in production

■ ABOVE *The chiselled jaw and narrow grille were genuine hot-rod throwbacks, although the "dodgem" bumpers were a concession to current safety laws.*

■ LEFT *If you went out on the prowl, the original Plymouth show car featured this natty trailer for your effects.*

PONTIAC

■ PONTIAC FIREBIRD

The first-generation Pontiac Firebird was sired by Chevrolet's Camaro, arriving some six months after it, and differing only in terms of trim, engine choices and the traditional Pontiac split-grille treatment of its nasal styling. It was restyled below the waist for 1969 and given a dose of safety equipment, while convertible versions were also listed.

The most classic of the early Firebirds was the 1969 Trans Am. It took its name from the Trans-American road-race series organized by the Sports Car Club of America, and began a whole dynasty of Firebirds with this name. Its special white-and-blue stripes paintwork, rear spoiler, beefed-up chassis and 335–345bhp Ram Air power made it distinctive and much better on the tarmac than standard Firebirds.

An all-new Firebird arrived as a mid-1970 model with a distinctive style that lasted through 1981, minor restyles occurring for 1974, 1977 and 1979. Again there was a high-performance

■ LEFT *This is where the Firebird story first began: a sister model to the Chevrolet Camaro with a traditional Pontiac split-grille nose.*

Trans Am model, which was a highly marginal seller to start with (only 2116 sales in 1971), but became the most popular Firebird of all by the end of the decade (more than 93,000 were sold in 1978). There were also standard, luxury Esprit and Formula models.

The Firebird almost died in 1972 when General Motors began asking serious questions about the future of the performance-car market. Luckily it was decided to keep it going and the

PONTIAC FIREBIRD (1971–81)	
Engine	6-/V-six/V-eight-cylinder
Capacity	3785–7456cc
Power	105–345bhp
Transmission	4-speed auto 5-speed manual
Top speed	96–125mph (154–201kph)
No. built	1,061,719

■ LEFT *There was no mistaking the snout of the second-generation Firebird. This is a 1972 Trans Am, the high-performance model of the range.*

■ ABOVE *The 1974 Firebird was restyled with Federal laws in mind. The car pictured is a Trans Am 455 Super Duty.*

■ ABOVE *Towards the end of its life, the second-generation Firebird sprouted decoration (as this 1980 Trans Am shows) but lost power.*

■ ABOVE *The third-generation Firebird series arrived in 1982. This is a line-up from 1987, when the 5.7 litre V-eight reappeared.*

■ LEFT *The Trans Am name-plate continued to denote the top-of-the-range performance version.*

Firebird did extremely well for GM.

Power dropped steadily through the 1970s due to increasingly strict US government emission controls. Still, the Firebird never succumbed to pressure to lose its optional V-eight power, and a turbocharged 301 cubic inch (4936 cubic centimetre) version added a bit of spice for the 1980 model year.

For the third-generation, 1982 Firebird, again the basic bodywork was shared with Chevrolet's Camaro, but Pontiac stylists designed a distinctive chiselled, cowled-headlamp nose for the 'Bird. Base, S/E and Trans Am models were listed, while a return to the big 350 cubic inch (5740 cubic centimetre) V-eight arrived for 1987, also powering a top-level model called the GTA with

its distinctive spoiler and skirts. With 245bhp in its most powerful guise, the Firebird could manage 0–60mph (0–96kph) in just 5.4 seconds.

Falling sales and a lack-lustre image in the face of ever-improving imported competition characterized the final years of this long-running design. It was not

finally replaced until 1993, when the latest Firebird was unveiled (again closely based on the new Chevy Camaro but featuring a sharp, eagle-like nose, which varied slightly according to model). Initially available only as a coupé, an attractive-looking full convertible was added in 1994.

■ ABOVE *Quintessentially American, the Firebird (seen here in Trans Am guise) offered coupé style and V-eight power for a bargain price.*

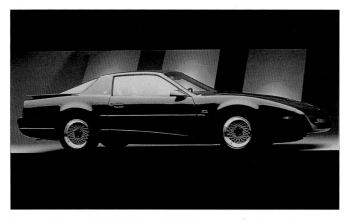

■ ABOVE *This is a 1991 Firebird GTA. Two years later the series was replaced by a new fourth-generation Firebird.*

PORSCHE

■ BELOW *Although it was first launched in 1963, essentially the same 911 design was still being produced in 1979.*

■ PORSCHE 911

Today's Porsche 911 shares only a few nuts and bolts with the original edition of 1963, yet few modern classics have such a strong hereditary line and identity. The original Porsche 911 was to have been called the 901 until Peugeot reminded Porsche that it had the copyright on all model numbers with "01" in them, and so the magical formula was born.

Styled by Ferry Porsche's eldest son Butzi, it is still recognizable today, although spoilers and fat arches altered its elegant profile throughout the 1970s. The development potential of the flat-six engine, with one of the most distinctive growling engine notes on the road, seems

limitless: it grew from just 2.0 litres to 3.6 litres in the latest versions, while power leapt fom 125bhp to 408bhp in the latest Turbo – leaving aside the 450bhp of the 911-based 959.

For drivers, the best of the "classic" 911 bunch was the 2.7 RS Carrera of the 1970s, a lightweight homologation special with stiffer suspension and a hallmark duck-tail spoiler. There have been some surprisingly mild variants, too, such as the Sportomatic with its semi-auto clutchless gear-shift and the 912, a budget model using the four-cylinder engine of the old 356.

■ LEFT *When Porsche launched a convertible version of the 911, it became instantly popular. This is a Carrera Cabriolet.*

■ BELOW *Porsche brought turbocharging into the modern age. Its 911 Turbo was a hugely powerful supercar, easily the fastest-accelerating production car of its day.*

Tail-happy handling has always been part of the 911's mystique, but much of that was cured early on when the wheelbase was lengthened. For modern 911 owners, talk of "lift-off (trailing-throttle) oversteer" is largely bar-room bravado. In any case, for those who harboured serious doubts about the handling, in the 1990s Porsche offered a four-wheel-drive model called the Carrera 4. More to the point was the car's superb steering and progressive,

powerful brakes, which gave the driver such vivid road-feel.

Those who get hooked on the 911 rarely go back to other cars. The legends about build quality and reliability are all true, and longevity is another strong suit since all 911s have been built out of non-rusting galvanized steel since the mid-70s. The 911 image has changed over the years though: for the buyer of the 60s and 70s, the 911 was the choice of the seasoned connoisseur; by the mid-80s it had become a yuppie icon, a rolling symbol of fast, flash cash. For some, including Porsche, this image has lingered a little too long.

The Porsche 911 is an abiding legend

■ ABOVE *The characteristic whale-tail rear spoiler of the Turbo found its way on to most versions of the 911 during the 1980s.*

■ RIGHT *Oversteer was always part of the 911 mystique, although the limits of its roadholding were always very high up the scale.*

that has defied all attempts at replacing it. By rights it should have been killed off by the 928 in the mid-70s but somehow sales never slackened off: the worthy but uncharismatic 928 had none of the 911's enduring appeal and Porsche has no plans to do away with its classic rear-engined coupé. After all, it has been the company's meal ticket through some tough times. In 1997 the 911 was replaced by an all-new flat-six-engined coupé with water-cooling. The name? 911. . .

PORSCHE 911 (1963–)	
Engine	6-cylinder
Capacity	1991–3600cc
Power	125–408bhp
Transmission	4/5/6-speed manual semi-auto
Top speed	130–183mph (209–294kph)
No. built	Approx. 430,000 (to date)

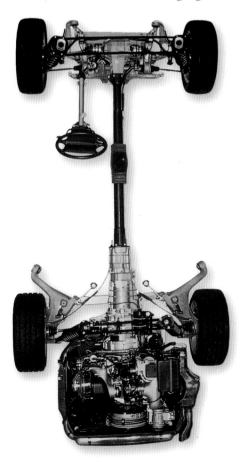

■ LEFT *Porsche introduced a four-wheel-drive system in the Carrera 4 in 1989 for sure-footed handling. Note how far behind the rear axle the six-cylinder engine is.*

■ ABOVE *The 911 evolved through several incarnations. This is a Carrera RS model, a stripped-out version with a 260bhp version of the classic flat-six engine.*

PORSCHE

■ PORSCHE 928

The whole of Porsche's glowing reputation was based on a format that it had used since 1948, namely a rear-mounted engine. The 924 of 1975 was its first-ever front-engined car but, since this was an Audi cast-off, it is fair to say that the 928 was the first car conceived by the Porsche team to have a front engine.

The 928 was always intended as a range-topping supercar, but secretly Porsche hoped it would prove to be a natural successor to the rear-engined 911. In the end, of course, it never did displace its more sporting sibling, and the 911 remained the seminal Porsche. In truth, the 928's main success was in attracting a new class of buyer to the Porsche brand, someone who might otherwise have elected to buy a Mercedes SLC or Jaguar XJS, for this was more of a grand tourer than an outright sportscar.

Porsche built an all-new 4.5-litre V-eight for the 928, which was fabulously

■ ABOVE *The flop-forward headlamps and highly rounded styling of the 928 met with some controversy.*

■ ABOVE *The wrap-around facia gave the impression of completely cosseting the driver. The standard of finish and level of luxury were of a very high order.*

■ ABOVE *Porsche originally harboured ideas that the 928 might one day replace the long-lived 911, but instead it slotted in as a top-of-range grand tourer.*

PORSCHE 928 (1977–95)	
Engine	V-eight-cylinder
Capacity	4474–5399cc
Power	240–350bhp
Transmission	5-speed manual 4-speed automatic
Top speed	143–171mph (230–275kph)
No. built	Approx. 35,000

■ LEFT *The GTS was a run-out (final) version, and the pinnacle of a long line of 928s.*

smooth and flexible but ultimately not as quick as the 911. There was a choice of rear-mounted manual transmission or, more commonly, Mercedes-built automatic. An attempt to give it some more power was made with the later 4.7-litre 928S (which had an extra 60bhp at 300bhp).

In character, the 928 was ruthlessly efficient rather than exciting, a trait that its clean but uninvolving styling seemed to exacerbate. It was also very comfortable, at least for the two front passengers; rear seat space was available, but very limited. Lavish equipment levels matched its "soft" image. Handling could not be faulted, and it was as forgiving as the 911 was tricky at its limit.

■ ABOVE *The front-mounted V-eight engine gave the 928 a very different character from more traditional Porsche models: powerful yet unruffled and refined.*

■ BELOW *In its ultimate guise, Porsche tried to give the 928 more sporting appeal, with fatter wheels, lower suspension and lower-profile tyres.*

■ ABOVE *With its 5.4-litre 350bhp engine, the GTS was the fastest and most rewarding of all 928 models, but always a real rarity.*

Power jumped again in 1986 with the launch of the S4. Its 5.0-litre power-plant now had a twin-cam head, 32 valves and a maximum output of 320bhp: the 928 was finally coming of age. The S4 restyle altered the nose and tail sections.

The best versions of all were saved for last, however. To counter criticisms that

this was not as sporting as some rivals, Porsche offered a GT version with an extra 10bhp, electronic limited slip differential and sports suspension (which improved handling but made the ride harder). The package became even sharper with the 1992 GTS, now sporting a 5.4-litre 350bhp engine, wider wheels and a more vigorous feel.

After a production run of 18 years, the 928 was retired in 1995. The model was not as successful as Porsche had initially hoped, but it had provided a useful lesson: traditional Porsche people stuck with what they knew and liked – the 911 – and the Stuttgart firm meddled with this fact of life at its peril. It has never looked back.

PORSCHE

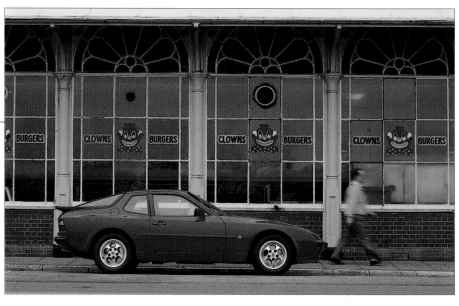

PORSCHE 924/944

The Porsche 924 was conceived in the early 1970s as a joint project with Volkswagen/Audi, to be designed by Porsche but produced and marketed by Volkswagen using as many stock VW parts as possible. The engine was the fuel-injected 2.0-litre unit from the Audi 100 – also found in the VW LT van – and, while the rear transaxle was new, the gears inside were Audi, too.

It was only when the fuel crisis began to bite hard, and sales of the ugly-

■ BELOW *In Carrera form (a 1980 limited edition), the 924 was very powerful and boasted a dramatic body kit that presaged the 944.*

■ ABOVE *In profile, the 944 was very similar to the 924, but its flared wheel-arches were an instant give-away that this had pukka Porsche power.*

duckling VW-Porsche 914 began to flag, that Porsche realized it was faced with the prospect of having no cheap sports-car to sell in the second half of the 70s. With the 911's future also uncertain, Porsche decided to take over the project as a pure Porsche model, with production subcontracted to VW.

Launched in 1975, the 924 was an instant success. However, this was no 911: the van-derived engine could be raucous when pressed, even if it endowed the 924 with brisk acceleration and a 125mph (201kph) top speed in its long-legged fifth gear. More impressive was the handling, the perfect 50/50 weight distribution giving the 924 a well-balanced poise that allowed even novices to drive quickly and safely, with

PORSCHE 924/944 (1975–93)	
Engine	4-cylinder
Capacity	1984–2990cc
Power	125–211bhp
Transmission	4/5-speed manual 3-speed auto
Top speed	125–160mph (201–257kph)
No. built	122,304/163,820

■ RIGHT *Many people were surprised to find Porsche producing a front-engined four-cylinder car, and indeed the 924 began life as an Audi project.*

■ RIGHT *This is a full line-up of 944 models at Porsche's Stuttgart facility.*

precise, informative and light steering – not unlike a 911's – allied to slight roll angles. The gearbox was pleasant to use and a few 924s were even built with automatic transmission.

The 924 Turbo of 1978 hardened the model's performance image in the late 70s. Its 170bhp came courtesy of a KKK turbocharger. Top speed surged from 125mph (201kph) to 141mph (227kph), and acceleration was almost in the supercar class with 0–60mph (0–96kph) in 6.9 seconds. Stiffer suspension and better brakes meant the handling was even more polished. Cooling slots in the nose and discreet spoilers singled this model out from the the ordinary 924.

In the 1980s, the 944, with a proper Porsche 2.5-litre four-cylinder engine – effectively half a 928 V-eight – finally shook off associations with the VW LT van, although the 924 itself lingered on until 1985. In fact, the 944 was a very different car with big wheel-arches, fatter wheels and tyres and a lower stance. It got twin cams in 1986, and was joined by a Turbo version in 1986, that was good for nearly 160mph (257kph). The last-of-the-line three-litre models came in both closed and convertible forms. Even then the model did not die: the 1993 Porsche 968, which lasted until 1995, was a radically evolved version of the 944.

■ LEFT *The 944 was undoubtedly one of the best-handling cars made in the 1980s, thanks to its wide stance and competent chassis engineering.*

■ LEFT *Even the basic 944S was a quick car, but in Turbo form the 944 was good for 160mph (257kph).*

■ BELOW *In many ways, the 944 Cabriolet was the most attractive 944 variant. Its hood (top) was simple and effective.*

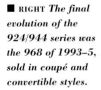

■ RIGHT *The final evolution of the 924/944 series was the 968 of 1993–5, sold in coupé and convertible styles.*

PORSCHE

■ PORSCHE 959

Porsche built the 959 with the intention that it should become a formidable Group B racing car, and it was shown at the 1983 Frankfurt Motor Show as the "Gruppe B". But when Group B cars were banned from racing in 1986, Porsche switched the emphasis of its design programme to create the ultimate road car.

It started by drastically reshaping the basic 911 body, using high-tech plastics and aluminium doors and front lid. The suspension was all new and multi-adjustable, while a clever system monitored tyre pressures on the move.

Then there was the engine, a monstrous twin turbocharged version of the familiar flat six. With only 2.85 litres, it developed 450bhp and could accelerate the 1450kg (3200lb) 959 from rest to 60mph (96kph) in an unbelievable 3.6 seconds, or 0–100mph (0–161kph) in a stunning 8.2 seconds.

The *pièce de résistance* was undoubtedly the transmission. Not only was four-wheel drive permanent, and not only did it have six speeds, but there

was also a choice of four computer-controlled traction settings to suit different conditions: thick snow/mud, ice, wet and dry. Even so, the rear-engined 959 was challenging to drive.

Only existing Porsche owners could buy the £155,000 ($261,000) car, and very quickly a "grey market" sprang up, boosting used prices to ridiculous levels. Since less than 300 were ever made, demand would always outstrip supply, and remaining examples are blue-chip classics of the first order.

■ ABOVE *The idea for the 959 was born as early as 1983 when this so-called Gruppe B prototype was displayed at the Frankfurt Motor Show.*

■ LEFT *The 959 sat low and squat on multi-adjustable suspension. It also had permanent (full-time) four-wheel drive, six speeds and selectable traction control.*

PORSCHE 959 (1987–88)	
Engine	6-cylinder
Capacity	2850cc
Power	450bhp @ 6500rpm
Transmission	6-speed manual
Top speed	197mph (315kph)
No. built	283

■ BELOW *Wild in every way, the 959 was loosely based on the 911, but its bodywork was drastically altered, featuring both plastic and aluminium body panels.*

■ ABOVE *Tremendous urge was tempered by phenomenal grip. Even so, driving a 959 was never a relaxing experience, thanks to the explosive power of 450 horses sitting in the tail.*

■ PORSCHE BOXSTER

After the death of Porsche's front-engined models (the 968 and 928), the Stuttgart firm was left with just one model once again, the venerable rear-engined 911. Having passed through such a painful period of front-engined cars, Porsche elected to take a new direction with its first all-new model in 18 years: the Boxster.

What distinguished the new Boxster was its engine position – in the middle of the car, driving the rear wheels. Porsche claimed that "the mid-engine provides ideal driving dynamics", and the world was forced to agree.

The new Boxster was fabulously entertaining to drive, balanced, responsive and surprisingly forgiving. Powered by a brand new 204bhp 2.5-litre six-cylinder "boxer" engine, in the best Porsche tradition, the Boxster was

as fast as it was smooth. Porsche claimed a top speed of 149mph (240kph) and a 0–62mph (0–100kph) time of 6.9 seconds, or slightly less if you ordered the attractive option of the Tiptronic S gearbox, which allowed gear-changes to be made from paddle controls on the steering wheel.

The four-piston mono-block brake caliper system was for the first time fitted to a road-going Porsche, and was claimed to have 100 per cent fade-free characteristics. It enabled the Boxster to pull up short from 62mph (100kph) in just 2.7 seconds.

Perhaps the Boxster's greatest allure

lay in its purposeful styling. Boasting the lowest drag coefficient of any car in its class (0.31), it was elegant, smooth and timeless. The striking headlamps were shrouded by durable plastic covers.

An enticing cockpit boasted instruments grouped in an arc, slightly overlapping each other. The electric soft-top could be lowered in just 12 seconds and stowed underneath a metal cover.

The Boxster undoubtedly represented a serious part of Porsche's future. Priced very competitively to do battle with the Mercedes-Benz SLK and BMW Z3, it also attracted a whole new generation of drivers to the Porsche marque.

■ LEFT *From within the engagingly styled interior, the electric soft-top could be folded down in just 20 seconds.*

■ ABOVE *Beautifully balanced in action thanks to its mid-engined layout, the Boxster was reasonably fast and boasted race-car braking ability.*

■ LEFT *The name Boxster was a joining of two Porsche classics, the "boxer" engine layout and the Speedster body style.*

■ BELOW *There was little room for doubt that Porsche created one of the most desirable of all sportscars in the Boxster, and yet this was its entry-level model.*

PORSCHE BOXSTER (1996–)	
Engine	6-cylinder
Capacity	2480cc
Power	204bhp @ 6000rpm
Transmission	5-speed manual
Top speed	149mph (240kph)
No. built	Still in production

RENAULT

■ RENAULT 5 TURBO

The idea of a car created specially to compete in rallies was Renault's. The 5 Turbo, introduced in 1978, spawned a string of copycat homologation specials like the Lancia S4 and Ford RS200, all sold for road use as well, because the rules stated that a minimum number had to be built. As a pioneer, the Renault was also the only rally car which made complete sense as a road car.

In fact, an impressive tally of nearly 5,000 Renault 5 Turbos were built because of customer demand. It's easy to appreciate why. The 5 Turbo had a centrally mounted turbo intercooled engine, which offered scorching acceleration, massive grip and endless handling entertainment.

Very little of the shopping (standard) Renault 5 (Le Car in the US) remained. Renault's Alpine factory bolted on

■ LEFT *The 5 Turbo launched the rally-spec homologation generation. In style and driving character it was a wild experience.*

■ ABOVE *The mid-engine looks tiny – in fact, it was only 1.4 litres – but it kicked out 160bhp for some screaming acceleration.*

■ ABOVE *Unlike the Gallic artscape of the Turbo 1, the Turbo 2's interior was based on that of the standard Renault 5 (Le Car).*

wildly flared wheel-arches, gaping cooling vents and big spoilers, and the doors, roof and tailgate of the first cars were in aluminium. The interior was a typically French mix of bold primary colours and avant-garde design.

Mechanically, the story was even more divergent. Racing suspension, big brakes and hugely fat tyres

complemented the heavily heat-shielded engine (which sat just inches from your ears, inside the cockpit).

From 1983, there was a Turbo 2 version with minor trim changes, a recognizably Renault 5-derived interior and a heavier all-steel body; in contrast to the first edition (of which 1,830 were built), some 3,167 Turbo 2s were sold.

■ ABOVE *In the massively flared arches sat very wide alloy wheels and tyres, which boasted huge grip.*

■ LEFT *Although its name and some body panels were derived from the Renault 5 shopping car, the 5 Turbo was a real mid-engined beast.*

RENAULT 5 TURBO (1978–86)	
Engine	4-cylinder
Capacity	1397cc
Power	160bhp @ 6000rpm
Transmission	5-speed manual
Top speed	125mph (201kph)
No. built	4,997

■ RIGHT *The 1984–91 GTA was the latest in a long line of Renault-based sportscars from Alpine, which was France's equivalent of Porsche.*

■ RENAULT ALPINE GTA/A610

Launched in 1984, the Renault Alpine GTA was the last of a famous line of rear-engined French sportscars using Renault V-six power in a steel back-bone chassis. Gunning for the Porsche 911 market, it offered superb driver involvement and high levels of grip (despite the tail-happy layout) but never managed to tempt many buyers away from Porsche.

They were certainly quick cars, particularly in Turbo form, topping 150mph (241kph) and turning in 0–60mph (0–96kph) times in the six-second bracket. Drivers loved the GTA for its feel and responsiveness, yet it was a comfortable, quiet long-distance machine. Despite its exotic looks, it was surprisingly practical, with usable rear seats and rust-free plastic bodywork. The Douvrin V-six engine – straight out of the big Renault 25 – offered no reliability problems either, and the overall quality of the cars was acceptable, if not in the 911's league.

In 1991, the GTA evolved to become the A610 with a few styling tweaks that somehow robbed the crisp-edged shape of character but gave it broader showroom appeal: pop-headlights are the quickest way of identifying the new model. The power of the Turbo model was hiked up to 250bhp thanks to a

■ ABOVE *The unusually styled interior raided the Renault parts bin for its switchgear.*

larger 3.0-litre engine, and top speed rose to 165mph (265kph) with no turbo-lag. The double-wishbone suspension was tweaked to cure any hint of the twitchyness suffered by the older model. With the inclusion of power-steering, parking the A610 wasn't such a muscle-building exercise either.

The GTA and A610 Alpines were hailed as classics while still in production, but always lived in the shade of the Porsche 911. Production ended in 1995, with no successor.

RENAULT ALPINE GTA/A610 (1984–95)	
Engine	V-six-cylinder
Capacity	2458–2975cc
Power	160–250bhp
Transmission	5-speed manual
Top speed	146–165mph (235–265kph)
No. built	17,450

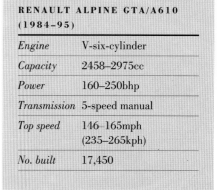

■ ABOVE *An expanded 3.0-litre V-six engine sat in the tail. It had 250bhp on tap.*

■ LEFT *In Turbo form the GTA was exceptionally fast. The rear-sited V-six engine inevitably caused tail-happy manners, but the GTA was grippy nonetheless.*

■ RIGHT *The A610 Turbo stepped up a rung: a 160mph (257kph) top speed and improved handling made it a Porsche rival.*

RENAULT

■ RENAULT ESPACE

Other car manufacturers can lay claim to having invented the people carrier, otherwise known as the Multi Purpose Vehicle (MPV), but Renault was the first to produce an MPV specifically created from the ground up as such and make it popular. It revolutionized the car market and the repercussions of its success are still being felt, with every major manufacturer producing a rival.

The origins of the Espace actually began with the French sportscar constructor and aerospace leader Matra. In the late 1970s, it was allied to Simca-Talbot and produced a proposal based on the Horizon for a radical "one-box" people carrier. But Matra was sold on to Renault and with it went the MPV project. Renault immediately recognized

■ ABOVE *With a restyle in 1991, the Espace moved on to ever-greater success.*

its potential and brought its new Espace to production in 1984, the same year as Chrysler Corporation's minivans.

The first and most striking feature was the shape, an exceptionally neat and integrated design with a long, steeply raked windscreen. In construction it was equally different: a steel-skeleton frame clothed with plastic panels.

The single most significant factor in the Espace equation was its interior. The fact that it was spacious, airy and cleanly designed was secondary to its tremendous adaptability. There were three rows of seats for up to seven passengers in all, and each of these seats could be removed to increase luggage space. The front seats could

■ ABOVE *Tremendous adaptability was the Espace's strength: the front seats could swivel around, and you could fold down a central seat to make a picnic table.*

swivel round to face the others, and the central one could fold to make a table. Picnic-goers and mobile office workers were happy and Renault never looked back, dominating the European MPV market with successive Espace cars.

■ ABOVE *Up to seven seats could be fitted in the Espace, and then removed individually at will to turn it into a load-lugger.*

RENAULT ESPACE (1984–91)	
Engine	4-cylinder
Capacity	1995cc
Power	103–120bhp
Transmission	5-speed
Top speed	106–111mph (171–179kph)
No. built	147,960

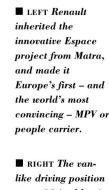

■ LEFT *Renault inherited the innovative Espace project from Matra, and made it Europe's first – and the world's most convincing – MPV or people carrier.*

■ RIGHT *The van-like driving position was criticized but it gave wonderful visibility.*

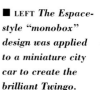

■ RENAULT TWINGO

One of the first things that Renault's new design chief Patrick Le Quément did when he joined the firm was to let it be known that Renault would be taking the lead in design terms, producing the best innovative new cars. The Twingo was the perfect expression of this ideal.

Le Quément skilfully extended the idea of the "one-box" design pioneered by Renault's Espace to the smallest car in the range. The line from the front bumper to the top of the windscreen was one elegant curve, broken only by the characterful hooded headlamps and bonnet (hood) cooling vents.

The hatchback Twingo may have looked cute from the outside but its cabin was its best feature. The digital instruments were sited in a pod in the centre of the dash, and all the switchgear was in contrasting colours and a tactile material. There was a huge amount of space, made all the more practical by the four individually reclining and sliding seats. Optional extras included a full sliding sunroof and air-conditioning.

Considering the avant-garde look of the Twingo, it was mildly disappointing to find old-world mechanicals underneath, taken directly from the antiquated Renault 5. The engine was harsh and the

■ LEFT *The Espace-style "monobox" design was applied to a miniature city car to create the brilliant Twingo.*

■ ABOVE *Little eyebrows over the headlamps and interesting air vents in the bonnet (hood) added character to the design.*

■ ABOVE *The Twingo was the ideal city car: very compact, nimble and economical.*

road behaviour nothing special. It took until 1996 for Renault to fit a modern engine in the form of a brand-new 1149cc unit with more power and extra zing. An automatic version dubbed Easy was launched at the same time.

The Twingo rose to become the best-selling car in France as buyers rushed to share in its chic, and a whole culture seemed to spring up around it. The millionth example was built in 1997.

RENAULT TWINGO (1992–)	
Engine	4-cylinder
Capacity	1149–1239cc
Power	54–58bhp
Transmission	5-speed manual 3-speed automatic
Top speed	93mph (150kph)
No. built	Still in production

■ RIGHT **Très jolie** – *the Twingo endeared itself to French buyers, who elevated it to the Number One best-seller in 1995.*

■ FAR RIGHT *Interior packaging was impressive, and the rear seats could slide fore-and-aft individually. Note the centrally mounted digital dash.*

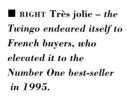

RENAULT

RENAULT SPORT SPIDER

So-called niche cars began to assume tremendous importance in the 1990s. Sales of mainstream models went down while low-production models sold proportionately more. Usually, niche cars were merely cleverly positioned conventional designs, but that is not a description you could apply to Renault's amazing Sport Spider.

The recipe was exciting, and wildly out of the ordinary for a major company like Renault. Here was a car built for one purpose only: pure driving enjoyment. The brief called for a lightweight, mid-engined sports two-seater, which was so pure in its ethos that it made do without a roof.

Indeed, the first Sport Spider made do without even a windscreen. The design team, led by the brilliant Patrick Le Quément, sculptured a radical shape, which incorporated a solid wind deflector where a windscreen might have been. Later on, a version was offered with a windscreen and wiper in

■ ABOVE *Renault was amazingly ambitious and adventurous with its Sport Spider: mid-engined, roofless and even devoid of a windscreen!*

■ BELOW *The styling was by Patrick Le Quément's innovative team at Renault. Although a return to the theme of the Lotus 7, it was unashamedly modern in appearance.*

■ ABOVE *A deliberately sparse cabin reflected the lightweight, bare-boned nature of this stripped-out road racer. Note the exposed aluminium basis (framework).*

place, but you still got no side windows or roof. That didn't seem to matter, because owners got the chance to drive and enjoy a car which had the look and feel of an advanced concept car.

The Sport Spider was equally radical in construction. The chassis was made of lightweight aluminium, which was also extremely rigid. The suspension was by race-inspired, rose (spherical)-jointed double wishbones, and the huge vented disc brakes came from the A610 supercar.

For its power, Renault opted to fit the sizzling 150bhp two-litre engine of the Clio Williams. That was sufficient to take it to 62mph (100kph) from rest in just 6.9 seconds.

■ RIGHT *The Sport Spider was also meant for racing, and Renault organized a one-make series, which supported British Touring Car races in 1996.*

Overall the Sport Spider was incredibly quick, both in a straight line and through corners. At 1740lb (790kg), it may not have been as light as a Lotus Elise, but it was certainly no heavyweight. It cornered with almost no roll.

The umbrella organization that created this unique car, Renault Sport, also ran a racing series exclusively for the Sport Spider. Race cars got more power (175bhp), so the action was fast, furious and incredibly exciting, and attracted many talented drivers and large viewing audiences.

This was perhaps the main point of the project. Renault knew the Sport Spider was not going to be a strong seller. It cost much more than rivals like the Lotus Elise and Caterham 21, and it was obviously too impractical to be used on a daily basis. Production volumes (at Renault's Alpine works in Dieppe) were tiny but the publicity gained for Renault's radical design work was huge – and its courage in putting such a machine into production at all was widely applauded.

■ ABOVE *In practice, most Sport Spider customers opted for the version with the full windscreen.*

RENAULT SPORT SPIDER (1995–)	
Engine	4-cylinder
Capacity	1998cc
Power	150bhp
Transmission	5-speed manual
Top speed	134mph (216kph)
No. built	Still in production

■ RIGHT *This image suggests that the Sport Spider was somehow acceptable in rain. True, you had a windscreen wiper on this version, but no roof or side windows.*

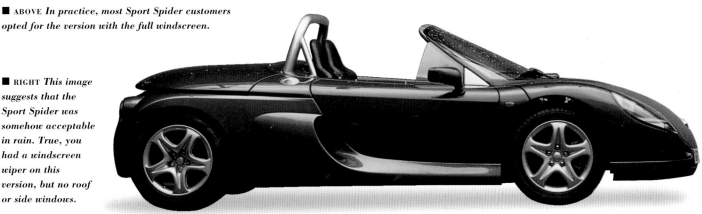

ROLLS-ROYCE

■ ROLLS-ROYCE CAMARGUE

The Pininfarina-styled Rolls-Royce Camargue, Crewe's flamboyant 1970s super-coupé, was a car for kings, princes, diplomats and superstars, a hedonistic two-door with no true rival. There was little to match it for size in the coupé stakes, and nothing approaching its price: the Camargue was the most expensive car on the market at its launch in 1975, 50 per cent dearer than a Corniche convertible.

Pininfarina was the natural choice for styling this new flagship, having done one-off designs on various Bentleys and Rolls-Royces in the 50s. Sergio Pininfarina even moderated his usual fee, but the styling got a luke-warm reception from some quarters. Farina did the interior, too, and designed a new dashboard using standard Silver Shadow instruments but with square black plates similar to an aircraft cockpit.

Launched in Sicily in 1975, the 120mph (193kph) Camargue was the first Rolls-Royce to have curved window glass and the first ever designed to metric dimensions. Mechanically, the car used a slightly more powerful 6.75-litre alloy Rolls pushrod V-eight engine and the usual independent suspension and complex hydraulic systems for the four-wheel disc brakes and self-levelling suspension.

■ BELOW *The Camargue was one of Rolls-Royce's most exclusive models. Over an 11-year period, only just over 500 were made.*

■ ABOVE *If you wanted the most expensive car in the world in 1975, the Rolls-Royce Camargue was your choice: a two-door coupé from the "best car company in the world".*

The star technical attraction of the £29,000 ($48,850) Camargue was its superb split-level air-conditioning system, which cost as much as a Mini and had the cooling capacity of 30 domestic refrigerators.

Each Camargue took six months to make, at a rate never higher than one per week. Unsurprisingly, the Camargue's best market was the USA (280 cars); 75 went to Saudi Arabia, while in Europe the car's best market was its native Britain with 136 sold.

■ ABOVE *Pininfarina also styled the interior, which was a palace of leather and wood, topped off by the most sophisticated air-conditioning system yet seen in a car.*

■ ABOVE *The clean and simple styling was done by Pininfarina, and was good enough to hide the model's considerable bulk.*

■ ABOVE *Fit and finish were superlative, while the detailing was quintessentially British, with hand-stitching and chrome handles.*

ROLLS-ROYCE CAMARGUE (1975–86)	
Engine	V-eight-cylinder
Capacity	6750cc
Power	Not quoted
Top speed	120mph (193kph)
No. built	534

ROVER

■ **LEFT** *Rover's David Bache admitted to using Ferrari's Daytona as inspiration. For a luxury saloon (sedan), the SD1 looked extremely sporty.*

■ ROVER SD1

With the P6 saloon (sedan) car range Rover had scored an undoubted winner, as European journalists recognized when they awarded it the very first Car of the Year award. Its successor, the so-called SD1, won it again in 1977.

For a Rover, the new SD1 3500 was pretty radical. Gone were all traces of chrome and all wood dashboards, which were seemingly permanent fixtures on Rover's past. Gone was the traditional, sober saloon layout in favour of a hatchback. And the interior (with its separate "box of instruments") was anything but conservative.

The architect of the SD1 shape was Rover's David Bache, and he had the probity to acknowledge the Ferrari Daytona as a direct influence: the

prominent mid-riff indentation and narrow headlamps were unmistakable. As a result, the 3500 looked distinctly sleek for 1976.

As launched, the 3500 had Rover's familiar V-eight engine. In other respects it was a mixture of old and new: the live rear axle and drum brakes were hardly ground-breaking, but the MacPherson strut front suspension sharpened up the handling considerably. Less powerful 2000, 2300 and

2600 six-cylinder versions followed.

The best model of all was the 1982 Vitesse with its 190bhp fuel-injection engine, lowered suspension, spoked alloy wheels and tailgate spoiler. Although it was rare (less than 4,000 were built), the Vitesse added a true performance edge to the SD1 range, which was replaced in 1986.

■ **ABOVE** *Rover departed from its traditions with the interior. Most notable was the separate binnacle housing all the instruments.*

■ **ABOVE** *The most powerful SD1 model of all was the Vitesse, with its 190bhp fuel-injected V-eight, lowered suspension and tailgate spoiler.*

■ **ABOVE** *The range of SD1 engines started with a 2.0-litre four-cylinder unit and went up to the popular 3.5-litre V-eight.*

■ **LEFT** *The ultra-quick Vitesse was a fitting end to an innovative chapter in Rover's long history.*

ROVER SD1 3500 (1976–86)	
Engine	V-eight-cylinder
Capacity	3528cc
Power	155–190bhp
Transmission	5-speed manual 3-speed automatic
Top speed	125–135mph (201–217kph)
No. built	113,966

S A A B

■ SAAB 99 TURBO

Sweden's aerospace leaders are very well known for their motor cars, and the string of models Saab has produced for over 50 years have always been unconventional, highly distinctive and instantly recognizable. The 99 Turbo was a model that launched Saab into a new era.

Saab's traditional front-wheel-drive layout remained, but the engine was new, jointly developed by Triumph and Saab. When it came to extracting more performance from this engine, Saab adopted turbocharging technology. Turbos were still a novelty in 1977, and Saab made the turbocharger an art-form of its very own. Long after other makers had abandoned this route, Saab plugged away with it as a performance and emissions device.

As a result of turbocharging, the standard fuel-injected 2.0-litre engine's power was boosted from 118bhp to 145bhp, very high for an engine of this size in 1977. New heights of performance were achieved – 0–60mph (0–96kph) in nine seconds, 125mph (201kph) top speed – though Saab never did iron out drastic turbo lag (the time it took for the turbo to cut in once the throttle had been pressed), nor a tendency to ferocious take-offs.

■ ABOVE *Fitting a 145bhp turbocharged engine into the unassuming 99 bodyshell created one of the performance icons of the 1970s.*

Saab pioneered the birth of the popular turbo car with the 99, and it became something of a cult car. Its ruthless turbo speed was quickly duplicated by others such as Audi and many Japanese makers, but none made the formula quite as attractive as Saab.

GTF 489W

■ LEFT *Under the forward-hinging bonnet (hood) was Saab turbocharger technology. The Swedish company made the turbo a real speciality.*

SAAB 99 TURBO (1977–80)	
Engine	4-cylinder
Capacity	1985cc
Power	145bhp
Transmission	4-speed manual
Top speed	125mph (201kph)
No. built	10,607

■ ABOVE *The 99 Turbo was angled toward safety: hence the impact (energy-absorbing) bumpers and headlamp wipers.*

■ RIGHT *No one could describe the 99 as a handsome car, but it was utterly unique.*

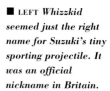

SUZUKI

■ SUZUKI SC100 WHIZZKID

When your traffic jams are in danger of becoming full-scale preserves, you are forced to do something drastic. The traffic jams of Tokyo and Osaka are the worst in the world, and the Japanese government's solution was to offer tax and parking breaks for owners of very small cars, called K-class cars.

Suzuki was the first company to offer a "K" car (in 1955), and its offerings have always been among the best. One interesting departure was the Cervo of 1972. This was a rare attempt to introduce some zing into the species. It was a two-plus-two coupé based on the rear-engined Suzuki Fronte saloon, measuring just 126in (320cm) long. It used a tiny 539cc two-stroke engine developing 28bhp. Its top speed of 65mph (105kph) was hardly thrilling, but then this was always intended to be a city car first and foremost.

For export Suzuki transformed the Cervo to become the rumbustious SC100 GX, which was known in Britain by its nickname, Whizzkid. The old two-pot engine was replaced by a 970cc four-cylinder Alto engine developing 47bhp, still sited in the tail. Now the little coupé really flew: its top speed jumped

■ ABOVE *The SC100's minute size can be gauged from this shot of one next to a Princess limousine. It was just 10ft 6in (320cm) long.*

■ ABOVE *It was the SC100's narrowness that was surprising to western drivers, but it was designed to conform to Japan's city laws.*

to 85mph (137kph), and there was sparkling acceleration and brilliant fuel economy to match.

It sold for a bargain price, too, and at this level no European maker had ever offered the SC100's lavish list of equipment: rev counter, reclining front seats, cigar lighter, front disc brakes and all-round independent suspension. Suzuki's British importers sold all the cars they could from 1979 to 1982, and now it has minor classic status.

■ LEFT *Whizzkid seemed just the right name for Suzuki's tiny sporting projectile. It was an official nickname in Britain.*

SUZUKI SC100 WHIZZKID (1979–82)	
Engine	4-cylinder
Capacity	970cc
Power	47bhp @ 5000rpm
Transmission	4-speed
Top speed	85mph (137kph)
No. built	894,000 (7,539 UK Whizzkids)

■ FAR LEFT *In action the Whizzkid was a real joy. Its 1.0-litre engine gave it nippy acceleration, but it was dodging through heavy traffic that was most fun.*

■ LEFT *The engine was sited in the tail, making passenger accommodation tight. Giugiaro was responsible for the styling.*

S U Z U K I

■ LEFT *It only had three cylinders and 658cc at its disposal, but a turbocharger assured that the Cappuccino was nippy and great fun to drive.*

■ SUZUKI CAPPUCCINO

If Cappuccino means a hot frothy coffee brew that gives you a lift when you need it, then Suzuki's car truly lived up to the name. The little Cappuccino sportscar began life as a show car in 1989, intended to show what could be done within Japan's "K" class mini-car regulations.

The reaction was so good that Suzuki went into production in early 1992 at the very limited rate of 200 per month. It was a car dedicated to the eccentric Japanese market, but there were still some exports to certain markets such as the UK.

The Cappuccino may have been a tiny car – just 130ins (330cm) long and 55ins (140cm) wide – but it was big on character. The rounded curves were reminiscent of the Austin-Healey Frogeye Sprite. The tail was cut off so

that you could almost stretch out a hand from the cockpit and touch the rear bumper.

The Cappuccino's *pièce de résistance* was its ingenious three-piece folding hardtop roof, which could be put into no less than five positions: fully enclosed; with one targa panel removed, both removed for "T"-bar motoring; all roof panels out but the rear-window section in place, or with the rear part folded down

for the complete open-air treatment.

Considering its 658cc three-cylinder engine, this was a surprisingly rapid little machine: if you removed the 87mph (140kph) top-speed limiter, it was capable of reaching 110mph (177kph) and sprinting from 0–60mph (0–96kph) in about nine seconds. It also handled incredibly well, sounded great and was amazing fun, all for a price that embarrassed any other sportscar.

■ ABOVE *The little Suzuki sportscar was designed around Japanese city car rules – just 130in (330cm) long and 55in (140cm) wide.*

SUZUKI CAPPUCCINO (1992–)	
Engine	3-cylinder
Capacity	658cc
Power	64bhp @ 6500rpm
Transmission	5-speed
Top speed	87mph (140kph)
No. built	Still in production

OTHER MAKES

■ SEAT

Spain's only home-grown marque started life as a branch of the Fiat empire in 1953, though it made several models unique to its own market. The most interesting of these was the Sport coupé of 1975–80, a small Fiat 128 3p rival. In the 1980s, Seat shed its Fiat chains and was bought by VW, which developed the marque as its sporty, Latin brand.

■ SKODA

The Czech-made Skoda marque can be traced back to the last century and has an illustrious history. By the 1970s, however, it had become a bit of a joke with its poorly made, wayward-handling rear-engined cars. The 1970–81 S110R coupé was the only vaguely "classic" model, although *Autocar* called the later 136 Rapid a "mini-Porsche". After a take-over by VW, quality and design improved.

■ STUTZ

An American industrialist bought the famous pre-war Stutz name in 1969 and launched a Virgil Exner-styled coupé to revive the long-lost marque. It was based on a Pontiac Grand Prix and was partly made in Italy. The tastefulness of the design might have been questionable but the model hit a chord in Hollywood and Arab markets. Various body styles were offered, including convertibles, saloons (sedans) and a mammoth Royale limousine.

■ SUBARU

Hill farmers loved the Subaru because it combined saloon (sedan) car urbanity with unstoppable four-wheel-drive transmission. Subaru built on this all-wheel-drive reputation with a range of interesting cars, culminating in the curious XT sports coupé, the Legacy saloon and the stunningly fast, rally-winning Impreza Turbo. Quality was always high on the agenda.

TALBOT-SUNBEAM LOTUS

■ TALBOT SUNBEAM LOTUS

"Put a Chrysler Sunbeam in your life" went the glib ad campaign for the new supermini from Chrysler in 1977. Within two years the group had been sold to Peugeot, which renamed all Chrysler models as Talbots, including the Sunbeam.

This thoroughly unexceptional hatchback was based on the Hillman Avenger, but that did engender one strong advantage: unlike most superminis, this model had rear-wheel drive and therefore exploitable handling. In short, it was ripe for a pump up in volume.

So the Sunbeam Lotus was born. Lotus had a history of engineering exciting road cars for mainstream makers (witness the Ford Lotus Cortina), and it did a wonderful job on the Sunbeam. Into the engine bay went Lotus's 2.2-litre twin-cam engine, whose 150bhp made this one of the fastest of the brat pack of rally-orientated specials around at the time: 121mph (195kph) top speed and a 0–60mph (0–96kph) time of 7.4 seconds.

Lotus also specified a five-speed ZF gearbox with first gear canted over to the

left in true racing style. The suspension was lowered and stiffened and brand new wide alloy wheels were created. The live axle and rear drum brakes may not have been very sophisticated but the set-up was certainly effective, as Henri Toivonen found out when he won the World Rally Championship in a Sunbeam Lotus.

The Sunbeam Lotus felt special, too, with its black (later also blue) paint, silver side stripes and prominent Lotus badging. Its career was cut short in 1981 when the plug was pulled on the whole Sunbeam range.

■ LEFT *While the Talbot Sunbeam was an instantly forgettable hatchback, the Sunbeam Lotus was a memorable performance car.*

■ BELOW *The Lotus 2.2-litre twin-cam engine was a comfortable fit. Its 150bhp power output made the Sunbeam the quickest hot hatch around.*

TALBOT SUNBEAM LOTUS (1979–81)	
Engine	4-cylinder
Capacity	2174cc
Power	150bhp
Transmission	5-speed manual
Top speed	121mph (195kph)
No. built	2,308

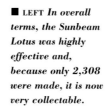

■ LEFT *In overall terms, the Sunbeam Lotus was highly effective and, because only 2,308 were made, it is now very collectable.*

■ RIGHT *Although it was based closely on the standard Sunbeam, the interior had a special rally-style feel to it.*

TOYOTA

■ LEFT *A Japanese Ford Mustang might be a good description of the first series Toyota Celica coupé.*

■ TOYOTA CELICA

In Toyota's sprawling range of models, the Celica stands out as a model that has consistently had integrity, style and a certain panache. In the Toyota scheme of things, it has always slotted in as the four-seater coupé model and for the first generations it was based on the Carina saloon (sedan) floorpan.

The first Celica appeared in 1970 with exactly the right balance of Coke-bottle styling and good proportions. For the first three years, the shape was always a notchback, but from 1973 an attractive new Liftback rear-end was also offered.

Various engines were used, the most popular being the 1600 and 2000,

■ ABOVE *In Liftback style, the Toyota Celica looked stylish, and it is a rare popular Japanese car with true classic credentials.*

■ ABOVE *Engines offered in the first-generation Celica range from a 1600 OHV up to a 2000 OHC, which developed 130bhp.*

TOYOTA CELICA (1970–77)	
Engine	4-cylinder
Capacity	1407–2289cc
Power	86–130bhp
Transmission	5-speed manual 3-speed auto
Top speed	102–112mph (164–180kph)
No. built	1,500,000

which were available in overhead-valve, overhead-cam and twin-cam forms. The best models were the GT versions with their extra power and sports equipment.

Toyota made sure, in true Japanese style, that every Celica was lavishly equipped. Even the most basic model had five gauges, a cigar lighter and stereo – real luxuries in those days.

The first-generation Celica was

replaced in 1977 by another stylish model, and then again in 1981. In 1985, the fourth-generation Celica became very much more stylish, with its smooth shape, pop-up headlamps and airy cabin, while a convertible version was new to the range. The 1989 edition sold as well as ever, and the Celica – now in its sixth generation – is a much-valued name in the Toyota portfolio.

■ ABOVE *The fifth-generation Celica was controversial in appearance but continued to forge ahead in the sales charts.*

■ RIGHT *This is a fourth-generation Celica, the first to be offered in a convertible body style.*

■ TOYOTA MR2

Twelve years after the launch of the mid-engined Fiat X1/9, Toyota came up with the first credible rival, the MR2, in 1984. Many expensive and exotic cars used the layout, but on affordable sportscars it had previously been the exclusive province of Fiat and, perhaps, the Pontiac Fiero in America.

MR2 stood for Midships Recreational 2-seater. By plundering the corporate parts bin Toyota created a good-value, sure-fire winner. It had a smooth, responsive twin-cam engine matched to immaculate mid-engined poise, a combination nobody could touch in the affordable sportscar arena. If traditionalists were suspicious of the

■ LEFT *Nothing less than a miniature Ferrari was how many press writers were unashamed to describe Toyota's brilliant MR2 sportscar.*

slightly bland angular styling – not to mention Toyota's questionable pedigree as a maker of exciting cars – then one drive around the block in the 120mph (193kph), 30mpg (48kpg) MR2 would almost certainly win them over.

Without doubt this was a very special car, justifying its reputation as a "mini-Ferrari". To keep its appeal broad Toyota made sure the MR2 rode like a saloon (sedan), was acceptably quiet and had a saloon-car driving position, not a low-slung sporty one that might have been off-putting. About the only black mark was the lack of cockpit space.

From 1986 there was a T-bar version with a removable roof section. In Japan, there was an even more exciting 145bhp supercharged model, but that was not imported to Europe because it would only run on unleaded fuel. It was sold in North America however, and there was a rather dull single-cam model for the home market.

The original MR2 has inspired two more generations of mid-engined Toyotas – and indeed Britain's mid-engined MGF – and looks set to become a sportscar classic of the next century.

■ LEFT *The MR2 badge came to mean everything enjoyable in handling terms.*

■ ABOVE *Thanks to its mid-mounted engine, the MR2 had not only sporting performance but also balance and poise.*

■ ABOVE *The standard 1.6-litre engine developed 130bhp and was sited, crucially, amidships.*

■ ABOVE *A new-generation MR2 replaced the squarish first series in 1989, expanded both in size and appeal.*

TOYOTA MR2 (1984–89)	
Engine	4-cylinder
Capacity	1587cc
Power	130bhp @ 6600rpm
Transmission	5-speed manual
Top speed	120mph (193kph)
No. built	166,104

TRIUMPH

■ TRIUMPH DOLOMITE SPRINT

The Triumph brand could be described as the BMW of the British car industry, since its strength lay in creating high-quality saloons (sedans) and sportscars with appeal for the enthusiastic driver. No other car summed this up so well as the Dolomite Sprint.

It was the engine that set the Sprint apart from most other British saloons of the 1970s; 16-valve technology was unusual in 1973, and Triumph's overhead-cam unit pioneered 16V technology two decades before it became *de rigueur*. The engine was simple, retaining a single chain-driven camshaft – and the design was so clever that it won a Design Council Award in 1974.

Certainly the engine was punchy and effective: 0–60mph (0–96kph) in under nine seconds was blistering for a saloon car in 1973, and embarrassed many so-called sportscars such as the MGB. The parent company, British Leyland, was keen to promote its sporting image and entered it for many races; a Sprint won the British Saloon Car Championships of

■ ABOVE *Triumph was a name associated with high-quality sporting saloons (sedans), and its Dolomite Sprint was the best of them all.*

■ LEFT *The 16-valve head on top of the 2.0-litre engine was ahead of its time in 1973, allowing 127bhp.*

TRIUMPH DOLOMITE SPRINT (1973–80)	
Engine	4-cylinder
Capacity	1998cc
Power	127bhp @ 5700rpm
Transmission	4-speed manual 3-speed auto
Top speed	115mph (186kph)
No. built	22,941

■ LEFT *The Dolomite Sprint lasted until 1980, and there was no direct replacement for its combination of rear-drive handling, keen performance and classic style.*

■ RIGHT *Italian stylist Michelotti was responsible for the stylish shape, even though it looked a little outdated by the mid-1970s.*

1975 and 1978, and many rallying successes were also scored.

The four-speed gearbox was derived from the TR6 and could be had with optional overdrive (standard from 1975). Alternatively, you could choose an automatic (which was very rare, with only 1,634 built). Other significant changes over the standard-issue Toledo/Dolomite were larger brakes,

■ RIGHT *In handling terms the Sprint was very sharp around corners, yet it was equally at home cruising down the motorway.*

■ ABOVE *Conservative in style, the interior was a rather messy array of classic dials in a wood facia.*

twin headlamps, a vinyl roof, front spoiler and alloy wheels (the first time any British production car had boasted these as standard).

The Dolomite Sprint had a rounded character. It was rapid and urgent when pressed, yet refined and relaxed when cruising in overdrive top. The handling was sharp at all times, mild understeer transferring into power oversteer if you provoked the car around bends.

The character of the interior was typically British: a full-width wood dashboard, hard-wearing trim and a profusion of traditional gauges.

Overheating, head gasket problems and poor-quality control marred an otherwise brilliant car. Also, it was poorly timed, being launched just as the Arab–Israeli conflict forced petrol shortages in Britain, and thirsty cars like the Dolomite Sprint fell out of favour.

An interesting Dolly Sprint variant was the 1975 Panther Rio built by a British specialist. This was a real mini-Rolls-Royce with hand-beaten replacement panels and a leather-and-walnut luxury interior. However, at three times the price of the Dolomite Sprint, only a handful were ever made.

■ RIGHT *Thanks to its advanced engine, the Sprint was a real performer; a 115mph (186kph) top speed was very healthy for a small saloon.*

When the Dolomite left production in 1980, that was sadly the end of the line for old-style Triumphs, and on the death of the model the Canley and Speke plants that had made it were closed. The following year the Honda-based Acclaim scotched any remaining pride in the marque, and it died three years later.

TRIUMPH

■ LEFT *Shocked was the only description of the public's reaction to the TR7. Harris Mann's styling was highly controversial.*

■ TRIUMPH TR7/TR8

The long line of TR-badged Triumph sports cars stretches back to the TR2 of the early 1950s and boasts some of the most charismatic sporting machines among its family. For many the ultimate TR7 was the runt of the litter, a quirky, unappealing product of the depressing British Leyland years of the 70s.

Certainly the TR7 was controversially styled: its lines were penned by Harris Mann (who also has the Austin Allegro to his credit). Build quality was never up to much: they tended to break down and catch fire, and the fixed-head model in

particular had very little appeal. Yet there is much to be said in favour of the maligned TR7. It sold in greater quantity than any other TR model, and in due course it became a rather attractive sportscar, at least in convertible form.

The original plan had been to make a drop-top TR7, but concerns about American legislation possibly banning open cars led Triumph to launch the new sportscar in fixed-head form only in 1975. For lovers of the machismo of Triumph TR straight-six power disappointment lurked, for British Leyland opted to fit a mere four-cylinder

■ LEFT *TR8 models were quite rare and much sought-after by aficionados.*

■ ABOVE *The TR7 enjoyed some success in rallying. With a V-eight engine in place, it was undoubtedly the quickest rally car around.*

■ RIGHT *With age the TR7 matured into a much better car. Sadly, the 16-valve Dolomite Sprint engine never made it into a production TR7.*

engine (the 105bhp Dolomite 1850 unit), driving through a Morris Marina four-speed gearbox. It was frankly not a sporting package at all.

Despite this, export sales went pretty well, especially in America (British sales did not begin until May 1976). Some of the criticisms were addressed with the adoption of a Rover SD1 five-speed gearbox in 1976 and lowered suspension the following year. But it was not until the drop-top model was added in 1979 that the TR7 turned the corner and became a real sportscar.

Still there was not enough power for many tastes. Triumph fitted its fine twin-cam Dolomite Sprint engine to its rally cars, but road cars were denied this option. Instead a stunning Rover V-eight-powered version was offered for export

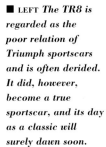

■ LEFT *The TR8 is regarded as the poor relation of Triumph sportscars and is often derided. It did, however, become a true sportscar, and its day as a classic will surely dawn soon.*

■ BELOW *With a Rover V-eight engine fitted, the TR7 became the TR8 and made some inroads into the American market.*

■ ABOVE *The interior was a typical 1970s concoction of black plastic. The drop-top looked particularly neat when folded.*

TRIUMPH TR7/TR8 (1975–81)	
Engine	4/V-eight-cylinder
Capacity	1998/3528cc
Power	105/137bhp
Transmission	4/5-speed manual 3-speed auto
Top speed	110–120mph (177–193kph)
No. built	112,368

only, dubbed the TR8. This model was actually quite rare (only 2,497 were made) and soon private owners were doing their own V-eight installations on TR7s, a fad that assumed epidemic proportions since the performance was so much better: 137bhp in "soft" tune meant 120mph (193kph) instead of 110mph (177kph) and 0–60mph (0–96kph) in 8.4 seconds. These figures could be greatly enhanced by tuning the V-eight engine to even higher levels.

Production finally ended in 1981, and few enthusiasts mourned the death of the TR7; far more sad for them was that this event marked the demise of the great Triumph sportscar. The TR7 was a car that never fulfilled its potential but which has recently started to gain a following. Its distinctive style and bargain prices make it a surprisingly attractive sportscar and a sure-fire candidate for future classic status.

T V R

■ TVR 3000S

TVR is one of those very British specialist car-makers, producing highly individual sportscars against all odds of success. The company's convoluted history goes back as far as 1947, and by the late 1970s it was firmly established as an iconic sportscar-maker.

The 3000S was the ultimate expression of a line of TVR sportscars stretching back to the 1957 Grantura. The TVR formula was very traditional: a separate chassis, glassfibre body, Ford V-six engine and luxuriously trimmed cabin. However, the idea of a convertible was new to TVR, and the 1978 "S" was its very first drop-top.

Based closely on a one-off produced for TVR boss Martin Lilley, the 3000S shared most of its specification with the fixed-head TVR 3000M Taimar, including the chassis and mechanicals. The bodywork was much lower, the doors were new and the tail was revised to incorporate a boot (trunk) lid. The lower scuttle line (hood line) also forced the instruments to be repositioned, with the rev counter (tachometer) now facing the passenger! Another traditional-style feature was removable soft side screens.

■ BELOW After more than 20 years, TVR's first convertible model was the 3000S, based on the 3000M seen in the background.

TVR 3000S (1978–79)	
Engine	V-six-cylinder
Capacity	2994cc
Power	142–265bhp
Transmission	4-speed
Top speed	133–150mph (214–241kph)
No. built	258

■ ABOVE Proving that the formula of a good-value, open-topped two-seater sportscar never died, TVR made a relaunched S model from 1986 until the mid-1990s.

The 3000S lasted for just one year, when a brand-new model range took over. In that time, a mere 258 cars were made, including 13 turbocharged cars. The 3000S Turbo is the most classic of all the earlier TVRs, having incredible performance and rarity on its side. The S was so sorely missed that in 1986 TVR relaunched it in revised form.

■ ABOVE In character and form, the 3000S recalled the great days of British rag-top roadsters like the Austin-Healey 3000.

■ ABOVE In action, the TVR was keen thanks to its Ford-derived V-six engine. With an optional turbocharger, it became a brutal machine.

■ RIGHT *With the Cerbera, TVR took a bold new direction in 1994. Here was its first two-plus-two model for a decade, its first all-new engine ever, and its most sophisticated project ever.*

■ TVR CERBERA

The Cerbera, named after a creature from classical mythology, was first seen at the 1994 Birmingham Motor Show. The long, low two-plus-two coupé may have drawn on other TVR models for its styling inspiration, but the outcome was the best model TVR had ever produced.

TVR's dynamic approach to design meant that, from debut to production readiness, the Cerbera took little over two years. Especially challenging was the all-new AJP V-eight engine, the first engine designed and developed entirely by TVR. It was initially used in racing TVR Tuscans but was refined enough to pass tough emissions tests. Like all other power plants used in TVRs, the AJP sounded raw and urgent, yet was also remarkably smooth.

The 4.2-litre engine developed a monstrous 350bhp and could rev as high as 7000rpm. Unencumbered by aerodynamic weakness, the Cerbera was capable of staggering performance: 0–60mph (0–96kph) in 4.0 seconds and up to 185mph (298kph) top speed. An even more thunderous 4.5-litre GT version was shown in 1996 – it had no less than 440bhp.

The Cerbera's chassis was quite capable of dealing with all that power. Its handling was safe yet exploitable and fun, while the ride quality was firm yet comfortable.

Undoubtedly one of the car's best features was its interior. The cabin was a haven of curves, which were almost sci-fi in the way their loops swathed the passengers – all four of them, at a push. The leather-stitched console incorporated classy black-on-white dials, while the underslung cluster of dials below the steering wheel worked very well. The Cerbera has become a fitting top-of-the-range model in TVR's line-up.

■ LEFT *The muscular, almost hot-rod appearance was widely admired, and neat details like the hidden electric door "handles" made it unique.*

■ BELOW *Not only was the design work stunning, the new Cerbera was one of the fastest cars of its day: 185mph (298kph) from TVR's AJP V-eight engine.*

TVR CERBERA (1996–)	
Engine	V-eight-cylinder
Capacity	4185cc
Power	350bhp @ 6500rpm
Transmission	5-speed
Top speed	185mph (298kph)
No. built	Still in production

■ ABOVE *The interior was equally innovative. The sculpted dashboard looked fabulous and the siting of an instrument cluster under the steering column worked very well.*

T V R

■ TVR GRIFFITH

TVR progressed into the 1980s with a new chairman at the helm, businessman and true enthusiast of the marque Peter Wheeler, who succeeded in turning TVR's fortunes around in no uncertain terms. Wheeler quickly realized what his customers wanted and concentrated his efforts on making convertible two-seaters with glassfibre bodies and brawny Rover V-eight engines.

The angular Tasmin series of 1980–91 was successful, if not exactly pretty, but the car it led to was undeniably a masterstroke. The Griffith had its roots in the TVR Tuscan racer

■ ABOVE Power slides were part and parcel of the Griffith package. With 280bhp on tap and no traction control system, care was always required.

■ LEFT The Griffith marked a radical break away from TVR's past into a bold and highly successful future. Mature styling and increasingly powerful V-eight engines headed the move.

first seen in 1988, which used the familiar TVR tubular chassis, uprated suspension and a monster 400bhp V-eight engine. Tuscans were raced in one of the quickest and most exciting one-make series in the world but were never officially homologated for road use.

The spirit of the Tuscan resurfaced in the new Griffith, a pukka road-going car launched at the Birmingham Motor Show in 1990, but not actually available until late 1991. The Griffith name harked back to the magnificently hairy Ford V-eight powered TVRs of the mid-

1960s. The justification for exploiting that heritage was certainly there, since the first edition of the new Griffith sported a V-eight engine based on the unit still used in the Range Rover, and developing either 240bhp or 280bhp.

In looks, the Griffith was far removed from TVRs of old: instead of angular and slightly gawky lines there were swoopy curves everywhere, a profile unbroken by styling adornments and clever air ducting at the leading edges of the bonnet (hood) and doors. Other neat styling details included a lack of

■ ABOVE Few other cars could match the character of the Griffith's leather-and-wood sculpted interior.

exterior door handles, evocative aluminium knobs in the cabin and a removable solid-centre roof section. Perhaps the most impressive aspect of the Griffith was that it was almost totally designed and produced in-house. Considering the brilliance of the end product, this was a remarkable achievement for such a small size company.

Testers were immediately impressed by the Griffith's character: an almost forgotten formula of raw V-eight power, rear-wheel drive and a rich, burbling exhaust note that was like no other car. Some even compared its overall impact to that of the E-Type Jaguar in 1961, since the TVR offered a similarly intoxicating brew of luscious curves, superior performance and exceptional value for money. No other sportscar offered so much for so little, and TVR grew in size and importance on the back of Griffith sales.

If the press was impressed with the Griffith, it was rapturous about the 1993 Griffith 500, whose engine grew in size to five litres and which developed no less than 345bhp. Now you could expect

■ RIGHT *The powerful Griffith boasted one of the greatest exhaust notes in motoring.*

a 0–60mph (0–96kph) time of a little over four seconds and mid-range punch and low-speed torque the like of which was simply not available elsewhere.

TVR followed up the Griffith with other models such as the cheaper Chimaera and even more potent Cerbera, but neither had the impact of the original, svelte Griffith, which remains one of the most popular models in the Blackpool manufacturer's repertoire.

TVR GRIFFITH (1990–)	
Engine	V-eight-cylinder
Capacity	3947–4997cc
Power	243–345bhp
Transmission	5-speed
Top speed	152–163mph (245–262kph)
No. built	Still in production

■ LEFT *The gauges had to be recalibrated in a Griffith to suit its phenomenal performance – up to 163mph (262kph) top speed. Cabin architecture was widely admired in TVRs.*

■ ABOVE *The innocuous-seeming "500" tag on the end of the Griffith name hinted at its new 5.0-litre V-eight engine and its 345bhp of raw power.*

VAUXHALL

■ VAUXHALL LOTUS CARLTON

In March 1989, news filtered through that Vauxhall was cooperating with Lotus in the development of a high-performance version of the Carlton saloon (sedan) (known as the Opel Omega outside Britain). When it became clear that General Motors was not going to follow the lead set by BMW and Mercedes-Benz in limiting top speed to 155mph (249kph), a minor media storm broke out. The new Lotus Carlton, said the press, was irresponsible: its top speed of 176mph (283kph) was more than anyone should ever be doing.

The controversy over the Lotus Carlton's speed was spurious. Any number of cars from Porsche, Ferrari or Aston Martin were capable of going much faster than this. The germ of the problem in the media's eyes was that the Carlton was a family car, capable of seating four adults in comfort. In practice, this was the Lotus Carlton's unique selling point, since no other supercar could transport so many so fast. In truth, it was all a storm in the proverbial teacup, since the volume of

■ ABOVE *A four-seater saloon (sedan) with a Vauxhall badge that was capable of 176mph (283kph) – it could only be the Lotus Carlton.*

■ LEFT *The prominent Lotus badging betrayed the work done to this 3.6-litre six-cylinder engine, which developed 377bhp.*

VAUXHALL LOTUS CARLTON (1989–92)	
Engine	6-cylinder
Capacity	3615cc
Power	377bhp @ 5200rpm
Transmission	6-speed manual
Top speed	176mph (283kph)
No. built	440

■ LEFT *Apart from a body kit, rear spoiler and five-spoke alloy wheels, this could have been any member of the rather ordinary Carlton/Omega family.*

cars sold was tiny; General Motors wanted to sell 1,100, but, in fact, only 440 were built because of the effects of the recession on sales.

The heart of the new supersaloon was its Lotus-developed 3.6-litre six-cylinder 24-valve engine. With its twin turbochargers, catalysts and advanced electronic management, it had huge power and torque. This, together with a Corvette ZR-1 six-speed gearbox, gave performance that was simply sensational. The Carlton accelerated faster than a Ferrari Testarossa and could reach 160mph (256kph) in under a mile.

Not only did it go fast in a straight line, it cornered and stopped with great finesse – a car with the Lotus badge on it should behave in no other way. Self-levelling dampers controlled the suspension superbly, providing handling of an order that belied the car's bulk. *Autocar* magazine described the braking as "the best we've tried on a road car".

Far from being a nervous, temperamental sportscar, the Lotus Carlton was benign and extremely safe. It would happily idle around town and was forgiving if abused. You could also go

■ LEFT *As well as being exceedingly quick, the Lotus Carlton was fun around corners and extremely safe into the bargain.*

shopping, since the boot was huge – and the rear seats folded to increase capacity.

Passengers were supremely cosseted. You got leather seats, a leather steering wheel, polished wood and pleated cloth trim, plus head restraints all round, six-speaker CD hi-fi, air-conditioning, electric windows and a sunroof. The

Lotus Carlton looked the part too. Its body kit comprised a deep front spoiler, wheel-arch extensions, aerodynamic side skirts, a new rear bumper and a boot spoiler; and there was just one colour, Imperial Green. The price was certainly high at £48,000 ($80,840) but entirely justified by the car's rarity and specification.

■ LEFT *Apart from the Lotus badging, 180mph (290kph) speedometer and extra electrical equipment, this could have been an ordinary saloon (sedan) car dashboard.*

■ ABOVE *This was a very comfortably trimmed car, with standard leather, polished wood and a host of equipment.*

■ RIGHT *In the tail-pipes of the Lotus Carlton was a whiff of the political controversy that surrounded its high top speed.*

VOLKSWAGEN

■ VOLKSWAGEN GOLF GTI

Based on the best supermini the mid-1970s had to offer, the VW Golf GTI was the father of the modern hot-hatch brat-pack, setting the standards for two generations to come. When the first Golf GTI appeared in 1975, who could have guessed that production figures would pass 1.35 million by the time the car reached its 20th birthday? Certainly not Volkwagen itself, which only envisaged a short run of 5,000 units for the sporty hatchback in those gloomy years following the fuel crisis.

The first prototypes were fitted with the 80bhp carburettor engine from the Audi 80 GT, but by the time the car appeared at the 1975 Frankfurt Motor Show it was sporting fuel injection for an output of 110bhp. The first model had a four-speed gearbox driving through the front wheels.

Outwardly there was very little to mark the GTI out from the standard Golf: discreet badging, side stripes, a chin

■ RIGHT *GTI became the term used to describe the hot-hatch generation, which was kicked off by this car, the Volkswagen Golf GTI, in 1975.*

■ BELOW *At first, the Golf GTI was considered a low-volume production special, but as the years progressed drivers recognized its greatness and bought it in huge volumes.*

■ ABOVE *Apart from the subtlest of spoilers and very minor trim differences, the GTI looked like a standard hatchback – the ultimate in understatement.*

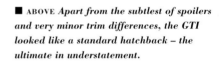

spoiler and plastic wheel-arch lips. The car was an instant hit, mixing punchy performance and tenacious knock-about handling from the firmed-up strut suspension with the practicality of a well-built three-door hatchback body of well proven durability. Production figures leapt from just over 10,000 in 1976 to 31,000 in 1977 and an amazing 42,000 in 1978.

The first right-hand-drive cars were not launched until July 1979, and that year multi-spoke BBS alloy wheels and a five-speed gearbox became part of the specification. There was a popular cabriolet version of the GTI, but the handling suffered from the extra weight involved in the strengthening of the Golf shell. The drop-top MkI body shape lasted right up until 1992.

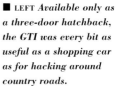

The best of the MkI GTIs was the 1800 model, replacing the 1600 in 1982. Power went up only marginally, but there was 8lb ft (10.8Nm) of extra torque, produced 1500rpm lower down. You could spot an 1800 by its new wider alloys, twin headlights and steel sunroof.

The GTI has lived through two generations since the demise of the MkI in 1985. The shape has been gradually rounded-off and the power – and luxury – increased. The 16-valvers of the mid-1980s packed 139bhp and came complete with electric windows, sunroof, central locking and driver's seat height adjustment. The facelifted 1990-model-year cars had deeper spoilers and power steering. The most coveted of all the MkIIs is the Rallye, a 5,000-off limited edition four-wheel-drive Golf using VW's Syncro system allied to a 1756cc supercharged engine. Built as a homologation special for rallying, the Rallye spawned the front-drive but supercharged G60. This was built on normal GTI production lines – unlike the Rallye, which was produced in Belgium.

■ LEFT *Available only as a three-door hatchback, the GTI was every bit as useful as a shopping car as for hacking around country roads.*

■ BELOW *The Mk1 convertible body style lasted right up until 1993.*

The concept continued in the MkIII Golf, either as a 155bhp 2.0-litre or the blockbuster 140mph (225kph) VR6 complete with super-sweet 2.8-litre V-six power – and that is a guaranteed future classic.

VW GOLF GTI MK1 (1975–85)	
Engine	4-cylinder
Capacity	1588–1781cc
Power	110–112bhp
Transmission	4/5-speed manual
Top speed	115mph (185kph)
No. built	350,000

■ LEFT *As a convertible, the GTI caught the mood of the 1980s, even if ultimately it was not as sharp-handling or rigid as the saloon.*

■ ABOVE *As a lightweight car with a powerful 1.6 or 1.8-litre engine, the GTI was a stormer, and its leech-like behaviour around twisty bends won it many friends.*

VOLKSWAGEN

■ RIGHT *The first-generation Scirocco was like a sharp-suited coupé version of the Golf, and in GTI form became a performance icon.*

■ VOLKSWAGEN SCIROCCO/CORRADO

Having relied on the rear-engined Beetle and various derivatives for four decades, Volkswagen underwent a complete revolution in the 1970s. It followed the lead taken by its sister company Audi in adopting front engines and front-wheel drive, completely renewing its model range and revitalizing its prospects.

The first of the new generation was the 1973 Passat, the most significant was the 1974 Golf, but the best was the Scirocco, launched two months before the Golf. The Scirocco was developed alongside the Golf and shared many common elements: platform, power trains, suspension and so on. Yet the Scirocco had style, and it also had clarity of purpose as an enjoyable coupé.

Italy's Giugiaro did a superb design job according to the folded-paper school of design. The shape was crisp, taut and light, and the rising glass line was utterly distinctive. For Volkswagen, the Scirocco was a specialist car, so it asked Stuttgart-based firm Karmann to build it. There was a large range of models, starting with

■ RIGHT *The second-generation Scirocco was styled in-house by VW and perhaps lost some of the Giugiaro charm of the first series.*

lowly 1100 and 1300 versions (though these were not widely exported). Far more satisfying were the larger-engined 1500 and 1600, but the best of all were the models powered by the 110bhp Golf GTI engine. These were variously badged GLI, GTI and Storm and became minor icons of performance motoring, not surprisingly with a top speed of

114mph (183kph) and a 0–60mph (0–96kph) time of 8.9 seconds. The Scirocco was an even better handling car than the Golf.

Automatic transmission was optional on all but the base models and the GTI engined versions. Four-speed manual was standard, although the very last 110bhp models got five speeds as

■ LEFT *All Scirocco models offered keen driving manners with a healthy dose of both style and practicality.*

■ ABOVE *The 1985 16V version of the Scirocco was quite a stormer, having 139bhp at its disposal.*

■ RIGHT *The GTX was a 111bhp mid-range model with a sporting close-ratio five-speed gearbox.*

standard. In 1981 an all-new Scirocco was launched, although to many it was a retrograde step. It had a blander profile, disappointing ride and handling.

Officially the 1989 Corrado was not a replacement for the Scirocco, which was perhaps auspicious because it was a far better car in all respects. The shape returned to the sharp, compact purposefulness of the original Scirocco, but it was underneath where the most impressive work had been done.

Put simply, the Corrado had one of the best front-wheel-drive chassis ever made. Neither the standard 136bhp 1.8-litre engine nor the supercharged 160bhp G60 engine did it justice; drivers had to wait until the 1992 VR6, with its blistering 190bhp 2.8-litre V-six engine, to exploit the chassis to the full: it was fluid, composed, controlled and extremely quick. By the time Corrado production finished in 1995, VW had made half a million.

■ ABOVE *With one of the best front-wheel-drive chassis ever, the Corrado was capable of stunning speeds around corners and, with the right engine, in a straight line, too.*

VOLKSWAGEN SCIROCCO MK1 (1974–80)	
Engine	4-cylinder
Capacity	1093–1588cc
Power	50–110bhp
Transmission	4/5-speed manual 3-speed auto
Top speed	89–114mph (143–183kph)
No. built	504,200

■ ABOVE *The Corrado was altogether a step up: every department had been improved.*

■ RIGHT *Fast, responsive, well-built and very good value, the Scirocco was a bestseller throughout the 1970s and 80s.*

VOLVO

■ VOLVO C70

Volvo design chief Paul Horbury said that he knew he had succeeded with the new C70 when he parked an example outside a prominent Californian hotel, and the valet attendants left it there for show rather than parking it in the parking lot underground.

Volvo's image in the 1970s and 80s was one of staid dreariness. The C70 was symptomatic of the company's turn-around. For its first sports coupé since the '60s it formed a co-venture with UK-based TWR (which engineered the chassis) and the result was the most desirable Volvo ever.

■ ABOVE *With the C70, Sweden's leading car-maker entered new territory, doing battle with Mercedes and BMW coupés.*

VOLVO C70 (1996–)	
Engine	5-cylinder
Capacity	2319–2435cc
Power	193–240bhp
Transmission	5-speed manual 4-speed auto
Top speed	137–146mph (220–235kph)
No. built	Still in production

■ ABOVE *The extremely handsome design of the C70 was penned by Volvo's British-born design chief Paul Horbury.*

■ RIGHT *In full convertible form, the C70 was yet another new departure for Volvo: never before had it offered a series (production) drop-top model.*

■ RIGHT *The C70 was as effective in action as it was great to look at. Its turbocharged five-cylinder engine and chassis dynamics engineered by TWR guaranteed it fine manners.*

The C70 borrowed much of its technology from the 850R saloon (sedan), including its 240bhp turbocharged five-cylinder engine driving the front wheels. Since it was lighter and more aerodynamic, the C70 posted even better performance figures than the 850R: 146mph (235kph) top speed and 0–60mph (0–96kph) in 6.7 seconds.

The cabin reflected functional Scandinavian themes, with a huge choice of colour schemes and tasteful, luxurious decoration. The ten-speaker

■ ABOVE *Volvo's new executive-class coupé looked like a convincing alternative to the best coupés in its class.*

■ ABOVE *Described as "typically Swedish", the C70 interior was a paragon of tasteful luxury. Full four-seater convertibles have always been rarities.*

hi-fi was among the best available anywhere in the world. Even more attractive than the coupé was the full convertible version announced shortly afterwards at the 1997 Geneva Motor Show.

The C70 secured a starring role in the Hollywood film *The Saint* starring Val Kilmer. Through the TWR connection, two of the first "customers" for the new Volvo were Formula 1 racers Damon Hill and Pedro Diniz, who both received a C70 as personal transport.

■ RIGHT *Even with its hood (top) raised, the C70 managed to look aristocratic and stylish.*

SECTION TWO
A-Z of Dream Cars

The pure dream car was born in 1939, when General Motors presented the Y-Job. This was not a car designed for general consumption, but one created by a styling department as an "ideas" car, a sleek, chrome-adorned sculpture designed to inflate passions and inspire imaginations.

The true golden age of dream cars was the 1950s, when the fantastic was normal and bizarre shapes and schemes were required. The aftermath of flying cars, nuclear-powered cars and gyroscopically controlled two-wheeled cars left America having had too much, and so the European design houses became the home of dream cars in the 1960s and 1970s. Here we bring dream cars right into the present day and beyond as we marvel at the creative genius behind some of the greatest cars ever designed.

ALFA ROMEO

■ BELOW *The incredible BAT series was created by Bertone. BAT 5 (left of picture) was unbelievably way-out for 1953, BAT 7 (foreground) was yet more outlandish, while BAT 9 (background) was merely extraordinary.*

Traditionally, Alfa Romeo has aligned itself to the major Italian carrozzieri (design houses) when it comes to design work. It has favoured Bertone, Pininfarina and Zagato, but many other independents have been drawn to the magic that is Alfa Romeo, and Alfa itself has occasionally produced a few of its own dreams in the metal.

Flying saucers and BAT-mobiles

After the Second World War, Alfa Romeo encouraged experimental bodies on its chassis. The Disco Volante ("flying saucer") race cars were a collaboration with Touring, for example, but of all Alfa Romeo's dream cars, the most spectacular were undoubtedly the incredible BAT series – BAT standing for Berlina Aerodinamica Tecnica. All were designed by Franco Scaglione of Bertone. The first in the series of three was the so-called BAT 5, which in 1953 was as way-out as they come. The aim was to create the most aerodynamic shape possible on an Alfa Romeo 1900 chassis, and with a claimed Cd figure of 0.23, it certainly was. The faired-in wings, sideways-popping headlamps and

hawk-like nose were striking enough, but it was the rear-end that got all the attention. Two huge, inward-curving wings rose fantastically around a long central rear "tunnel".

Things got even more outrageous with the BAT 7 prototype of 1954. The rear wings began at the windscreen pillars and became so curved-in that they almost touched each other over the razor-sharp central fin. Huge slots in the

fins equalized side pressure, and an even more aerodynamic Cd figure was claimed. By the time the third and final BAT 9 arrived in 1955, the rear wings had been clipped back to vaguely modest proportions, and there were now side fins from door to tail. After three successive years of making Turin Show crowds swoon, the BAT series was retired. All these cars have since been restored to a glorious condition.

■ LEFT *Ital Design was responsible for the 1969 Iguana prototype, based on the near-racing-specification 33. It was at one point scheduled for a production run but this didn't materialize.*

■ ABOVE *The 1971 Caimano was designed by Giugiaro and featured very angular lines, a flop-forward canopy, pop-up headlamps and an air brake. It was based on the Alfasud.*

■ LEFT *Proteo was the name of this Alfa Romeo Centro Stile prototype. It clearly prefigured the general profile of the later GTV production car.*

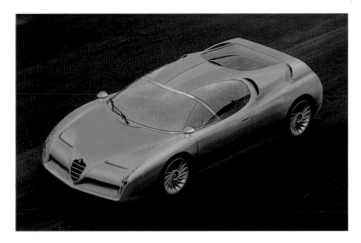

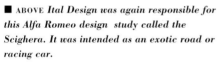

■ ABOVE *Ital Design was again responsible for this Alfa Romeo design study called the Scighera. It was intended as an exotic road or racing car.*

■ BELOW *Walter de Silva's masterful hand created the stunning Nuvola, an exercise in a classically inspired sports coupé.*

■ ABOVE *A long bonnet (hood), short tail and classically curved cabin excited public passions.*

Iguana, Spider, Proteo and Nuvola

Ital Design developed another spectacular Alfa concept car, the Iguana prototype of 1969. This was intended to enter production in a small series but it never did. Based on the 33 Stradale mid-engined chassis, it was notable for its brushed-steel body (ten years before the De Lorean) and sharp nose treatment.

■ ABOVE *Simple, stylish and sporty: the Nuvola's wood-and-chrome interior looked both backwards and forwards in time.*

To many eyes the 1994 Spider and GTV production models looked like show cars. To prepare the public for the radical shape of these newcomers, Alfa Romeo designed the Proteo prototype in 1991. This had the rising belt-line and bonnet (hood) cut-outs for the headlamps, which made the Spider/GTV so distinctive, but was based on the 164 and featured four-wheel drive, four-wheel steering and removable glass roof panels.

Alfa Romeo's design boss Walter de Silva was responsible for the striking Nuvola concept car shown at the 1996 Paris Salon. For its inspiration, this handsome car looked back to the great days, not only in its proportion and detailing but also in that it had a separate chassis, in theory allowing any body shape to be designed around it.

Alfa's own shape was extremely elegant: a long, classic bonnet, low, tapering rear, recessed lights and lots of chrome. Despite the retro flavour, it was also ultra-modern: 300bhp aluminium V-six engine, four-wheel drive, six speeds and glorious 18in (45.7cm) alloy wheels. Sadly, despite the precedent set by the Proteo, the Nuvola looked unlikely to become a production model.

AUDI

The Audi name is one of the oldest in the German motor industry, but its post-war career did not begin until Volkswagen bought the Auto Union combine, and the Audi name was revived in 1965. Audi has always been associated with front-wheel drive (and later four-wheel drive) quality saloons (sedans) and coupés.

The brand had just the right qualities for extending the Volkswagen-Audi Group's interests in bold new directions: sportscars, supercars and dream cars, but it was only with the Quattro that Audi finally became a truly aspirational marque.

Quattro Spyder, Avus Quattro

Without a doubt, the Quattro Spyder was the star of the 1991 Frankfurt Motor Show. It also signalled the way ahead for Audi in its exclusive use of aluminium in the bodyshell: this lightweight route would ultimately be used for the A8.

■ ABOVE *The Quattro Spyder was a four-wheel-drive mid-engined supercar. Its major significance was the use of aluminium in the bodyshell and a roof-line that inspired a generation of VW/Audi products.*

■ ABOVE *Emphasized by its unpainted finish, the aluminium structure of the Avus was ultra-smooth and lightweight, so that this 6.0-litre V-twelve car was capable of 211mph (339kph).*

Equally arresting was the dramatic shape (penned by Erwin Hammel) – all the more so for its bright orange colour scheme. Fitted with a mid-mounted 2.8-litre V-six engine and four-wheel drive, it was claimed to do 155mph (249kph) and reach 60mph (96kph) from rest in less than six seconds.

A mere two months later, at the Tokyo show, Audi upstaged every other concept car with its Avus Quattro, very similar in shape to the previous Spyder but finished in glorious polished aluminium. The quicksilver showstopper recalled the racing heritage of the great Auto Union record-breakers of the 1930s. The specification was breathtaking: a 6.0-litre 60V 12-cylinder engine arranged in three banks of four cylinders and developing 509bhp, four-wheel drive and six speeds. Audi claimed an amazing top speed of 211mph (339kph) and 0-60mph (0–96kph) in just three seconds.

TT and TTS Roadster

The name chosen for Audi's next-generation 1990s sportscars recalled the world's oldest motor race held on public roads, the Isle of Man TT. Destined to become a production model, the TT was first shown as a concept car at the 1995 Frankfurt Motor Show.

■ BELOW *Undeniably Germanic in form and function, the TT coupé recalled in spirit its ancestors of the 1930s, the great Auto Union racers.*

■ LEFT *Polished aluminium detailing reflected the use of aluminium in the doors, bonnet (hood), boot (trunk) and engine. Circular dials and red leather trim completed a classy cabin.*

■ BELOW *At the 1995 Tokyo Motor Show Audi presented the TTS roadster, probably even more desirable than the TT coupé. Note the hood (top), held taught like a parachute.*

■ RIGHT *Strong, simple lines epitomized Audi's philosophy of design, while its high performance potential was realized by a turbocharged 210bhp engine.*

A group of young Audi designers created the TT as a car they desired to own, but was accessible to a wide public. Hence, existing Audi technology was used wherever possible: the five-cylinder turbo engine from the A4, and Audi's four-wheel-drive system was used. The 150bhp engine was claimed to produce a very fast top speed of 140mph (225kph).

In style the TT was described as "Germanic" and a vision of the Audi brand. The curves recalled Bauhaus design and pre-war Auto Union racing cars. The show cars' silver paint emphasized the Teutonic element and also betrayed the choice of aluminium for the engine, doors, bonnet and boot (hood and trunk).

The two-plus-two interior was functional and sporting. Traditional sportscar themes were pursued, such as circular dials, leather upholstery, aluminium grab handles supporting the centre console, even exposed rivets securing many metal items. Following quickly on the heels of the TT hatchback coupé show car, at the 1995 Tokyo Motor Show Audi presented the TTS roadster. The most obvious changes were the open top, only two seats, larger wheels and thong-laced leather seats. Under the bonnet, the engine was a more powerful "concept" evolution of the A4 1.8-litre turbo engine, developing no less than 210bhp – good for 149mph (240kph) and 0–60mph 0-96kph) in six seconds.

The most exciting part of the TT/TTS twins story was that Audi planned to put the models into production before the end of the century at a plant in Hungary. This meant that they would be ready to compete with such rivals as the Porsche Boxster and Mercedes-Benz SLK.

■ RIGHT *Both the TTS and its fixed-head TT brother were scheduled to go into production by the end of the century.*

BERTONE

Alongside Pininfarina, Bertone is the greatest design house in the world. Its history stretches back to 1912, when Giovanni Bertone founded a *carrozzeria* in Turin. Bertone's great days began in the 1950s, and it became the first port of call for numerous manufacturers seeking the right design for their new products.

Nuccio and his wicked children
Giovanni's son Giuseppe "Nuccio" Bertone steered the company through its greatest era, boasting a propensity for spotting brilliant young talent: such

great names as Giugiaro, Gandini, Michelotti and Scaglione all served their apprenticeships at Bertone. No one doubts the brilliance of Bertone's production designs such as the Alfa Romeo Giulietta Sprint and Giulia GT or the Lancia Stratos, nor its capacity for manufacturing for Alfa, Fiat, Volvo and others. Bertone also badged several models under its own name, such as the Fiat-engined 850 Coupé, Ritmo Cabriolet and Freelimber off-roader.

The most striking category of Bertone designs were undoubtedly his show cars,

■ ABOVE *Nuccio Bertone was unquestionably one of the most profoundly influential figures in the car world, with a brilliant eye for design talent and an unending capacity to surprise. He died in 1997.*

■ RIGHT *The Marzal was an adventurous step forward in four-seater supercar design. It directly inspired the production of the Lamborghini Espada, although not with the Marzal's glass gullwing doors.*

which he called his "children", and especially those "wicked children", which were controversial or inspired comment. Bertone was rarely interested in practical innovations in his show cars: these were pure dream machines.

Marzal and Carabo
Bertone produced many special bodies in the 1950s on the chassis of Alfa Romeo, Jaguar, Aston Martin and Maserati, but he did not really get into his stride as a producer of dream cars until the late 1960s. One of the most striking of all was the 1967 Lamborghini Marzal, a very novel concept car, which directly inspired the later Espada series production car. Bertone's scheme for a four-seater Lamborghini called for enormous gullwing doors with surfaces almost entirely of glass. This solved the problem of entry to the rear seats and drew attention to the idea. So did the all-silver upholstery!

■ LEFT *The Stratos HF prototype of 1970 was just 33in (84cm) high. The windscreen opened for the passengers to enter, and the steering wheel folded away for easier access.*

■ OPPOSITE *With the Lamborghini Bravo, Bertone experimented with the use of glass as an integrated part of the design.*

■ ABOVE *The Villager was a typical product of the early 1970s fad for beach/leisure vehicles.*

■ RIGHT *Bertone designed the X1/9 for Fiat, and his own Dallara radical show-car interpretation was intended for racing in the Group 5 class.*

A year later, the Carabo marked another mould-breaking shape: something between a wedge and an arrow. The visual equivalent of a Doppler effect was created by the fluorescent red nose and green tail. The upward-hinging doors anticipated Bertone's Countach by four years, and gave the car its name – Carabo is a contraction of the Italian for "beetle".

Stratos, Bravo and Sibilo

With the 1970 Lancia Stratos show car, Bertone teetered on the edge separating car design from pure sculpture. This amazing machine was designed with a completely free hand and was a car of extremes. It was so low that the driver had to flip up the windscreen and walk in over the front end. To see out, you looked through small windows placed directly behind the front wheels – there was no rear visibility at all. To access the mid-mounted engine, a triangular shape panel hinged upwards like a piano.

The 1974 Lamborghini Bravo (based on the Urraco) integrated elements like the lights, air intakes and rear quarter-lights into the design of the car itself. Another feature was the dark glass, which appeared to form a seamless pane. This theme would be refined with the 1978 Sibilo, an exercise based on the Lancia Stratos. Here the distinction between the metal and glass surfaces was blurred, creating the impression that the body was hewn from a single piece. Inside, the Sibilo's steering wheel was a single solid piece, and the dashboard featured digital instruments set very far back directly in the driver's line of sight.

BERTONE

■ ABOVE *Bertone built his Navajo show car on an Alfa Romeo T33 racing chassis, complete with a flat-12 engine. The use of front and rear wings aided downforce.*

■ RIGHT *Along with many others, Bertone must have been disappointed by the styling of Jaguar's XJS. This is his re-interpretation, called the Ascot.*

Rainbow and Athon

Many observers felt that Bertone's Ferrari Dino 308 GT4 was a disappointingly boxy production design. Perhaps to address such criticism, Bertone produced the Rainbow in 1976, based on the mid-engined 308. The name came about because the solid roof could pivot to the vertical and drop down behind the seats, so making the car perfect for rain or sun. The angular lines were uncompromising: there were literally no curves to be seen other than the wheels and exhaust pipes. This model had the distinction of being advertised in the exclusive American Neiman Marcus store catalogue in 1979 but, with a price tag of $200,000, it scared any customers off.

Extending Bertone's reputation for creating pure dream cars, the 1980 Athon was an uncompromising roadster based on the Lamborghini Urraco. It typified Bertone's penchant for bold, squarish shapes joining together to form a whole, themes that would be extended by such cars as the Alfa 6-based Delfino and Citroën BX Group B-based Zabrus.

Bertone's Corvette-based Ramarro won many awards and one designer described it as "representing Bertone's soul". Its hard, geometric shape was emphasized by a completely blacked-out

■ ABOVE *The name Rainbow was chosen for this Ferrari-based car because of its potential for use in rain or sun. This show car was unusual in that it was actually offered for sale to special order.*

■ RIGHT *Bertone began taking new dream-car directions with the 1983 Delfino, a three-box coupé based on the Alfa 6.*

■ LEFT *The name Sibilo means "hiss" or "whizz" in Italian, accurately conveying the combined senses of speed and the blurring of the line between metal and glass surfaces.*

■ BELOW *The 1986 Zabrus predicted future shapes like the Alfa Romeo 145. Its basis was the fearsome Group B rally Citroën BX.*

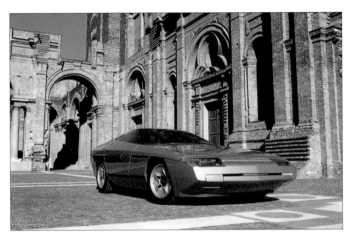

■ ABOVE *Using Chevrolet's Corvette as a basis, the Ramarro was long, low, cleanly finished and sleek.*

■ RIGHT *Bertone's interiors were typically highly sculpted, simple and clean. This is the Athon's exotic cockpit.*

glass top, but not everyone thought the shape had the timeless quality of previous Bertone efforts.

The 1988 Genesis was a people carrier with a difference: it had a 455bhp Lamborghini V-twelve engine mounted between the front passengers. There was space for five people, the rear three sitting in "arrow" formation. Its style and layout were controversial, and the point of having a V-twelve engine was undermined by a long-legged three-speed automatic gearbox.

■ BELOW *The 1980 Athon, based on a Lamborghini Urraco, was a widely admired roadster show car.*

BERTONE

■ ABOVE *Marking a return to the impact of the great show cars of the 1970s, the Nivola used a Corvette ZR1 engine.*

■ RIGHT *"People carriers" were never so radical as Bertone's startling Genesis. The gullwing doors suited its mechanical basis – the Lamborghini Countach V-twelve!*

Nivola, Rush and Blitz

For the Nivola of 1990 (its name recalled the great Italian race driver Tazio Nuvolari), Bertone turned to the Chevrolet Corvette ZR1 for its motive power – and, like all Bertone's show cars, it was a full runner. The bright-yellow concept car featured a targa roof, which stowed above the engine, and hydropneumatic suspension. Most bizarrely of all, it had massaging vibrators in the backs of the seats, claimed to relieve the stress of long

journeys! Perhaps they were needed, for the Nivola measured an expansive 78in (1.98m) wide.

At the 1992 Turin show, Bertone presented two concept ideas. One was part of Fiat's Cinquecento concept display, an outlandish two-seater 4x4 buggy called the Rush. The other was the Blitz electric sportscar. The Blitz was described as a car/bike cross-over.

The sportscar angle was not out of place in an electric car since power response is near-immediate in electric vehicles.

Karisma and Slalom

Despite its rather tacky name, the 1994 Karisma was a fine-looking car based on a Porsche 911 platform. It revived the gullwing four-seater theme pioneered by the 1967 Marzal, and deliberate

■ RIGHT *The exposed front wings and near-tandem seating position echoed Bertone's intent that the Blitz should be a motorcycle/car cross-over.*

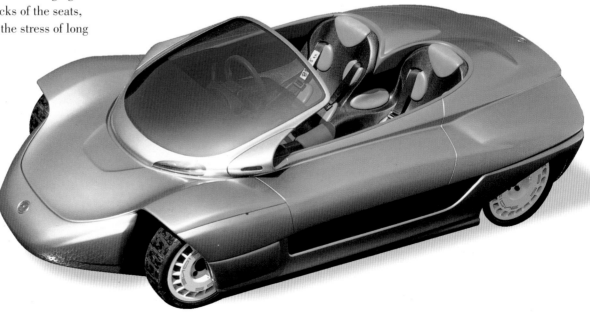

■ RIGHT *With its big gullwing doors and four-seat interior, the Porsche-based Karisma was a spiritual successor to the Marzal, seen in the background.*

reference was made to this early Bertone design. The leather-trimmed interior had full seating for four adults, and the gullwing doors were claimed to "allow dignified entry".

A startling shade of orange – said to be inspired by Bertone's favourite champagne, Veuve Clicquot – at least made the 1996 Slalom stand out, not that it needed to with its sports-coupé shape and audaciously designed stacked front and clipped-in rear lights. Adjustable rear seats made the two-plus-two interior fairly practical. Based on the Opel/Vauxhall Calibra Turbo 4x4 floorpan, it was also surprisingly effective to drive.

Nuccio Bertone died in 1997, but left behind him a design and manufacturing empire with the highest reputation, 1500 staff and dozens of clients from around the world. Perhaps his most important characteristic was an ability to spot talent: Marcello Gandini and Giorgetto Giugiaro, the two greatest car designers of recent years, both served as apprentices under Bertone.

■ ABOVE *The orange paintwork of the Opel Calibra-based Slalom was said to be inspired by Nuccio Bertone's favourite champagne.*

■ ABOVE *Rush was the name of this fun-packed, little, two-seater sports off-roader, based on Fiat's tiny Cinquecento.*

■ ABOVE *The Lancia Kayak was undoubtedly more accomplished than Lancia's own later coupé effort, the Kappa.*

CHRYSLER

From Thunderbolt to Turboflite

After GM's Buick had produced the Y-Job, the world's first ever "dream car", in 1939, the first to follow up the idea was its rival Chrysler. Two years later its styling chief Alex Tremulis created the Thunderbolt, a bulbous retractable-top two-door with push-button controls.

After the war, Chrysler collaborated with the Italian design house Ghia to create such dream cars as the Plymouth XX-500 and Chrysler K-310 in 1951. A man called Virgil Exner emerged as the head of styling for Chrysler and directed a whole string of unusually smooth shapes by American standards, notably the Firearrow series of 1953–54, the 1954 De Soto Adventurer and the ill-fated 1956 Norseman, which sank the Andrea Doria.

The Ghia connection resulted in the striking 1956 Dart, an impressively clean, aerodynamic car (claimed to have one third the drag of conventional cars) with probably the tallest rear fins ever seen. The steel roof was designed to slide back into the rear compartment.

■ ABOVE *Under the tutelage of Virgil Exner, Chrysler produced some extraordinary show cars. This Plymouth Special was seen in the 1957 film,* Bundle of Joy.

■ BELOW *By 1965, the first American dream-car golden age was already over, as this tame Plymouth VIP shows. Its main feature was a cantilever roof and rear "office".*

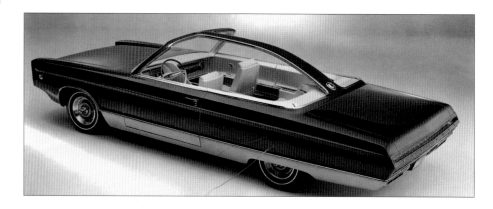

■ LEFT *If you are wondering how you got into the outlandish 1961 Turboflite, when you opened the door, the whole roof and glass lifted up like a clamshell.*

By 1958, Exner's direction had lost its way a little, the Imperial d'Elégance being anything but elegant. The 1961 Dodge Flitewing advanced an interesting solution for a hardtop coupé: the windows opened outwards and upwards automatically on exit. The Turboflite went one better: the whole roof and glasshouse lifted up as one for entry.

Lamborghini revives the dream

Throughout the 1960s Chrysler experimented in the dead-end of turbines, handlebar steering and even

■ LEFT *A liaison with Lamborghini produced the 1987 Portofino, a dramatic mid-engined four-seater with Lamborghini V-eight power.*

■ LEFT *Plymouth's Speedster show car was only 10in (25.5cm) longer than a Mini. It had a mid-mounted 2.0-litre engine.*

■ ABOVE *One of Chrysler's most daring show cars was the Plymouth Slingshot, designed for optimum acceleration.*

vacuum-operated ashtrays. As the years progressed, the dream cars got more predictable; the 1965 Plymouth VIP was typically unadventurous, and Chrysler seemed to have a rude awakening from its dream state.

It took until the 1980s for Chrysler (along with other American manu-facturers) to rejoin the dream train and re-establish the American tradition for producing other-worldly machinery.

Perhaps it was Chrysler's purchase of Lamborghini in 1987 that set the ball rolling, although the rise of designer Tom Edle and president Bob Lutz had a huge influence. Certainly its immediate action to create a co-project, which would demonstrate the abilities of the new alliance, produced one of the great show cars of the 1980s. At the Frankfurt Motot Show in the autumn of 1987, the Portofino was displayed. Chrysler described it as the "ultimate mid-engined touring sedan", and most were

inclined to agree. Using a 250bhp Lamborghini Jalpa V-eight engine, this imposing machine featured seating for four, a clamshell bonnet and boot (hood and trunk), and four Countach-style doors, which opened upwards for entry.

The Plymouth Speedster of 1989 was remarkable for its size: at 130in (330cm) long, it was minuscule by American standards, but this marked an attempt to link motorcycle and sportscar themes for the youth market. The result

included a small air deflector, central pop-up headlamps and an interior trimmed in wetsuit rubber.

The wild styling of the 1991 Chrysler 300 show car picked up on Viper themes and catapulted them into the arena of a 17ft-long four-door sports saloon (sedan). Under the long bonnet sat the 8.0-litre V-ten Viper engine, and in front of it was an Allard-style grille. The rear doors were "suicide" (i.e. rear-hinged).

■ RIGHT *Extreme light weight and optimized aerodynamics were behind the Aviat, whose aerospace bias was notable.*

CHRYSLER

■ ABOVE *The name Back Pack suggests outdoor use, and that is precisely what this Plymouth concept car was designed to do.*

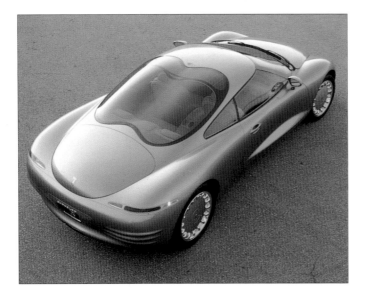

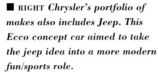

■ ABOVE *The double-curvature rear glass of the Thunderbolt was extremely effective. The cab-forward design permitted ample space for four passengers.*

■ RIGHT *Chrysler's portfolio of makes also includes Jeep. This Ecco concept car aimed to take the jeep idea into a more modern fun/sports role.*

Other 1991 show debuts were the Jeep Wagoneer 2000 (a huge estate car (station wagon) with massive 20in (50.8cm) wheels) and the Dodge Neon (a compact saloon (sedan) with sliding doors, fabric roof and a three-cylinder two-stroke engine).

Chrysler increasingly investigated "cab forward" design, and the most extreme expression to date was the 1992 Cirrus; it genuinely did point the way toward Chrysler's future saloon output, although the pillarless construction sadly did not.

From Expresso to Jazz

The 1994 Expresso was a curious taxi-styling exercise described as "Happy Face". Seen from the sides, the windows formed eyes and the bold side accent became a smiling mouth. Making sure you remained happy inside the car was a computer games console and an LCD entertainment module.

Also at the 1994 Detroit show was the Venom, a revival in spirit of the great muscle-car years of the 60s. Its matt-black bonnet (hood), chiselled nose and scooped body sides may have looked evocative but the reality underneath was less intoxicating: it was based around a Neon with a 3.5-litre V-six engine taken from the LH saloon.

Challenging GM's Ultralite in the aerodynamic, low-weight stakes was the

LEFT *Undeniably handsome, the Thunderbolt reflected a new design ethos at Chrysler, the so-called "cab-forward" approach.*

■ RIGHT *This is the 1995 Eagle Jazz show car, whose design traits such as large-diameter wheels and snubbed nose predicted future trends but could not revive the Eagle nameplate.*

Aviat. Looking remarkably similar to the Ultralite, it was claimed to weigh less than 2000lb (900kg) and have a Cd figure of 0.20, thanks to clever ducting at the front and almost jet-plane-style exits in the tail.

For 1995, Chrysler produced a stunning retro-coupé, which owed more than a nod to the 30s Bugatti that shared its name – Atlantic. It was a two-plus-two based around a Viper chassis and was styled by Tom Gale as an expression of the coupé art form. Power

came from two Neon engines joined together to make an eight-cylinder block, with an estimated power output of 325bhp.

Inside, the Atlantic bristled with cushioned leather, rosewood and classical, Swiss-watch-style dials.

When Chrysler's subdivision, Eagle, presented the Jazz at the 1995 Detroit show, pundits instantly recognized this as the future of the model's styling: a bold, snubbed nose, a very long wheelbase and a striking two-piece hatchback tail.

■ ABOVE *For the Atlantic, two Chrysler Neon four-cylinder engines were joined together to make a single 325bhp V-eight with a glorious architectural feel.*

■ RIGHT *The ostentatious Atlantic was made into a proper running car, although, unlike the Viper on which it was based, it looked unlikely to reach production.*

■ RIGHT *The Atlantic was an unashamed throw-back to the design world's glory years of the 1930s. It even shared its name with the car that inspired it, Bugatti's sublime Atlantic coupé.*

CHRYSLER

■ LEFT *The Chrysler LHX was a highly advanced-looking luxury saloon (sedan) concept. Its flowing lines were echoed in later production models, though the low roof-line proved impractical.*

■ BELOW *The more aggressively styled sister to the LHX was the Dodge Intrepid ESX. It had a diesel/electric hybrid engine.*

Pick-ups and concept cars

The Dakota Sidewinder, seen in 1996, reflected an American passion for pick-ups, taking it to the extreme. Chunky, open-topped with a narrow hot-rod-style windshield and a Viper GTS-R 600bhp engine under the bonnet (hood), this was bound to make an impression. The "gas" pedal was marked "Go" and the brake pedal "Whoa"! Perhaps even more outrageous was the Dodge T-Rex, a 6-wheeler based on the Ram pick-up and sporting a 500bhp V-ten engine.

At the opposite extreme. Chrysler presented a China Concept Car, created to satisfy a request from the Chinese

■ LEFT *The engaging little CCC was intended as a vehicle for China, although Chrysler hinted that its all-plastic body (surely inspired by the Citroën 2CV) could have a wider impact on production processes.*

authorities to tender for a new "people's car". The CCC seemed an up-date of the Citroën 2CV, even down to its Bauhaus glass treatment and full fabric roof. Sadly production looked unlikely.

Perhaps Chrysler's most important concept cars for many years appeared at the 1996 Detroit show: the stunningly sleek and sensual LHX and ESX. These were not guts-and-glory sportscars, merely four-door luxury saloons (sedans), but they succeeded in getting everyone excited. The ESX was the more aggressive, despite its diesel/electric hybrid power. The LHX was more traditional and flowing, with a huge

■ LEFT *Imposing in every way, the grand Phaeton measured over 21 ft (5.4m) long and had enormous 22in (55.8cm) aluminium wheels.*

■ BELOW *The Jeep Icon interior had an exposed, pared-down, almost industrial feel to it.*

■ RIGHT *The "dual-cowl-phaeton" style means separate front and rear compart-ments, even two windscreens. The opulence of the rear compartment was unstinted.*

cabin featuring rear-seat airbags and entertainment centre. Its fuss-free, almost pancake-flat shape drew admiring comment from all quarters and some themes appeared in the 1998 model year Concorde/Intrepid production cars.

From Copperhead to Phaeton

A return to sportscars marked the 1997 Detroit show, and the Dodge Copperhead was an exciting 2.7-litre V-six two-seater. It took its name from the Copperhead snake; the dashboard was said to mimic the shape of the snake's head.

Chrysler concepts did not stop there, as it also showed the Pronto small family car, Jeep Icon (the first monocoque Jeep, and very trendy-looking), the Dakar and

– probably the most spectacular of all – the Phaeton. This leviathan measured 5.4 metres long and was powered by a 5.4-litre V-twelve engine. It was a modern homage to the great "dual-cowl-phaeton" style typified by the 1940 Newport parade car. The rear passengers had their own windshield, and even their own set of instruments. This was a car conceived to titillate the fancies of a mythical future generation of *concours*

d'élégance devotees, a sad evocation of champagne-glass applause being pushed by Chrysler in its literature.

If there was one thing Chrysler had proved, with its cab-forward revolution and projects like the Viper and Prowler, it was that dream cars need not be confined to an upper stratum strangled by *haute couture* but could genuinely percolate through to the real world, and reach a truly wide public.

■ RIGHT *The Jeep Icon shown in 1997 boasted lightweight unit-body construction, while its youthful looks promised much for the future.*

CITROËN

Experiment is the very life-blood of Citroën, as innovations have made their way into its road cars years before other manufacturers come up with similar solutions. One has only to think of the great *Traction-avant* (front-drive) DS, GS, CX and SM to realize how advanced, how individual, was Citroën's technology.

Karin, Xenia and Eole

Falminio Bertoni was the leading light behind Citroën's glory years, but for its birth into the pure dream-car era it appointed a new design chief, Trevor Fiore. His first work was the Karin, presented at the 1980 Paris show. Its pyramid shape was utterly unique, and a reflection of a logical driving position with the driver seated in the middle. This was followed the next year by the Xenia, a rather more conventional hatchback, which nevertheless showed crisp, clean lines.

It was the arrival of American Art Blakeslee that shaped Citroën's real future. Steeped in Peugeot-Simca-

■ LEFT *The Activa was Citroën's 1988 vision of an advanced executive car. Sophisticated technical features were managed suspension, four-wheel drive and four-wheel steering.*

■ RIGHT *Activa 2 was a two-door development of the Activa theme, with a fully active suspension system, which made it into production in the Xantia road car.*

■ BELOW *In 1996, Citroën invited students to design a city car for the 21st century. Norwegian Per Ivar Selvaag's extraordinary proposal was adjudged to convey Citroën's cultural values in a radical package.*

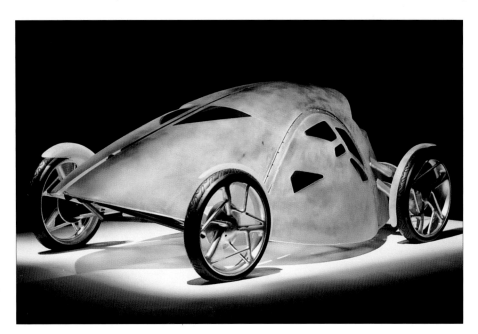

Chrysler values, he began with the ECO 2000, an ultra-economical small car project, and built up to the Eole. Named after Aelos, Greek god of the wind, Citroën's 1985 exercise was a car designed to cheat the wind. Based on CX components, it was a full four-seater claimed to have a Cd figure of just 0.19, achieved by using flexible body panels, cooling flaps and suspension that lowered as speed increased.

Activa, Citéla and Xanae

The name Activa was used on Citroën's flat-riding Xantia production car, but it first appeared in 1988 on an advanced four-door prototype. This had four-wheel drive and four-wheel steering,

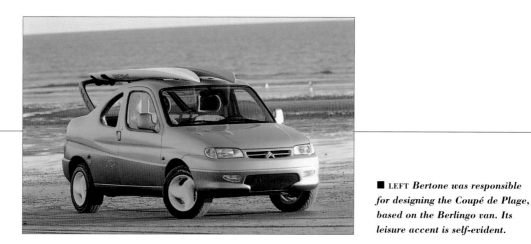

■ BELOW *Although it looked like a three-wheeler, Citroën's 1991 Citéla electric city car prototype in fact had a pair of narrow-set rear wheels.*

■ LEFT *Bertone was responsible for designing the Coupé de Plage, based on the Berlingo van. Its leisure accent is self-evident.*

"managed" suspension, highly advanced aerodynamics and a 220bhp V-six engine.

The 1990 Activa 2 was a two-door coupé development of the theme with full active suspension and advanced electronics. However, some industry observers reckoned it looked a little too much like Ford's production line Probe for comfort.

The Citéla of 1991 was an idea for a city electric vehicle, and it was an extremely compact car (just 116in (296cm) long). The rear wheels were set very close together, and the sodium cadmium battery was claimed to last 600,000 miles (966,000km).

Xanae was the name given to a very attractive family car concept vehicle presented at the 1994 Paris Salon. Predicting the way Renault would go with its Scenic, the Xanae was a one-box mini-MPV. It had one door on the left, and two pillarless doors on the right. The quite radical transparent roof was an unbroken continuation of the windscreen.

■ RIGHT *The concept of a compact "people carrier" was given a futuristic slant with the 1994 Xanae. The side doors hinged in opposite directions and the front seats swivelled.*

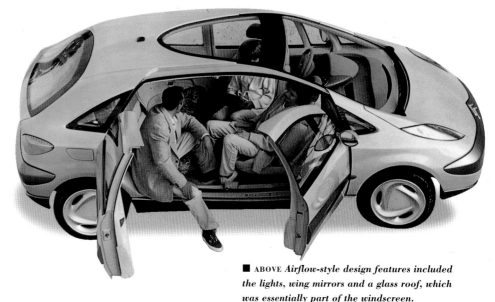

■ ABOVE *Airflow-style design features included the lights, wing mirrors and a glass roof, which was essentially part of the windscreen.*

DAEWOO

Korean firm Daewoo had a problem of image: it was never one of experimentation, more of solid marketing success based on hand-me-downs from other makers. It addressed this by hiring Ital Design to come up with a concept car for the 1995 Geneva Motor Show. The Bucrane was a comparatively low-key debut, but this was intentional.

■ ABOVE *Ital Design was hired to come up with the Bucrane to give Daewoo a new design credibility. It was a four-seater coupé with V-six power.*

■ ABOVE *The name "No.1" hints that this was Daewoo's first self-produced concept car, an open roadster presented at the Frankfurt show in 1995.*

■ BELOW *A "No.2" was a novel exercise in the small one-box family-car idiom. Notable was the very low glass waistline.*

The Bucrane was a two-box four-seater coupé based on the mechanicals of its top-line model, a licence-built version of the Honda Legend. This meant a front-mounted 240bhp V-six engine and automatic transmission.

The styling was soft and mildly retro, but devoid of any real beauty. Its main features were heavy side scallops as engine air outlets and thick rear pillars forming a rear roof spoiler. The glazed roof and sweeping expanses of glass (the rear one was described as "lentil-shaped") gave it an airy feel inside. The temptation to fit a large chrome-plated grille was easily succumbed to.

In retrospect Daewoo was probably happier with the end product than Ital Design, and it began a fruitful association between the two firms (the Italian *carrozzieri* styled the later Lanos and Leganza ranges). The Bucrane had also freed Daewoo from its image as a builder of outdated designs, and established it as an innovator.

From Mya to Joyster
Daewoo improved its design credentials by acquiring, in 1994, the IAD design offices in Worthing, Britain, and by founding a design centre in Bavaria. The first fruit of this new direction was the 1996 Mya concept car. Based on the floorpan of forthcoming Daewoo cars, it was partly realistic, partly dreamy. The gullwing doors, for instance, looked totally impractical for a four-seater car, but the soft, mature and sporty lines enhanced Daewoo's credibility.

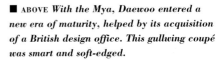

■ ABOVE *The Mya's cabin reflected a youthful design input, featuring highly textured surfaces and stylized controls.*

■ RIGHT *The Korean giant Daewoo's ambitions were laid bare with the Shiraz, an impressive-looking concept car hinting at a possible future presence in the Mercedes/ Jaguar class.*

■ ABOVE *With the Mya, Daewoo entered a new era of maturity, helped by its acquisition of a British design office. This gullwing coupé was smart and soft-edged.*

Daewoo stepped up its concept-car visions in 1997 with the launch of a whole vault of dream cars. These included the mundane (such as the Lanos Cabriolet and the small-car pairing of the Matiz and Mantica), but also provided a glimpse of enticing future possibilities.

The Shiraz, for instance, was a new departure for Daewoo: a V8-engined limousine to rival Mercedes and Jaguar. Designed by stylists in Britain, the Shiraz looked surprisingly sophisticated, even elegant. The interior featured silver and wood veneers and paddle switches on the steering wheel to change gear.

Rear-seat passengers were treated to tables, which folded out to reveal PC units and a printer/fax output.

Other new directions included the Tacuma, a medium-sized leisure-type people carrier, and the DEV 5, a small,

electrically powered car, which was capable of reaching 75mph (121kph). Most exciting of all Daewoo's dream cars must be the Joyster, a highly characterful and compact (13ft (4 metre long)) two-seater roadster designed by Ital Design. Its lines perhaps recalled the Ghia Focus (which is no bad thing), and it featured vertically stacked lights front and rear and a very distinctive front grille in which the traditional Daewoo fan was flanked by curious panels drilled with holes of differing sizes.

■ RIGHT *The best of all Daewoo concepts was undoubtedly the Joyster, an extremely neat sports two-seater designed by Ital Design. Note the curious front-grille treatment.*

DAIHATSU

Considering its position at the lower end of the Japanese market, Daihatsu has an impressive record of dream and show cars to its credit. These cars go far beyond the self-defined limits of its road-car programme.

Weird dreams

Daihatsu never followed convention. This was proved over and over again by such weird, but fun, concepts as the 1987 Urbanbuggy (an MPV/off-road/buggy cross-over) and the 1985 Trek (a single-seater "box" with a canvas camping-tent top, telephone, TV, spade and winch). With the 1989 Sneaker, a curious little goblin of a car with seating for three, Daihatsu even cast a little bit of magic: the Sneaker lowered a fifth wheel from its rump and rotated itself into tight parking spots.

In 1991, a maturing face was in evidence with the highly appealing X-021, a smooth, retro-styled roadster in the Mazda MX-5 Miata vein. That meant a front-mounted engine (a 1.6- litre 16V 140bhp "four"), rear-wheel drive and an open two-seater cockpit. It was novel in that it had an aluminium space frame, plastic bodywork and race-derived suspension – all expensive items, so it is not surprising that the very pretty X-021 did not make production.

Wacky concepts

Just as impressive was the 1993 Personal Coupé, which, although it was based on humble Charade front-wheel-drive mechanicals, looked neat and was a distinct prospect for production. The same could not be said of the Ultra Mini of the same year, whose main strength was managing to fit four seats into a 98 in- (250cm-) longcar. Its 660cc engine sat under the rear seats. Likewise the Multi Personal 4 was a light-hearted but ultimately daft sports-utility with an interior, which it was claimed was fully washable. Yet another 1993 concept car was the Dash FX21, a very neat electric/ petrol hybrid four-door saloon (sedan).

Daihatsu's crazy Midget III show car of 1995 almost reinvented the Citroën 2CV with its bug-eye headlamps, high roof-line, tiny (659cc) engine and overall charm. Based on a single-seater pick-up, it added rear bodywork and two

■ LEFT *The Midget was a production single-seater pick-up, and the Midget III added a pair of rear seats too.*

■ RIGHT *It was a shame that the handsome X-021 never passed the dream car stage. 140bhp and aluminium/plastic construction sounded enticing.*

rear seats to make a three-seater. Even more ridiculous was the Town Cube, literally a cube on wheels, designed as a joke around the maximum permitted size for Japan's legal class of micro-cars. For the 1997 show round, Daihatsu previewed its vision of a future compact car, the NCX. A capacious, five-seater interior resulted from a long-cabin, short-nose ethic, and the 1.0-litre three-cylinder engine was claimed to produce amazing fuel economy. It proved that, while Daihatsu specialized in small cars, its ideas were actually broad-ranging and consistently forward-looking and experimental.

■ ABOVE *The 1995 Town Cube was really an in-joke: a vehicle designed around the maximum size limits for microcars.*

■ LEFT *Smart, understated and appealing, the 1993 Personal Coupé was a novel idea for a 1.0-litre compact coupé.*

FORD

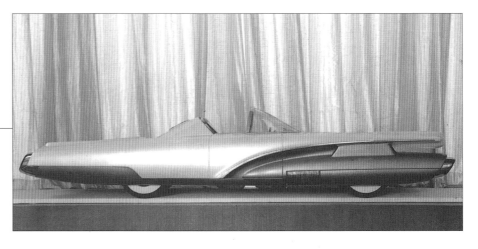

Perhaps it was Henry Ford's prosaic image as a provider of popular cars that delayed Ford's entry into the dream-car arena. Whatever the reason, Ford lagged behind Chrysler and General Motors in the razzmatazz world of futuristic ideas.

Ford's first dream car

Probably the first true Ford dream car was the X-100 of 1953, which anticipated the torpedo styling themes of later Fords like the 1961 Thunderbird. Another indication of Ford's new directions from the same year was the Mexico – only a scale model, but the result of wind-tunnel testing and an important pointer to future trends. Ford claimed 50 engineering firsts for this car, including a moisture-sensitive cell on the roof, which automatically closed the plastic sliding roof panel.

More extreme was the 1956 Mystere, at once the most amazing and most repulsive of dream cars. Its excessive chromework, double headlamps and heavy body accents appeared in production Fords in years to come, but mercifully the lifting bubble canopy,

swinging steering wheel and gas turbine power did not.

One of the most famous of all 1950s dream cars was the Lincoln Futura of 1955, if only because it was later modified to become the Batmobile in the popular TV series of the 60s. When the double-bubble canopy housed the caped crusaders, its kicked-up tail fins evoked just the right bat-like connotations.

Ford suffers hangover

Ford worked its way through many contorted schools of styling such as the Z-back roof (in the 1957 La Galaxie). It went on to become increasingly unhinged as it proposed a nuclear-powered dream car called the Nucleon in 1958, a gyroscopically controlled two-wheeled car called the Gyron in 1961, a three-wheeled flying car called

■ **LEFT**
Aerodynamics was one of the obsessions of the 1980s. The Probe IV may have been exceptionally wind-cheating but its wheel spats (skirts) and window cut-outs were utterly impractical in the real world.

■ **ABOVE** *It took until the 1980s for Ford to come back to the dream-car arena with an aerodynamic two-door concept car called the Probe.*

■ **RIGHT** *It wasn't realized at the time, but this odd-looking 1981 creation, the aerodynamic Probe III, was basically the forthcoming Ford Sierra. It prepared the public for a radical production shape.*

■ OPPOSITE *Details surrounding this 1956 ⅜ scale model, called X-1000, were extremely vague, like a poorly remembered dream. Ford said the engine could be front or rear mounted, and that the car might even fly!*

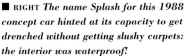

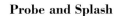

■ RIGHT *The name Splash for this 1988 concept car hinted at its capacity to get drenched without getting slushy carpets: the interior was waterproof!*

■ LEFT *The Probe V marked a return to the good old days of gimmickry. The sliding doors and engine cover prove as much.*

Probe and Splash

Future Ford Probe show cars were far more adventurous. The 1983 Probe IV was an amazingly aerodynamic yet practical hatchback. Its Cd figure of 0.15 was spectacular, achieved by wheels covered by urethane "membranes", meticulous airflow management and a spoiler at the base of the windscreen. The ultimate Probe V of a few years later extended the aerodynamic theme still further.

Uniting sportscar and pick-up truck themes was the purpose of the 1988 Splash. Looking like a space-age beach buggy, this striking two-seater had removable windows, roof and rear hatch. Its four-wheel drive, adjustable ride height and retractable mud flaps boosted its chunky off-road flavour, and the colourful weatherproof interior looked trendy enough for its intended youth market.

the Volante the same year and a vast six-wheeler called the Seattle-ite in 1962.

It should not be surprising that, after that lot, Ford's design team and the public had something of a dream-car hangover, and Dearborn's output of show specials petered out in the 1960s.

It took Ford's purchase of the Italian Ghia styling house to kick-start its dream-car programme again in the 1970s. Ghia's creations for Ford (such

as the Coins, Megastar and Action) are described in the pages devoted to Ghia. Ford's domestic US styling studios took longer to return to the dream-world.

Meanwhile, Ford's European subsidiary started a trend of creating show cars that anticipated future production models with the Probe III in 1981. It was all but identical to the Ford Sierra, only the aerodynamic appendages being really different.

■ LEFT *Lincoln's concept car for 1988 was the Machete, whose blade-edged shape perhaps presaged Ford's vaunted "edge-design" school. Note the narrow headlamps.*

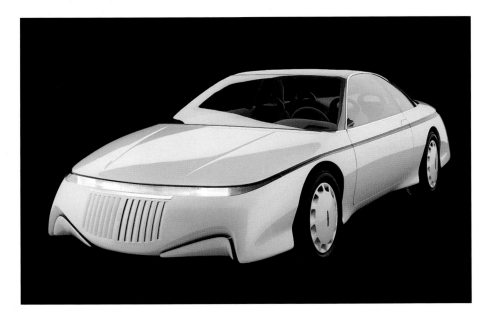

■ ABOVE *Inside the Machete, ultra-simple curves combined with digital electronics.*

FORD

■ RIGHT *"Edge design" was a term Ford used to describe its new corporate design identity. It meant the use of hard-edged surfaces seemingly colliding with one another, and emerged with the GT90 of 1995.*

The Contour, shown at the 1991 Detroit Show, was revolutionary in so many respects. Its engine was the first straight-eight since Pontiac's in 1954 and was mounted transversely to save space. The shape of the car was dramatic with steeply raked screens and a long cabin dominating. It was mounted on an aluminium chassis entirely bonded together. The headlamps were 1in- (2.5cm-) high arc discharge rods and there were two floating rear spoilers.

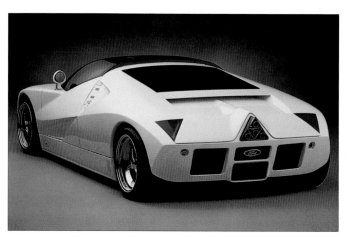

■ LEFT *The GT90's triangular surfaces were most marked from the rear. The large black central triangle is the exhaust outlet.*

■ LEFT *Drawing its inspiration from the GT40 race car of the 1960s, the GT90 was a very low, rakish, mid-engined supercar.*

■ ABOVE *Ford's designers applied "edge design" to a road-going IndyCar-inspired concept car called the IndiGo.*

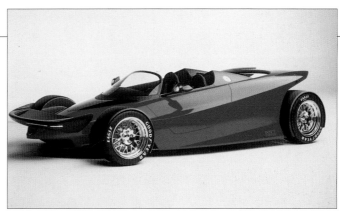

■ ABOVE *A black front spoiler and wings created a race-car feel on the outside, while the hi-tech construction and sequential six-speed gearbox did so under the skin.*

Edge design

To describe its fresh way of thinking in design terms, Ford coined the term "edge design". Before production cars like the Ka and Puma took to the streets, Ford displayed numerous concept cars at motor shows around the world, which dramatically demonstrated its new philosophy.

Edge design burst on to the scene with the revolutionary GT90 in 1995. The name hinted at the inspiration for the car, Ford's highly successful GT40 road/race car of the 1960s. In format, there were similarities: this was a very low, mid-engined two-seater with fantastic performance potential, but in truth the cars were very divergent.

The GT90 resembled a Stealth bomber in the way that its triangular flat surfaces intersected one another. Under the skin, its technology was bang up-to-date racing-car: a honeycomb aluminium chassis, carbonfibre body and space-shuttle-type ceramic exhaust. Powered by a quad-turbo 720bhp V-twelve engine, it was intended to be launched in a limited series of 100 cars, but the plan never materialized. Much more significant was the GT90's effect on the future of Ford design.

IndiGo racer

It was not just the name of the IndiGo that was clever (playing on its association with IndyCar racing). This was no mere show car but a concept designed from the outset to be feasibly manufactured at some point. Even though most people who worked in the trade accepted that this was too radical to be offered for sale, it was a driveable car.

Ford said that the IndiGo "captures the essence of the race-track and transforms it into a realistic design for the street". The styling was strongly race car in feel, from the bespoilered, narrow nose to the blacked-out wings, while its construction (carbonfibre, aluminium and glassfibre) also mimicked competition use.

A 441bhp 6.0-litre V-twelve engine – formed by mating two V-six units together – was estimated to give a top speed of 170mph (273kph) and a 0–60mph (0-96kph) time of under four seconds. The six-speed sequential gearbox was derived from race cars, and changes were made by pressing buttons on the steering wheel. Even the instrument panel on the dashboard was Formula 1 inspired.

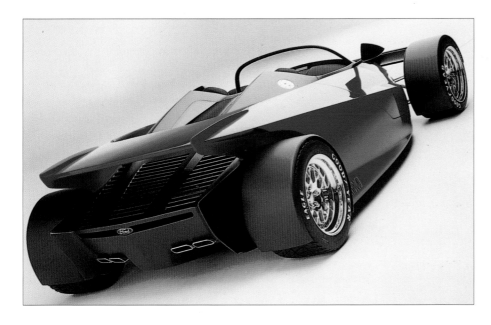

■ LEFT *In the centre of the car was a six-litre V-twelve engine with 441bhp at its disposal.*

FORD

Lincoln, meanwhile, forged ahead with its own L2K concept (in 1995), a possible future competition for the Mercedes-Benz SLK. Its blade-like shape (created by an affiliated design house called Concept Car Company) hid a 250bhp 3.4-litre V-eight engine. The following year came the Sentinel, a

startling expression of Ford's edge design ethos: a high waistline, wonderfully sculpted lighting, ultra-clean, flat shapes and elegant proportions. It was a huge car, but felt right, and was even made into a runner on a lengthened Jaguar platform.

■ ABOVE *Lincoln's L2K concept car was a V-eight front-engined roadster, pitching Lincoln into an area it had not explored before.*

■ LEFT *With a different set of wheels, the L2K was able to do the rounds of the show circuit with a dash of novelty.*

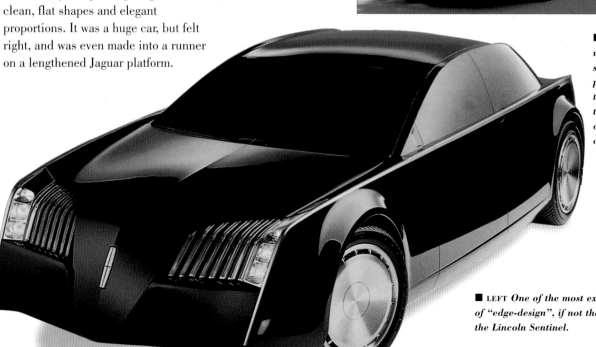

■ ABOVE *A very high waistline, clean shapes and good proportions made the Sentinel one of the most striking concept cars of 1995.*

■ LEFT *One of the most extreme expressions of "edge-design", if not the most elegant, was the Lincoln Sentinel.*

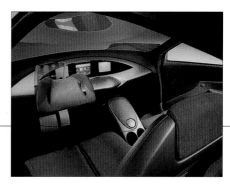

■ ABOVE *Computer animation and advanced voice-activated controls made the Synergy 2010's interior appear vastly different from today's cars.*

■ ABOVE *Synergy 2010 was an extremely bold styling statement, projecting ideas for a family car for the year 2010.*

The Synergy 2010 was Ford's idea of a family car for the year 2010, presented in 1996. As such, it featured two power sources – a 1.0-litre direct-injection engine feeding an electric motor – extremely lightweight materials (it weighed just one tonne (ton)), "air fences", which dictated the car's advanced, aerodynamic styling and voice-activated controls matched by computer-animated instruments. You could even call up the phone book by issuing a simple verbal command!

Just as the Ghia Saetta broke the path for the radical new Ka, so the 1996 Lynx dropped a few clues about the forthcoming Fiesta-based Puma coupé. One element that was lost in production was the odd twin roll-bar layout, which also formed the side window frames and guides for a fold-away roof.

Mercury's 1997 MC4 extended edge design to a mid-market four-seater. It looked good but still incorporated such dream themes as miniature "suicide" rear doors and a gullwing boot (trunk). More exciting still was the MC2 concept car shown at the 1997 Frankfurt Motor Show, in essence a new Ford Cougar. Here was the most successful and satisfying expression of edge design yet, a powerful combination of good proportions, aggressive angles and a lean profile.

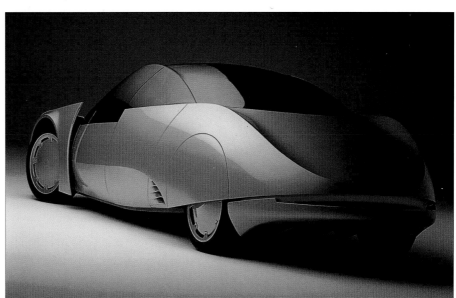

■ ABOVE *Extremely light weight and aerodynamic, the Synergy 2010 used a petrol/electric hybrid propulsion system.*

■ BELOW *Shown at the 1997 Frankfurt Motor Show, the Mercury MC2 was perhaps the most elegant "edge design" concept yet from Ford.*

GENERAL MOTORS

More than any other car-maker in the world, General Motors has embraced the dream-car theme with a vengeance. It was arguably the creator of the world's first dream car in the sense of a car created purely for advancing ideas rather than production realities: the Buick Y-Job of 1939 was a world pioneer. It had long, sleek lines, concealed headlamps and an electric top, which hid under a metal cover when lowered. The dream car had been born.

Harley Earl and Motorama

From then on, General Motors was the spiritual home of the dream car. The architect of this style revolution was Harley Earl, and it was his 1951 Buick Le Sabre that launched the jet-plane era

■ LEFT *One of the stars of GM's Motorama road shows of the 1950s was the Pontiac Club de Mer. This blue-anodized aluminium roadster was just 38in (96.5cm) high.*

of car design in America. Not only did it look fantastic, it bristled with innovation: cast-magnesium panels, a hood (top) that raised itself automatically when a sensor detected rain and heated

■ BELOW *The 1954 Buick Wildcat II had a glassfibre body. Note the "leaping-cat" bonnet mascot (hood ornament) and headlamps mounted by the windscreen.*

seats. The Buick XP-300 of the same year was also ahead, with sleek styling, locking side-impact bars, hydraulic seats and a methanol-powered engine.

Throughout the 1950s, GM laid on the flash, brash razzmattazz in giant mobile shows called Motoramas. The centre-pieces of these showy extravaganzas were always the latest creations of stylists obsessed with futuristic visions of a brighter, faster, bigger age. In the peak Motorama year (1956), GM spent £6 million ($10 million) on the shows and attracted two million spectators.

By then Harley Earl was the General's styling supremo. It was he who introduced the very idea of "style" into everyday motoring and the yearly changes of model, which are pursued in America to this day. Earl liked to introduce "concepts" at Motoramas, which might one day reach production. Some did, like the Corvette and Cadillac Eldorado Brougham, but most were, of course, far too way-out.

Firebirds and the Bonneville Special

These were the crowd-pleasers. The public swooned at the sight of cars like the Buick Le Sabre and XP-300. Most drastic of all, the XP-21 Firebird of

■ BELOW *Jet turbine styling and some genuine jet-fighter components gave the Pontiac Bonneville Special a science fiction spin.*

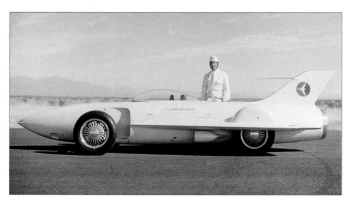

■ ABOVE *The 1956 Oldsmobile Golden Rocket featured roof sections that folded upwards when the door opened, while the seats swivelled and the steering wheel split in two to aid access.*

■ BELOW *Firebird II toned down the fighter plane extremes of the XP-21 in a body that could seat four people. Fins, turbines, a bubble roof and titanium bodywork kept the razzmatazz going.*

■ ABOVE *Nominally a feasibility study to ascertain the viability of gas turbine power, the XP-21 Firebird was essentially a shock publicity exercise.*

1954 was utterly sci-fi, its small jet-plane turbine propulsion being taken to extremes with a jet-fighter-style body: if you took away the wheels it really looked like a single-seater plane.

The Firebird evolved through two further generations. The Firebird II of 1956 had a central joystick and was claimed to have overcome the heat and noise-generation problems of a jet turbine engine. The more down-to-earth bodywork was in titanium, while passengers entered through a transparent canopy. The 1958 Firebird III returned to moon-rocket influences, sprouting aero-fins all over and boasting double bubble tops, a central lever for steering/braking/acceleration, cruise control, remote door-opening and "electroluminescent" instruments.

One of the best 50s dream cars was the 1954 Pontiac Bonneville Special. This was Earl's idea of a dreamy sportscar, full of glitz like fat chrome bonnet (hood) strips, chrome-mustachioed gaping grill, wrap-around screens, gullwing bubble-top and aircraft-style interior. It was the rear-end that was best, however: a Continental-style spare wheel cover with a turbine trim, flanked by jet-style tail lights.

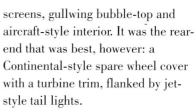

■ LEFT *Sci-fi met hi-tech in the Firebird III. Beneath the huge fins lay pioneering electronic controls. There was even provision for the car to drive itself via cables mounted under GM test tracks.*

GENERAL MOTORS

General Motors' output was prolific. In just one year (1954) no less than 12 different dream cars were paraded in front of the public. This was the golden age of the dream car, and GM was its golden child. GM stuck to "style" and "innovation" less than the outlandish themes of other US names, and often its show car ideas would become production realities.

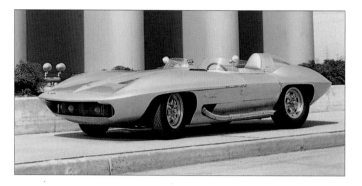

■ LEFT *GM styling supremo Bill Mitchell built the Sting Ray as early as 1959 as his own personal car. It inspired the later Corvette Sting Ray production car.*

■ BELOW *In 1962, the Mako Shark evolved from the Sting Ray. It was Corvette-based, and took shark-like styling themes to their conclusion.*

Rocket, Shark and Stingray Roadster

Highlights of the 1950s included the Buick Centurion, the remarkably clean Oldsmobile Golden Rocket, the 38in- (96.5cm-) high Pontiac Club de Mer, the

1957 Chevrolet Corvette SS (reminiscent of Jaguar's D-Type in many ways), and the jet-style Cadillac Cyclone.

General Motors lost none of its touch in the 1960s. Stylist Bill Mitchell drew inspiration from sharks in his 1962

Corvette Shark study: inlets for gills, exhaust pipes for fins, a pronounced snout and a graduated blue colour scheme. This followed the design of his own personal car, the Sting Ray Roadster, which also did the show rounds.

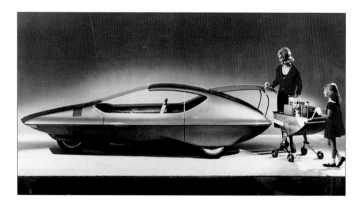

■ ABOVE *A paragon for suburban shopping bliss: the Runabout's front wheel could turn through 180 degrees to ease parking, while the tail contained two detachable shopping trolleys (carts)!*

■ ABOVE *To get into the 1967 Chevrolet Astro I, you popped a switch and the roof rose up, carrying the seats with it. It looked spectacular but was plainly a crazy idea.*

■ RIGHT *By the 1970s, the Golden Age of dream cars was over. In 1973, Bill Mitchell created this Pontiac Phantom show car as a swansong.*

Similar themes persisted in the 1963 Corvair Monza prototypes, transforming the beleaguered rear-engine Corvair into lithe sportscars, which undoubtedly influenced the next generation of sports shapes.

From Runabout to Aerotech

GM pursued other ideas too. Its Runabout was a vision of tomorrow's shopping car, a three-wheeler with two removable shopping trolleys (carts) built into the rear. The XP511 was a hybrid commuter trike with a huge clamshell canopy, and the Astro I incorporated a novel system of entry: the whole rear bodywork raised upwards, lifting the two seats with it.

Unlike the other US car manufacturers, GM never gave up its show car programme, pursuing dream themes into the 1970s with projects like the quad-rotor Chevrolet Aerovette and Pontiac Phantom.

The next major GM activity occurred from the mid-1980s on. GM concentrated on exceptionally exotic supercar projects like the Buick Wildcat of 1985, the Corvette Indy, the Pontiac Pursuit and, possibly the most extreme of all, the Oldsmobile Aerotech, with an amazing top speed in excess of 250mph (400kph).

■ LEFT *General Motors returned to the dream-car arena with a bang in 1985: the Buick Wildcat revived a famous dream-car name and catapulted it into the present day.*

Cadillac pursued a theme of luxury express transport. Following the 1988 Voyage, the more accomplished Solitaire of the following year was "one of the world's most aerodynamic vehicles" with a Cd of 0.28, the result of such wind-cheating additions as wheel spats (skirts) and faired-in headlamps. It was powered by a 6.6-litre V-twelve engine developed by GM and Lotus and featured electronic articulated doors.

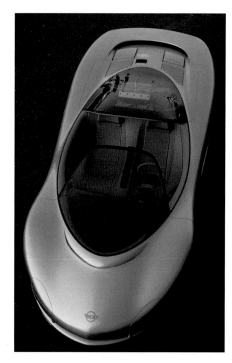

■ RIGHT *In 1986-87, the Oldsmobile Aerotech broke new world speed records: the short-tail car reached 257mph (414 kph), the long-tail an incredible 278mph (447 kph). And all from a 2.0-litre engine...*

■ ABOVE *The 1986 Corvette Indy concept car judged the spirit of the times to perfection, as an all-out mid-engined supercar of prodigious performance.*

GENERAL MOTORS

■ BELOW *The Pontiac Banshee of 1988 took its name from a mythical wild creature – and duly lived up to it.*

Stinger, Sunfire and Camaro

In 1989 came the Pontiac Stinger, an aggressively styled sports-utility vehicle. Adaptability was the name of the game here: all of its carbonfibre panels could be removed, as could the glass roof and the lower glass door panels (which could be replaced by a cool box and storage unit). Inside, four seats were adjustable six ways, while the rear passengers could elevate themselves by 15in (38cm) for a grandstand view over the roll-bar. Also

■ ABOVE *Impressive aerodynamism and a V-twelve experimental engine made the Cadillac Solitaire a limousine for dreamers. The Voyage is in the foreground.*

■ BELOW *Chevrolet's California Camaro was a vision of the future direction of GM's successful Camaro series.*

■ ABOVE *Pontiac's Sunfire was GM's expression of the cab-forward style espoused by Chrysler. The rear doors hinged from the back.*

supplied were a compass, phone, vacuum cleaner, stove, picnic table, umbrella and dustpan!

Pontiac's 1990 two-litre turbocharged Sunfire concept stole a page from Chrysler's cab-forward school of design in a two-plus-two coupé shape. One unusual feature was a set of "suicide" doors for the rear occupants, an idea dropped two decades earlier by every car-maker. The main point of interest, however, was the instrument binnacle: it was located in the centre of the steering wheel but was mounted to remain upright whichever way the steering wheel was turned.

The Camaro was always a badge that GM liked interpreting for the future. The California Camaro was typical: a far-sighted "running sketch in metal". A flamboyant use of glass, gullwing doors

■ LEFT *Impact was the name GM gave to its initial prototype for an electric sportscar. It actually entered production in little modified form as the EV1.*

■ BELOW *The Ultralite showed GM was thinking in many directions. Thanks to extreme light weight and smooth airflow, the Ultralite could reach 135mph (217kph) yet return up to 100mpg (160kpg).*

and a sharp-nosed treatment were notable features, while such fripperies as a vacuum cleaner in the console undermined its seriousness.

Experimental and Rageous

Chevrolet's CERV (Corporate Experimental Research Vehicle) projects stretched from the cigar-shaped 1960 single-seater to the 1990 CERV III, which built on the 1986 Corvette Indy. The CERV III was created with assistance from GM's newly acquired Lotus wing and used a heavily modified Corvette ZR1 engine producing no less than 650bhp, mounted centrally. Drive was to all four wheels through an automatic gearbox with six speeds, and the top speed was quoted as 186mph (299kph), with 0–60mph (0-96kph) coming up in 4.2 seconds. Active suspension, carbonfibre brakes and a Cd figure of just 0.274 were also

something GM wanted to shout about.

For the 1992 Ultralite, the claims were different: 100mpg (160kpg) economy and a top speed of 135mph (217kph). This was possible thanks to a carbonfibre body weighing just 420lb (190kg) and a Cd figure of 0.192. Yet it could still fit four adults.

The Sting Ray III (also 1992) pointed a little toward a new Corvette, with its longer wheelbase and shorter length.

Some regarded this concept car as superior to the C5 Corvette of 1997.

GM pioneered the productionization of a ground-up electric vehicle: the EV1 was launched in 1996. It all started life as the Impact concept car, an innovative and very sleek (Cd 0.19) coupé. Unlike any other electric car then developed, the Impact was a performance car, capable of accelerating to 0–60mph (0-96kph) from a standing start in under nine seconds. Its bonded aluminium spaceframe and composite body helped in keeping overall weight down.

With its Rageous concept car (1997), GM's Pontiac division created a Batman-style car described as a "sports coupé with the practicality of a sports-utility". Clearly an answer to Ford's edge-design thinking, it was a striking but not entirely happy mix of bold, folded edges and colliding shapes. Space inside was far better than in most sports coupés.

■ LEFT *General Motors built this Sunraycer solar-powered car to compete in long-distance sun-propelled competitions.*

GHIA

It is perhaps a sad reflection that to most people Ghia means a trim-level badge on their humdrum Ford. That all stems from Ghia's 1973 acquisition by Ford, but its history as one of the most illustrious Italian design houses stretches back to the early years of the 20th century. Ghia's main business was creating bespoke (dedicated) coachwork for high-quality Italian chassis, in which

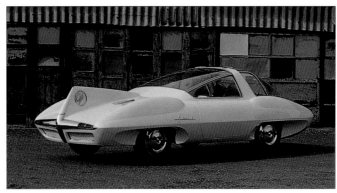

■ ABOVE *Virgil Exner was responsible for the extraordinary Selene II. The driver sat alone in a central position, while the passengers faced backwards and had a TV screen to watch!*

■ ABOVE *The 1959 Selene was a sleek, nose-heavy "people carrier" styled by Tom Tjaarda. This forward-control style was advanced by several designers, but its dynamic shortcomings consigned it to an early grave.*

it was extremely successful. These were the original dream cars – one-offs built for wealthy clients, certainly not "show cars" in the accepted sense.

In 1950, Chrysler sent a Plymouth chassis to Turin, and Ghia rebodied it to become the XX-500. Although it looked ponderous, it sparked an association that led to Ghia building many of Chrysler's 50s dream cars. Ghia got into its stride with some stunning coachwork, and the 1953 Fiat 1100 Abarth and Fiat 8V were trend-setting.

Aerodynamics and style

Undoubtedly, the 1955 Ghia Streamline (or Gilda) was one of the most spectacular shapes of the 1950s. Created in a wind tunnel at Turin Polytechnic, this long, radically finned

device mutated through several generations, still being displayed at shows with great succes as late as 1960. Aerodynamics were a Ghia speciality, as proven by the Nibbio record breaker, which reached 100mph (161kph) on

350cc. Ghia also made the beach-car milieu its own with a string of wicker-seated Fiats called Jolly, and manufactured its own range of sportscars with the Dual-Ghia Firebomb, L6.4, 450/SS and 1500.

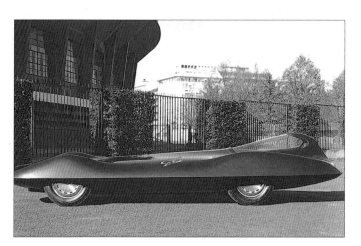

■ LEFT *At the 1961 Geneva Motor Show, Tom Tjaarda's IXG dragster was displayed. However, it was too streamlined to accept its intended Innocenti engine.*

■ OPPOSITE *The 1955 Turin show, where the world was enraptured by Ghia's incredible Streamline/Gilda, which boasted the largest tail fins of the era.*

■ RIGHT *The 1974 Coins was a vision of a future Ford Capri, although its bulbous styling (by Tom Tjaarda), three-abreast seating and single hatchback door for entry represented gimmickry, not advancement.*

A very talented man called Tom Tjaarda became one of Ghia's main stylists, and he made a big impression with the 1959 Selene, a sort of super-sleek forward-control "people carrier". Its follow-up, the Selene II of 1962, had a central driving seat and two rear seats facing backwards.

Then another brilliant stylist called Giorgetto Giugiaro joined Ghia from Bertone and designed many exceptional production cars. He also penned some attractive Ghia show cars, such as the Maserati Simun, the De Tomaso Pampero and the Oldsmobile Toronado Thor.

After its acquisition by Ford Ghia in 1973, Ghia was used as the European styling and prototype wing of Ford's global organization. Immediately, Ghia came up with a string of concept cars, inevitably based on Fords. Early examples were the Mustela (a Capri alternative), the Tuareg (an off-road Fiesta) and the Microsport (a truncated Fiesta-based sports coupé).

Radical wedges

Its best designs in the 1970s were also its most radical. The 1974 Coins was a striking curved wedge with a single rear-sited door. The 1977 Megastar was a Granada-based saloon (sedan), though you would never guess so from its amazing glass-house moulding (the front doors were 80 per cent glass). The Corrida was a chunky little safety-orientated sports coupé.

Probably the most striking Ghia show car of all was the 1978 Action, the most severe wedge shape ever seen. Designed by Filippo Sapino, it had a rear-mounted DFV Formula 1 V-eight engine and completely enclosed rear wheels.

■ LEFT *The Corrida was a pretty 1976 gullwing show car based on a Fiesta floorpan.*

■ BELOW *In 1977, Ghia showed the Megastar, a four-seater with a very swoopy glass waistline, based on Ford Granada parts.*

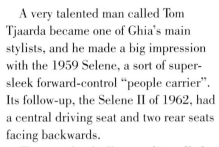

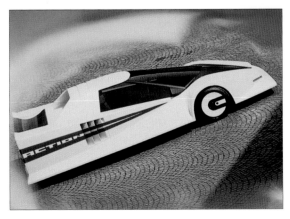

■ ABOVE *This car's name – Action – says it all. Styled by Filippo Sapino, its uncompromising wedge shape was highly dramatic for 1978, as was its Formula 1 power plant.*

GHIA

■ LEFT *Based on the Ford Granada, the Altair was a very successful design exercise.*

■ ABOVE *One of Ghia's most attractive concept cars was the Escort XR3-based Brezza. Its engine was mid-mounted.*

In the 1980s, Ghia continued as a prestige *carrozzeria*. Its Granada Altair project was dignified in its simplicity, while the Avant Garde and, in particular, the Brezza (both Escort-based) were delightful compact coupés. Ghia also produced an attractive body for the mid-engined AC ME3000.

A host of microcars followed: the five-seater but small Pockar, the Shuttler, the three-wheeled Cockpit and the Trio. It was a shame to many that more was not made of the Barchetta, a Fiesta XR2-based roadster, which might have been a

■ RIGHT *Ghia even flirted with the idea of a tandem two-seater three-wheeler called the Cockpit. The whole glass roof lifted up for access.*

■ BELOW *The British sportscar firm AC had connections with Ford, and this handsome 1981 Ghia reworking of its ME3000 sports car was once destined for production.*

modern Ford-badged answer to the MG Midget. Less successful was the seven-seater APV, a car which the then UK Prime Minister, Margaret Thatcher, famously wanted to be redesigned.

Via, Zig/Zag and Connecta

Much comment was attracted by the 1988 Saguaro, which predicted the softer, rounder styles of the 1990s in a sporty, four-door package. The 1989 Geneva showing was the Via, a "Ford Sierra Cosworth for the next decade". Designed by a team of British stylists – brothers Ian and Moray Callum, David Wilkie and Sally Wilson – it was a very smart and sleek four-door saloon with an intended specification that included a turbo V-eight engine and six-speed

■ ABOVE *Perhaps the Barchetta represented a missed opportunity, for this could easily have been a compact Ford roadster ahead of its time.*

■ ABOVE *The Zig and Zag were a jocular pair of extremely compact youth-oriented show cars. Zig was the sportscar, Zag the van.*

gearbox. One of its highlights was a fibre-optics system for navigating in fog; another was a fully detachable photo-sensitive glass roof.

An interesting pair of leisure cars was created for the 1990 Geneva Motor Show, both based on a cut-down Fiesta platform. The Zig was the more engaging of the Zig/Zag pair (the Zag was a van). Designed by David Wilkie, the Zig had a very short bonnet (hood) flanked by pinhole headlamps and a perspex (clear plastic)-shrouded cockpit. The Sally Wilson-designed interior was strikingly finished with dashboard instruments painted blue, green and orange and a rear-view mirror that sprouted, tentacle-like, from the facia.

■ ABOVE *The 1989 Ghia Via was a high-performance four-door saloon (sedan) with V-eight power and super-sleek styling.*

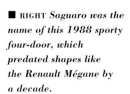

■ ABOVE *Ghia went microcar-mad in the 1980s with a whole string of city car projects. This one is called the Trio, because three people could be seated in it.*

■ RIGHT *Saguaro was the name of this 1988 sporty four-door, which predated shapes like the Renault Mégane by a decade.*

GHIA

■ ABOVE *The extremely lightweight Connecta marked a new direction for Ghia – electric power.*

■ RIGHT *Ghia styled this Lagonda Vignale-badged show car for Aston Martin. It revived the Vignale name-plate – Ghia having taken over coachbuilders Vignale in 1969.*

Having an Escort van as a basis might not sound very exciting, but Ghia's 1992 Connecta was an important show car: it was Ford's first electric show car. The body-shell was in lightweight carbon-fibre and could seat six people (four forward-facing, two rearward) in a length of only 166in (421cm).

Focus and Lagoda Vignale

One of the most radical and adventurous dream cars ever was the Ghia Focus, presented at the 1992 Turin show. Based on a shortened Ford Escort Cosworth platform, it was naturally a very rapid sportscar. But it was Taru Lahti's styling that made the biggest impression. Novel features included whale-like front stabilizers, interesting headlamp architecture, distinctive air intakes,

alien-like grab handles down the body sides, scalloped rear fins, central rear-exit exhaust and amazing "bubble" rear lights. The cabin was equally avant garde, combining organic shapes and natural materials with an exposed, stark treatment and curious, off-centre detailing. The Focus might have made production as a Ford but was judged too radical and too expensive.

Of the Lagonda Vignale shown at the 1993 Geneva show, much was said and even more expected, for this might have made a future four-door Aston Martin (Ghia and Aston were now owned by Ford). Moray Callum designed the Lagonda Vignale, which was variously described as "trend-setting", "marvellous" and "the ugliest car around" – it all depended on your viewpoint. There was certainly nothing retiring about this substantial saloon (sedan), least of all the grille, the high waistline, huge wheels and drooping tail.

Ford's design dynamo

Ghia cemented its reputation as Ford's think-tank with two concept cars launched at the 1996 Turin show. One

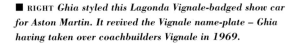

■ ABOVE *The Alpe was Ghia's vision for a competitor in the burgeoning sports-utility market sector.*

■ ABOVE *One of the most radically styled of all Ghia show cars was the 1992 Focus, which stood a strong chance of entering production. Note the intriguing side "rails".*

■ RIGHT *Based on an Escort Cosworth floorpan, the Focus was extremely accomplished in action. Note the curious "bubble" rear lamps.*

■ LEFT *The gauges reflected the Focus's forward-thinking yet classically inspired form. Organic forms melded with stylized detailing.*

was a clear signal of how the forthcoming Ford Ka would look: the radical Saetta's front end was shared with the Ka. In other respects, it was wildly different, Ford's prevailing edge-design mentality being taken to the limit. Dominated by a central roof rib, the silver-and-blue concept was bold in its geometric shapes, especially the rear lights. The other Turin debutant was the Alpe sports-utility, based on the Escort, with chunky, solid styling and a hint of off-road ability.

Today, Ghia's role is less as a creator of dream cars and more as a design dynamo in Ford's global empire, and a useful prototype-building facility in Italy's car design heartland. The Ghia badge persists on Ford products as an indicator of the highest level in its car ranges, but it is perhaps more fitting to remember the great legacy of the Ghia name by its impressive back catalogue of striking and innovative car designs. If only Ford had the courage to produce such brilliant creations as the Focus, the motoring world would be a better place.

■ BELOW *The 1996 Saetta fitted in with Ford's "edge-design" mentality, and prepared the public in for the radical small Ka.*

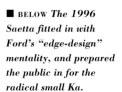

HONDA

Traditionally, Honda always shied away from producing concept cars, presumably because it viewed its mainstream cars as advanced.

Biting the dream-car bullet

Finally in 1991, Honda bit the dream-car bullet when it displayed a pair of models at Frankfurt.

These were the FS-X saloon and EP-X coupé. The FS-X (Futuristic Sports Experimental) was a bold and sleek

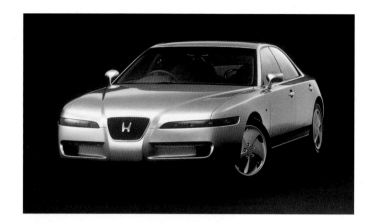

■ LEFT *Honda's first-ever concept car was the FS-X, a sporting saloon (sedan) with advanced engineering and a sharply styled aluminium body.*

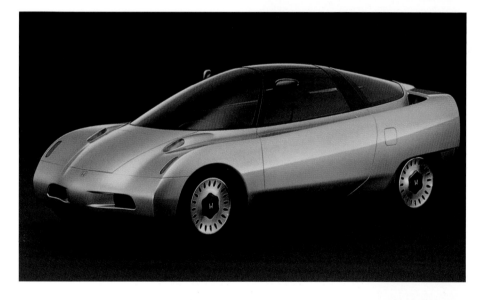

Electric and novel

For the 1993 Tokyo Show, Honda unveiled two further concepts. The first nailed its commitment to electric vehicles to the wall: the compact EVX predated the arrival of Honda's series production EV model, one of the first-ever ground-up electric cars. The second was the FSR, billed as "the ideal sedan for the 21st century". It was a technology car with such futurist goodies as active headlamps, radar braking, a message board for drivers following, reflective paint and a front-mounted camera for better visibility in adverse conditions. The wheel-arch

design clearly targeted at the Lexus and Infiniti luxury Japanese brands, which had had such success in America. Typically advanced in engineering terms, the FS-X sported a 3.5-litre VTEC V-six engine developing 280bhp, an all-aluminium body, four-wheel drive, liquid crystal sun visors and four airbags.

The little EP-X (Efficient Personal Experimental) was a curious, narrow tandem two-seater, also made entirely from aluminium. Powered by a 1.0-litre three-cylinder engine, it was claimed to be highly aerodynamic, efficient and safe if impractical.

■ ABOVE *Light weight, safety and aerodynamics were high on the agenda of the EP-X commuter vehicle.*

■ RIGHT *The EP-X was very compact, most notably in terms of width: the two passengers sat in tandem.*

■ LEFT *With its engine sitting inches to the right of the driver, the Side-by-Side sports racer was well named.*

treatment front and rear was novel, but the well-laid-out interior was more down-to-earth.

SSM stood for Sports Study Model, and this interesting 1995 show car was widely expected to enter production in modified form. It used NSX-style aluminium construction and ensured

sharp handling through its front-engine/rear-drive layout: Honda claimed a perfect 50/50 weight distribution front-to-rear. One novel feature on the car was a central "spur", which separated the driver's and passenger's compartments and was claimed to improve rigidity significantly.

The SSM's power was supplied by a 2.0-litre five-cylinder VTEC engine, driving through a new electronic sequential-shift automatic gearbox derived from that in the NSX. The instrument pack was an LCD display with a card-style ignition system and push-button starter.

Another novelty in 1995 was the Side-by-Side, a racing single-seater with a 650cc V-twin motorcycle engine mounted alongside the driver. Weighing just 380kg (840lb), it was fast, superbly balanced and a possible production prospect.

■ ABOVE *Angular shapes realized in aluminium pointed the way ahead for Honda design. The passenger and driver were separated by a metal bar.*

■ ABOVE *SSM stood for Sports Study Model. Although it first appeared in 1995, its appearance at shows for a further two years fuelled speculation about possible production.*

■ RIGHT *Coupés have always been a strong suit at Honda, and this aggressively styled four-seater shadows the American-market Acura CL.*

IAD

■ BELOW *The spectacular Venus was a dramatically wedge-shaped piece of sculpture, yet was fully functional, based around a Lotus Elite engine.*

International Automotive Design was founded in Britain in the 1970s, but its real glory days did not arrive until the 1980s. Eventually, it opened offices in California, Detroit, Tokyo, Paris, Frankfurt and Turin and became one of those quiet operations behind numerous mainstream products.

From Alien to Venus

After a few innocuous design studies, IAD burst on to the world scene with "an attempt to 'out-Countach' the Countach", as the designer of the Alien described his work at the 1986 Turin show. As an exercise in attracting international attention to the young British design company, the Alien was incredibly successful – crowds surrounded the car all through the show. Eventually, IAD attracted many big names, including Fiat, Mazda and Volvo, who beat a path to its door for design work.

The Alien was a stunning, waspish supercar with a F16 fighter-style glass

canopy over the passengers. Its handlebar steering and centre console reinforced the jet-plane impression.

Further concepts followed thick and fast. The Impact and Interstate were outrageous developments of the off-

roader/leisure vehicle (sports-utility) genre. Then came the Venus, audaciously launched at the hallowed Tokyo Motor Show in 1989, and later made fully functional for a Turin debut the following year. The canary-yellow Venus (designed by Michael Ani) used a Lotus Elite drive-train in another wedge-shaped body, dominated by a table-like plateau to the rear and ingenious wheel covers. These almost completely shrouded the wheels, and had a bold yellow accent across one-quarter of the circumference. IAD was flooded with Japanese work following the Tokyo debut.

Another highly impressive exercise was the Royale, an imposing luxury express (grand tourer) with mature lines. The interior was perhaps its most striking feature, decked out with leather and high-tech equipment, including one of the most sophisticated hi-fi systems ever seen on a car.

■ LEFT *The Venus, launched at the 1989 Tokyo Motor Show, made a big impact for British-based International Automotive Design.*

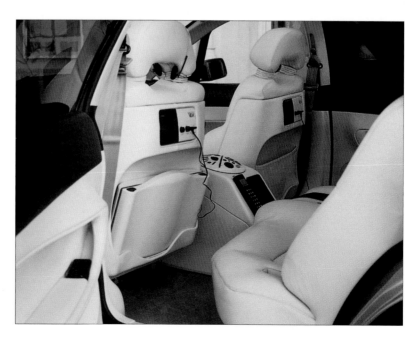

■ RIGHT *IAD's Hunter was a go-anywhere vehicle with a complete lack of any glass or weather gear.*

Its 1992 Lancia Integrale-based Magia prototype was extremely well received but a hoped-for production run with Lancia never materialized.

Calling it a Daewoo

In addition to production cars, IAD had considerable input into other manufacturers' show cars; for example, it created the 1989 SRD-1 for Subaru, a mix of five-door estate (station wagon) and low-slung sportscar styles, which ITAL design's Giorgio Giugiaro described as "right for the future". Also, it came close to entering production with one of the world's first viable electric hybrid cars, the LA301, but this effort was ultimately doomed.

IAD was eventually overcome by financial problems. Half the organization was acquired by British design and engineering company Mayflower, while the original Worthing design office came under Daewoo's control. IAD's talented design tradition therefore lives on in numerous Daewoo production and concept cars.

■ BELOW *With the Royale, IAD presented a mature-looking four-door executive-class saloon (sedan).*

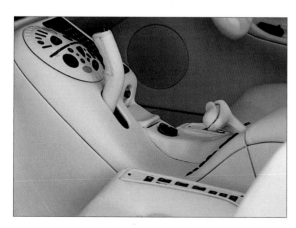

■ ABOVE *The intriguing white interior of the Royale featured advanced electronics, including an extremely powerful hi-fi system.*

■ RIGHT *Rear-seat passengers in the Royale were swathed in white leather and the latest in-car technology.*

ISDERA

German stylist Eberhard Schulz made his name in the 1970s with b+b, the famous and well-respected tuning-and-styling operation that produced so many upgraded Porsches. The pinnacle of b+b's work was undoubtedly the 1978 CW311 prototype, whose inspiration (the Mercedes-Benz C111) was clear. Fitted with a mid-mounted AMG-tuned 6.3-litre V-eight engine, many industry experts reckoned it had enormous promise.

■ ABOVE *Isdera's first project was the Spyder 033, which caused a stir with its decidedly Germanic styling and speedster-type roof arrangement.*

■ BELOW *The Spyder's cockpit was topped off by twin head fairings. Power came from a mid-mounted Mercedes-Benz engine from 2.3 to 3.0 litres capacity.*

Teutonic Spyder

In fact this promise was so enticing that Schulz set up a separate company to market a range of similar products. That was in 1983, and the first car to be produced was the Isdera Spyder 033.

The 033 mid-engined sportscar was as close to a dream car for the road as you could get. Its styling themes were very Teutonic: silver paint, strong forms coalescing into a muscular whole and an almost industrial theme throughout. Evocative head fairings nuzzled up behind the two passengers, who were

■ ABOVE *In cabin architecture, Isdera was very German. Colour schemes like this were all the rage in the 1980s, though hardly the highest expression of good taste.*

■ LEFT *Isdera's second model – and its most popular – was the Imperator. It looked very much like a development of Mercedes/Benz's CW311 concept car.*

the 1993 Frankfurt Show, the 112i Commendatore. Its development period was quite lengthy but resulted in a car that followed Isdera traditions, in other words the sort of supercar that Mercedes-Benz might have been making, if it hadn't had to deal with environmental issues.

The Commendatore was a fearsome beast. The predictable Mercedes V-twelve engine sat in the centre of a much more curvaceous body, but was tuned up to 400bhp. This meant a claimed top speed of no less than 212mph (341kph) and the sort of reliability you would never expect from other super-powerful sportscars.

protected from the elements only by a small wind deflector (there was no weather gear). They got in by hinging the doors upwards; the doors also took the wind shields up with them.

The 033 was powered by a Mercedes-Benz 2.3-litre engine. From 1989, this was replaced by a 16-valve 2.5-litre unit (195bhp) or a 3.0-litre six-cylinder.

Ferocious Dreams

Isdera's second model was the enclosed Imperator 108i, which was clearly derived directly from the b+b CW311 prototype, even down to its periscope for a rear-view mirror. The 108i had full gullwing doors and larger overall dimensions, and was altogether in a different league in terms of performance thanks to the fitment of the 5.6-litre V-eight engine from the Mercedes-Benz 560SEC. If you wanted even more

power, you could opt for the ferocious AMG 32V 6.0-litre engine: its 390bhp would take you to 188mph (302kph).

Isderas were built in tiny numbers: by 1990, less than 20 Spyders and no more than two dozen Imperators had been made. Not greatly increasing these numbers was a new model presented at

■ LEFT *The wedge-shaped profile of the Imperator was born in the 1970s but remained in production into the 1990s.*

■ BELOW *With an optional AMG 6.0-litre engine, the Imperator could reach a top speed of 188mph (302kph).*

ISUZU

The name Isuzu is known in the West mainly through its successful off-road vehicles and, even in Japan, Isuzu is the smallest and least prestigious of the domestic brands. It is all the more amazing, then, that the company should have such a brilliantly rich stream of design talent at its beck and call, and that it has produced, over the years, a startling string of concept cars.

4200R – star of Tokyo

Although hints of Isuzu's dream-car specialization were already evident in the COA series during the 1980s, no Isuzu dream car better illustrates its talent than the 4200R, which was the star of the 1989 Tokyo Show. Through its General Motors connections, Isuzu had close contact with Lotus in Britain, and it was Lotus that, via Isuzu's Brussels-based design office, essentially created the 4200R.

Julian Thomson was the designer of one of the cleanest shapes of this period: well proportioned, elegant, unfussy and

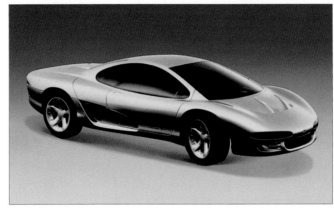

■ ABOVE *Isuzu began to impress with its COA series. This is the COA/III of 1987, a sports coupé with off-road levels of ground clearance.*

■ LEFT *The 4200R had a huge impact for Isuzu. Designed and engineered by Lotus people, it stole the 1989 Tokyo Show.*

free of gimmicks. Ex-Lotus man Simon Cox was more adventurous with the textured gunmetal interior, a two-plus-two cabin entered by four cleverly designed doors, the rear pair hinging clear of the body and sliding backwards.

The intention was that under the skin would lie a Lotus-developed version of

Isuzu's 4.2-litre V-eight quad-cam engine, producing 350bhp. Other technical highlights were four-wheel drive, Lotus active ride, a head-up display and navigation system. Sadly, the 4200R never made production, despite some encouraging noises.

Also at the 1989 Tokyo Show were two home-grown concept cars, the Costa and Multi-Cross, both based around the MU (Frontera) 4x4 platform. The Multi-Cross was a simple, rugged enclosed car with interchangeable doors and bumpers, while the Costa had a nautical theme.

Como – the F1 pick-up

Nothing could have been as nautical as the 1991 Nagisa show car, for this was actually a boat! In fact it was an amphibian, capable of cruising in the sea as easily as transporting its two passengers through the Tokyo rush hour – a completely daft notion.

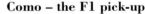

■ LEFT *Simon Cox created the startling Como, a car that combined supercar and pick-up styles over a Lotus V-twelve Formula 1 mechanical package.*

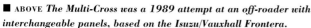

■ ABOVE *The XU-1 was a great 1993 exercise combining the rugged form of Isuzu's specialist off-roaders with sportscar-type scissor doors.*

■ ABOVE *The Multi-Cross was a 1989 attempt at an off-roader with interchangeable panels, based on the Isuzu/Vauxhall Frontera.*

No such derision awaited the Como, even though the idea of a Formula 1-powered pick-up may have seemed odd. Styled by Simon Cox, it used a mid-mounted Lotus V-twelve F1 engine and had a very short nose, gullwing doors and a pick-up rear deck. At the same 1991 Tokyo show but from Isuzu's California studio came the Terraza, an urban car powered by a ceramic engine and featuring a fifth wheel at the back for parking manoeuvres.

Group B rally cars, rally-raiders and the Citroën 2CV were all cited as influences by the designer of Isuzu's 1993 VehiCross, Simon Cox. Although its styling looked almost like science fiction, it was extremely well designed and thought out. Its chunky shape impressed executives so much that a feasibility study was carried out, and the VehiCross became a production vehicle with amazingly little modification within three years (bypassing the similar-looking but larger 1995 Deseo show car). There was no such happy fate in store for a dreamy fellow off-roader created by Californian stylists, the Trooper-based XU-1.

■ ABOVE *Is it a boat or a car? The Nagisa combined the two in one sublimely silly package.*

■ BELOW *Widely admired, the VehiCross was such a satisfying concept that Isuzu had the courage to re-engineer it for series production.*

ITAL DESIGN

■ BELOW *Giorgetto Giugiaro's very first project after forming Ital Design was the Manta, a mid-engined coupé based on Bizzarrini parts.*

Giorgetto Giugiaro's background in a family of artists helped him in his career as an "artist" of automotive forms. Even though his design career has encompassed such diverse areas as menswear, watches and pasta, his first passion has always been cars.

Giugiaro, the young art master
Aged just 17, Giugiaro joined Fiat's styling wing under Dante Giacosa and, two years later, accepted a job at Bertone and went on to become its youngest-ever head of styling.

In 1965, he left Bertone to head up Ghia and within three years had grown confident enough to set up his own consultancy with another ex-Fiat design and engineering expert, Aldo Mantovani. The office started in Turin but moved six years later to Moncalieri. Ital Design offered not only styling but also all the

services needed to bring a design to production, and soon manufacturers were flocking to his door.

As Ital Design, Giugiaro styled dozens of shapes for mass production, including the VW Golf, Maserati Bora, Lotus Esprit and BMW M1, all notable for an exceptional cleanliness of line. Ital Design has also produced some of the most admirable dream cars during its years, and has been highly influential in setting future trends.

Ital Design's very first project was the 1968 Manta, a dramatic coupé for the Italian specialist car-maker Bizzarrini. This was followed by sportscar designs

for Alfa Romeo (the 1969 Iguana and the 1971 Caimano), Abarth and Volkswagen (the VW-Porsche Tapiro and the Karmann Cheetah).

Boomerang and other prophecies
In 1972, the same year that Giugiaro designed the Esprit for Lotus, he also produced what many regard as his most extraordinary sportscar design, the Maserati Boomerang. This car, based on the Maserati Bora, pushed the frontiers of the accepted limits of car design. At only 42in (107cm) high, it was so low that the passengers were forced to become acrobats to get in, and the

■ LEFT *Geometric forms dominated the Boomerang and set Ital Design's agenda for two decades.*

■ RIGHT *Giugiaro cites the Tapiro as one of his most successful ever designs from a technical point of view.*

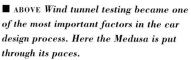

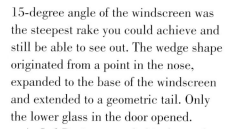

■ LEFT *The Lancia Megagamma of 1978 was a pioneer of the MPV form which grew up in the 1980s.*

■ ABOVE *Wind tunnel testing became one of the most important factors in the car design process. Here the Medusa is put through its paces.*

15-degree angle of the windscreen was the steepest rake you could achieve and still be able to see out. The wedge shape originated from a point in the nose, expanded to the base of the windscreen and extended to a geometric tail. Only the lower glass in the door opened.

As Ital Design extended its base of clients in the late 1970s, its concept cars became more prosaic, but the 1976 New York Taxi and the 1978 Lancia Megagamma were prophetic, proposing the idea of a compact, high-roof car with an adaptable interior layout – an MPV ahead of its time. In 1980, Giugiaro's Medusa showed a way forward in aerodynamics, proving it was possible to create a very clean four-door shape. This Lancia Montecarlo-based proposal boasted a Cd figure of just 0.263, then the most aerodynamic road car ever.

In 1984 Ital Design created the Etna for Lotus, which was at one stage earmarked for production. This was a supercar fitted with a stillborn Lotus four-litre V-eight 360bhp engine in the centre of the car. The contrast between its upper and lower halves was

emphasized by using thin, black-painted pillars, creating the impression of a transparent dome. The similar-looking Ford Maya from the same period was intended as a genuine production possibility and was full of practical features. It also had a removable targa top.

■ ABOVE *The Medusa proved that a long-wheelbase four-door design could be extraordinarily aerodynamic.*

■ ABOVE *With a front end almost indistinguishable from the Etna, the Ford-based Maya struggled to find its own identity.*

■ RIGHT *The Etna was built for Lotus in 1984, and should have become that company's first-ever V-eight supercar, but it was not to be.*

ITAL DESIGN

■ ABOVE *The main design feature of the Asgard was its extensive use of glass.*

■ LEFT *Outlandishly different, the Machimoto combined the joys of the motorcycle and car worlds. All passengers sat astride seats arranged in rows.*

Giugiaro struck out on a startlingly original course with the 1986 Machimoto, a hybrid of motorcycle and car elements. Although it looked like a cabriolet and used VW Golf GTI mechanicals, passengers sat astride twin rows of seats, rather like a motorbike, but the layout allowed seating for up to nine people. It could be steered either by a conventional wheel, by handlebars or by vertical hand grips. Another novelty was the prominent design of the wheel spats (skirts).

A similar feel recurred in 1996 with

■ ABOVE *The Aztec was a typically adventurous idea for a four-wheel-drive two-seater sportscar.*

■ LEFT *No less than three similar concepts were all based on Audi components: from front to back, the Aztec, Aspid and Asgard.*

the Formula series. This was a concept for multi-adaptable bodies to be fixed over the same structure. Giugiaro initially showed two ideas: the Formula 4 with its demountable speedster body and aero screens, and the Hammer with its open sides, split windscreen and more conventional seating. Neither was especially handsome but they both provided yet more evidence of his original thinking.

Aztec, Aspid and Asgard

More creativity arrived in a trio of designs produced in 1988. Each of the Aztec/Aspid/Asgard triplets shared a

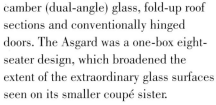

■ LEFT *A favourite theme of design houses is to propose their own interpretation of famous names, and this is Ital Design's Jaguar – the Kensington.*

■ ABOVE *More effort was expended on the Nazca than any other Ital Design concept car, but then this was a highly sophisticated BMW-engined supercar.*

common design theme and similar Audi mechanicals but had very different intentions. The most notable design element was the so-called "service centres" on either flank, which included sculptured gauges, read-outs for fluid levels and intricate compartments for tools and flashlights.

The Aztec was a four-wheel-drive two-seater with symmetrical but separate compartments accessed by doors, which hinged along a central point. The passenger's dashboard looked like the driver's, but the "steering wheel" was in fact a handle and the "instrument panel" was a screen to display car information on request.

The Aspid was identical to the Aztec up to the waistline and was a coupé version, which featured complex double-

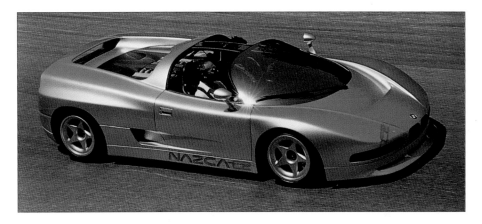

■ ABOVE *The Nazca theme was later developed by Ital Design to become the Spider, with an open roof.*

■ BELOW *The Nazca M20 boasted conventional doors with gullwing window flaps. Some observers would have liked to see the Nazca enter production as a BMW.*

camber (dual-angle) glass, fold-up roof sections and conventionally hinged doors. The Asgard was a one-box eight-seater design, which broadened the extent of the extraordinary glass surfaces seen on its smaller coupé sister.

With the 1990 Kensington, Ital Design suggested a future shape for a Jaguar saloon, and used Jaguar's V-twelve engine. The Jaguar chassis was left untouched but a modern yet recognizably "Jaguar" body was created. Interestingly, the windscreen was sited so far forward that it needed to be removed to dismantle the engine.

Nazca, Columbus and Firepoint
The Nazca of 1991 was probably the most talked-about of all Giugiaro's concept cars, and there was speculation that it might enter production as a BMW. Everyone remembered the

ITAL DESIGN

Giugiaro-styled BMW M1 supercar and the Nazca seemed to be the natural successor. It had a mid-mounted BMW V-twelve engine and styling, which inspired dozens of magazines to run cover stories. Entry was by conventional doors and flip-up side windows. Despite the fact that the Nazca went through two further evolutions, including a Spider version, BMW was adamant that it would not build such a supercar.

BMW did donate another V-twelve engine for the stupendous Columbus of 1992, which celebrated the 500th anniversary of the discovery of America. This was a huge machine: 19ft 6in (6

■ RIGHT *A BMW V-twelve engine sat underneath the immense Columbus, designed to whisk large parties of VIPs around at high speed.*

metres) long, 7ft (2.2 metres) wide and over 6ft 6in (2 metres) high. Its specification was equally grand: four-wheel drive, four-wheel steer, mid-mounted 300bhp engine and 20in (50.8cm) wheels. The interior was split into two compartments: the driver sat on a higher level with up to eight additional seats"below" in three rows.

In 1994, Fiat asked all the major Italian design houses to create a special body for the Punto (which was a Giugiaro design in the first place). Ital Design's interpretation was the Firepoint, a novel two-plus-two coupé with aircraft-inspired aerodynamics, such as the teardrop roof and reversed windscreen pillars. The side and rear windows could be removed, cleverly creating a roadster.

■ ABOVE *The electric-powered Biga was a minute little box capable of seating five people.*

■ BELOW *A V-ten engine sat amidships in the two-plus-two Cala prototype.*

■ ABOVE *Ital Design teamed up with Lamborghini to create the Cala, which was interestingly styled and could have become a production model.*

Cala and Legram

Lamborghini asked Ital Design to create a new two-plus-two targa sportscar that would slot in as an entry model below the Diablo, and so it created the Cala, which came tantalizingly close to production. The compact mid-engined two-seater used a brand new Lamborghini V-ten engine capable of phenomenal performance. Stylistically, its detail cues came from the Miura, though the overall shape was more of a wedge. Its advanced construction

■ RIGHT *Firepoint*
was the name given
to Ital Design's Fiat-
sponsored proposal
on the Punto.

consisted of an aluminium chassis
clothed in carbonfibre body panels.

The 1996 Legram was an almost
unrecognizable development of the
Formula "infinity project" begun by the
Formula 4. On the basic Formula
platform went an elegant sporting four-
seater body with an exceptional Cd
figure of just 0.25. A transparent dome
of glass stretched from the windscreen
base to the rear window, broken only by
aluminium cross-beams. Another
outstanding feature was the treatment of
the rear lights, which looked like
horizontal slits.

Ital Design's back catalogue of dream
cars is bewilderingly complete and
belies the relative youth of the company.
Equally impressive is the depth of its
engineering expertise and the extent of
its penetration into the design of
production models. In all cases, Ital
Design has been a trailblazer of ideas
and an initiator of clean design
principles and high-quality execution.

■ ABOVE *The idea behind the*
Formula project was to have
bodywork that was easily
interchangeable. This is the
Formula 4 sportscar.

■ ABOVE *The Legram proved that the*
Formula concept could produce a more
serious outcome. Note the intriguing use of
glass surfaces.

■ RIGHT *By changing a few of*
the upper panels, you could
create the Formula Hammer.
Some thought that this design
idea was seriously compromised.

MAZDA

Of all the Japanese manufacturers, Mazda has historically been the most adventurous in its production programme. Witness such extremes as the Wankel-engined Cosmo, the lithe RX-7 and MX-5 sportscars and the amazing AZ1 micro-gullwing coupé.

Alongside Nissan and Toyota, Mazda was one of the first of the Japanese show car originators, with cars like the 1970 RX 500. An early impact was achieved in 1981 when its MX-81 show car made its debut. The interest was the stylist, Bertone.

Mazda charted its direction with dream cars like the MX-03 of 1985. With the interesting MX-04 (1987) Mazda showed its ingenuity: this was a four-wheel-drive chassis shown with interchangeable bodywork – Mazda suggested roadster, coupé and buggy styles.

One of the three versions of the micro AZ550 Sports prototypes shown at the 1989 Tokyo show led to a production vehicle, the AZ1, a sports projectile designed within Japan's micro-car laws (maximum length 126in (320cm), maximum engine capacity 550cc).

Type A had a strikingly simple shape dominated by its glassy gullwing doors. Type C did not actually conform to the

■ ABOVE *Interchangeable bodywork provided the 1987 MX-04 with a choice of buggy or sports styles, the latter prefiguring the MX-5 production roadster.*

■ ABOVE LEFT *Mazda teamed up with Bertone to create its 1981 show car, the MX-81. Typically clean lines combined with a large glass surface area.*

■ LEFT *There was no steering wheel as such in the MX-81, merely an oblong "track" surrounding a TV display.*

■ ABOVE *Mazda's cute and tiny AZ550 Sports Type A actually became a production model (the slightly modified AZ1).*

■ LEFT *The AZ Type B was a funny little creation designed with removable roof panels for open-topped motoring.*

■ RIGHT *Despite being only just over 10ft long, the Type C AZ550 looked like a proper Group C racing-car.*

legal micro size requirements, but it was an amazing concoction looking like a toy-sized Group C racer, complete with a slanted front profile, large radiator intake and rear spoiler. Type B was perhaps the runt of the litter with its awkward humped lines.

Japanese Jekyll and Hyde

The 1989 Mazda TD-R was the first car to combine two potentially burgeoning fields, melding the apparently incongruous worlds of sportscars and off-roaders. Its nod to the sportscar world was its mid-engined two-seater layout, turbocharged 1.8-litre engine and ventilated disc brakes. Its off-roading alter ego emerged in permanent (full-time) four-wheel drive, minimal front and rear overhangs and deep sills. Joining Jekyll and Hyde was a novel wishbone suspension system, which could adjust the TD-R's ground clearance between 5in and 9in (130mm to 230mm).

Mazda's 1991 HR-X did not win any awards for styling, but that was not its main *raison d'être*. The HR-X pioneered a hydrogen-powered variant of Mazda's twin-rotor Wankel engine, which could

■ LEFT *Mazda's M2 division created a variety of special bodies, such as this M2 1008 coupé conversion for the MX-5. The headlamps are fixed behind cowls.*

also power an on-board hybrid electric motor. The bulky hydrogen tank was sited under the floor, but whatever its advantages, hydrogen looked an unlikely future power source, especially in such an outlandish shape as the HR-X's.

Centre stage at the 1995 Tokyo show went to the RX-01 prototype, a vision of a future, lighter, cheaper RX-7 sportscar. The rotary engine was retained,without the sequential turbocharging of the

contemporary RX-7, but with dry-sump lubrication and improved breathing – still good for 220bhp. It weighed only 2425lb (1100kg) and had aluminium suspension based on the MX-5.

Mazda was also unique in having an operation called M2, a dedicated design company based at its own office block in Tokyo. It created all sorts of alternative bodywork and engine modifications on existing Mazda cars, notably the MX-5.

■ ABOVE *Rotary power remained a Mazda forte, and the 1995 RX-01 provided a lightweight sportscar vision of its possible future.*

■ RIGHT *The TD-R successfully combined elements of sportscar and buggy themes: mid engine, four-wheel drive and variable ground clearance.*

MERCEDES

The C111 was not one project but five. This supercar blueprint was first shown in 1969, and was outside Mercedes-Benz's normal frame of reference.

A laboratory on wheels

Mercedes-Benz described the C111 as a "laboratory on wheels", and some were actually used on the road. Some of the features included gullwing doors, leather-trimmed cockpits and even air-conditioning.

■ BELOW LEFT *Breaking diesel speed records at Nardo in 1978: the aerodynamic C111/112 achieved an average top speed of 200mph (322kph).*

■ BELOW RIGHT *Mercedes-Benz show cars often anticipated forthcoming production cars. The F-200, despite its scissor-type doors and joystick controls, prefigured the new S-Class.*

The first example had a glassfibre body over a steel chassis and was fitted with a mid-mounted triple-rotor Wankel engine with fuel injection. That expanded to four rotors in the second generation C111 of 1970 – said to be good for 370bhp and 180mph (290kph). In its third form, a 3.0-litre five-cylinder turbodiesel engine was fitted, and the C111 immediately took all existing world speed records in the diesel class.

Further evolutions, with quite different bodywork, took more records: over 200mph (322kph) with a diesel engine (and 12 hours at an average 195.3mph (316kph)) and still more records with a 500bhp 4.8-litre twin-turbo V-eight.

There was a follow-up to the C111, logically called the C112. It appeared at the 1991 Frankfurt Show as a mock-up, by which time Mercedes-Benz was convinced that the market for such a supercar was not right – probably correctly, given Jaguar's experiences with the XJ220. The C112 would have been a stunning 6.0-litre V-twelve-powered mid-engined supercar. Mercedes even took orders for it (700 were received), but it returned them all.

Mercedes thinks small

As Mercedes-Benz began to diversify, it launched various concept vehicles to

■ OPPOSITE *Perhaps the most famous of all Mercedes-Benz concept cars was the C111, which first appeared in 1969 with a triple-rotor Wankel engine.*

■ ABOVE *Presented at the 1997 Frankfurt show, the F-300 Life-Jet was an amazing three-wheeler designed to lean into corners to simulate the behaviour of motorbikes.*

■ ABOVE *The AAV excited many show-goers because here, said Mercedes-Benz, was a clear indication of how the M-class (M320) off-roader would be.*

■ RIGHT *The stylish and highly textured interior of the AAV was typical of the boldness of concept cars.*

■ OPPOSITE *What might have been: the C112 was going to be a production V12 supercar but instead it was shown simply as a dream car in 1991.*

■ ABOVE *As the climate for supercars became more favourable in the mid-1990s, Mercedes-Benz and AMG built this stunning CLK GTR as a homologation road/race special.*

prepare the public for future changes. One example was the 1991 F100 MPV show car, paving the way for Mercedes' forthcoming V-class MPV.

The next obvious prediction of future models was the Vision, shown in 1993. For Mercedes-Benz this was a very radical concept, its first-ever small car. For the rest of the world it was also radical, featuring a ground-breaking layout of an engine sited so that it would move underneath passengers' feet in a head-on collision – good for driver and front-seat passenger safety, said Mercedes. By 1997 it was ready to launch the A-class, whose profile differed little from the Vision.

The same thing happened with the SLK (shown in concept form in 1994 and later somewhat diluted, particularly in the design of the headlamps and twin head fairings), the F200 (previewing the 1998 model S-class coupé) and especially the AAV, Mercedes' prototype 4x4, which fired so many imaginations – the eventual M-class road car was very staid in comparison. Perhaps most radical of all the designs was the F-300 Life-Jet trike, which leant into corners via computer control. Young, fresh and innovative, this exciting concept car brought to Mercedes a new sense of fun and experimentation.

MITSUBISHI

Mitsubishi burst into the dream-car arena with its HSR series which originated in 1987. Active ride, four-wheel drive and four-wheel steering may not have been very original in the concept car world but the fact that 295bhp and 186mph (299kph) were available from a 2.0-litre turbo engine certainly was.

A show-stopping car

Show-goers were impressed by the HSR's dramatically skirted shape, sophisticated electronics and novel seating, which swung out with the doors.

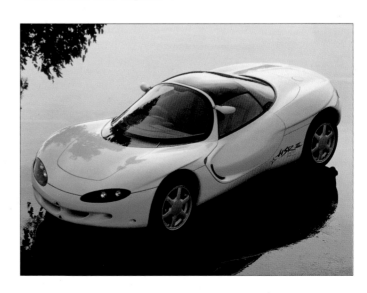

■ ABOVE *Mitsubishi's reputation for high-technology solutions reached new heights with the 1995 HSR-V, whose aerodynamics were claimed to have been inspired by dolphins.*

The stunning 1989 HSR II follow-up was officially only ever meant as a rolling test bed for technology and ideas, but the amazing shape attracted virtually all the attention, an aim that Mitsubishi surely intended, since it featured widely in corporate advertising campaigns. Mitsubishi called this project a Control Configured Vehicle, in other words a machine stuffed with computers and electronic displays. At various points around the body were flaps and wings whose position was controlled by computer so that airflow was optimized in any given situation.

■ ABOVE *Biodynamic suspension and an elastic (flexible) tail spoiler were two very '90s features of the HSR-IV.*

■ RIGHT *The HSR-III was strikingly styled and also technically advanced, with electronic suspension, four-wheel drive and four-wheel steer.*

■ ABOVE *This tiny bespectacled Lynx off-roader had an engine of just 660cc capacity.*

■ ABOVE *Some people likened the oddball mS 1000 saloon (sedan) to a modern-day duo-tone Morris Minor. Certainly it reflected a trend towards "retro" design.*

■ RIGHT *At the 1995 Tokyo Show, the Gaus offered a modern solution to adaptable luxury multi-purpose transport. The gullwing doors were more fanciful.*

Less noticed but perhaps more significant at the 1989 Tokyo Show was the RVR leisure car. Its novel retractable windscreen and targa roof were striking, and the latter made it into production in the Japanese-market RVR (Space Runner), which arrived in 1991.

The HSR evolved into a third generation in 1991. More compact but equally striking in its powerfully styled presence, the HSR III boasted electronically controlled suspension and traction control and a new 177bhp twin-cam 1.6-litre V-six engine. More far-fetched was the fitment of twin levers on the steering wheel in place of controls for the automatic transmission.

Inspired by dolphins

More outlandish 1991 Tokyo debutants were the mS 1000 and mR 1000 pairing. Catching the tidal wave of Japanese interest in all things "retro", the mS 1000 was an utterly bizarre two-tone curve-haven with a tiny chrome grille. It had two doors on the left and only one on the right, while the stubby little boot (trunk) led Mitsubishi to call it a "2.5 box" car. The mR 1000 looked more feasible: a two-seater targa-roofed runabout (commuter car), spoiled by flying buttresses at the rear and ugly tail lamps.

The proportions shrank even further in 1993 with the presentation of the tiny 101in- (257cm-) long, two-seater Mum, powered by a 500cc 30bhp engine, and the Lynx, an off-roader designed around Japan's micro-car regulations – meaning maximums of 660cc and a 130in (330cm) overall length.

By 1993 the HSR series was in generation IV, its styling ever more avant-garde, notably its elastic (flexible) aerotail rear spoiler. More significant was its "biodynamic" suspension, which became a production reality in the Galant.

Even more bells and whistles sprouted from the HSR-V in 1995, from elastic stabilizers to a vibrating under-floor, which was "a revolutionary way of reducing drag inspired by the skin of dolphins".

■ LEFT *Even by Japanese standards of miniaturization, the Mum was truly Lilliputian. It had a 500cc engine.*

NISSAN

Like most Japanese car-makers, it took Nissan almost two decades to refine its dream-car programme into something that was relevant and palatable for a worldwide audience. Early efforts, such as the 1970 126X, were characterized by dubious extremes and a certain lack of sophistication. However, Nissan did have some interesting ideas, including inflatable passenger airbags as early as 1971.

The dream car that catapulted Nissan into a more serious arena was the MID-4, which was a major Nissan project. It was first seen in 1985 as a Ferrariesque pure show car, but had matured by 1987 to look like a credible exotic rival for Porsche.

It was engineered around a 330bhp longitudinal 3.0-litre V-six twin-turbo engine and boasted four-wheel drive and four-wheel steering. There were serious noises about this becoming a production prospect as a new Nissan supercar, probably with a V-twelve engine and two-wheel drive, ready to do battle with Ferrari et al. That plan was scotched as the times did not favour such "hypercar" projects, although the production 300ZX of 1989 was hailed as "the first Japanese supercar".

The elegant 1986 CUE-X and ARC-X of 1987 also marked a new maturity.

■ LEFT *With a 330bhp twin-turbocharged V-six engine mounted amidships, the MID-4 promised much, although its styling was perhaps a little bland.*

■ ABOVE *The cleanliness of line and sensibility of proportion won many admirers when Nissan displayed its CUE-X in 1986.*

■ LEFT *The ARC-X of 1987 was a sophisticated precursor to Nissan's luxury-car programme Infiniti.*

Here was a pair of super-sleek, beautifully proportioned four-door saloons, which were also highly aerodynamic. The ARC-X featured four-wheel drive, four-wheel steer and a staggering array of electronics.

Pike dreams
Perhaps Nissan's most celebrated dream cars were the so-called Pike series of boutique models. Nissan set up a sub-division to manufacture special models,

■ OPPOSITE *The MID-4 was one of the more significant Japanese dream cars of the 1980s, as at one stage it was slated to become a production rival for Porsche and Ferrari.*

■ ABOVE *The first of the so-called Pike series was the curious Be-1, a retro-styled small car, which was so well received that it went into limited production.*

■ ABOVE *If the Be-1 evoked the 1960s, the Pao plunged further back to a utilitarian post-war era of flat glass, exposed hinges and sober lines. Again it was sold in small series.*

or "niche" cars in marketing language. The first of these was the Be-1, shown at Tokyo in 1985 and so well received that it went into production 18 months later. Its Mini-style round headlamps and retro-styling cues overcame the fact that it was based on the dowdy one-litre Micra, and it was widely admired.

Then in 1987 came the Pao (a 1940s-style runabout) and the humorously named S-Cargo, a bizarre arch-shaped van, which achieved tremendous popularity. Another design from this series (but destined not to go into production) was the 1989 Chapeau, a curious glass-house car, which looked somewhat like a telephone kiosk (booth) on wheels.

Perhaps the most charming of all the Pike cars was the Figaro, initially shown as a concept car but actually put into production. This heralded a new era of "retro" design in the car world, for here was a 1940s-style chrome-and-round-headlamps little car. Some details were appealing, like the electric canvas roof and chromed CD player; others were more dubious, like the all-white interior and toggle switches, which looked like Victorian cutlery. Also, it may have had the appearance of a sportscar but its 1.2-litre Micra engine and automatic transmission did nothing to make it behave like one.

■ LEFT *The humorously named S-Cargo was a brilliantly styled high-roof van.*

■ RIGHT *With the Figaro, Nissan exploited nostalgic yearnings for a different age. Production was very limited, and the 20,000 run was vastly over-subscribed.*

NISSAN

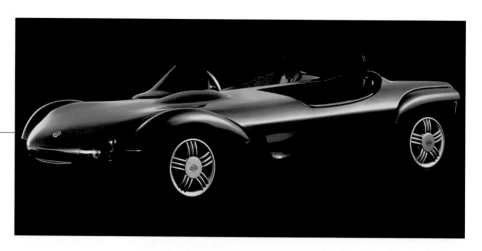

■ RIGHT *The Duad's name hints at its stepped passenger arrangement, dictated by the engine's position alongside the driver.*

■ ABOVE *This bold, retro, ultra-simplistic fascia comes from a 1989 concept called the Chapeau. While the interior was admirable, the exterior looked preposterously like a telephone kiosk (booth).*

■ ABOVE *The Rasheen brought a unique boxy style to the sports utility market. When it was shown as a concept car, western tastes were not motivated, but in production the Rasheen became a hot seller in Japan.*

From Boga to Duad

Nissan lost the plot a little with the 1989 Boga, its idea of a new city car. The concept was clever, to fit a four-door shell with luxury car space into an overall length of a supermini (compact), but the 1.5-litre Boga's style missed the

mark, and it perhaps got less attention than it deserved. Similar styling marred the 1991 Cocoon six-seater, whose party piece was a wake-me-up system: when it sensed that the driver was drowsy, it would spray a refreshing scent into the cockpit.

Nissan's 1989 UV-X was more down-to-earth, a neat one-box shape designed by Yoshio Maezawa, stylist of the 300ZX sportscar. Apart from being tipped to look like a future Bluebird (it didn't), its main feature was computer-controlled adjustable pedals and steering.

The 1991 TRI-X show coupé looked disappointingly back to the 1980s, and was clearly targeted at an American audience; this sort of thing reappeared in 1993 with the Marcello Gandini-styled AP-X. Much more engaging was its quirky Duad show car, which revived in spirit its 1987 Saurus. Intended as a modern interpretation of the immortal Lotus 7, it weighed merely 1035lb (470kg). Its quirkiness stemmed from the fact that the 1.0-litre engine was

■ LEFT *Although it looked perhaps like a dumpy VW Beetle, the FEV II had a more serious purpose, exploring city car possibilities.*

mounted alongside the driver, forcing the passenger's seat to be sited 15in (38cm) further back. Nissan hoped to launch the Duad as another in its Pike boutique series, but this never happened.

From Rasheen to Trailrunner

A different fate awaited the Rasheen, shown at Tokyo in 1993. This extremely box-like concept, described as "a totally new type of four-wheel-drive wagon",

actually made it into production. Its compact dimensions, practical Sunny mechanicals and characterful style endeared it to Japanese drivers, and led to a crew-cab-type (four-door pick-up) show car called the XIX in 1995.

Combining two-seater drop-top excitement with four-seater practicality was how Nissan described its 1995 AA-X, but the awkwardly colliding shapes looked uncomfortable, even if the idea itself was sound: to combine sportscar and family-car modes.

Nissan followed a happier path with its 1997 4x4 concept vehicle, the Trailrunner. Sporty styling crossed the bridge between the coupé and off-road worlds, and a unique design feature was a prominently displayed sliding spare wheel in the tail. Its 190bhp 2.0-litre engine and sequential six-speed CVT gearbox also promised a sporty temperament.

■ ABOVE *Nissan's designers were called upon to complete the R390 GT1 project in a short space of time.*

■ BELOW *To homologate the R390 for Le Mans in 1997, a tiny batch of road-going cars was built for discerning customers.*

OGLE

David Ogle founded his own industrial design company in 1954 and decided to branch out into car design (and indeed manufacture) in 1960 with a four-seater GT coupé based on Riley 1.5 mechanicals, but only eight were made. More successful was the pretty SX1000 coupé of 1962–64, an extremely curvaceous glassfibre body based on Mini parts.

Ogle also designed the very handsome SX250 body on the chassis of the Daimler SP250. This was shown at the 1962 London Motor Show and impressed British specialist company Reliant so much that it was modified to become the

■ LEFT *The use of heat-absorbing glass was quite advanced for its day. Ogle essentially invented the sports estate (station wagon).*

■ BELOW LEFT *Tom Karen has headed Ogle Design since 1962. The car pictured was once owned by HRH Prince Philip.*

■ BELOW RIGHT *Ogle Design was the leading British independent design house in the 1960s. This is its Triplex GTS estate, based on the Reliant Scimitar, itself an Ogle design.*

Reliant Scimitar coupé. Ogle then took the Scimitar and made a Triplex GTS estate (station wagon) special with a rear-end made of Triplex heat-absorbing glass. This car became the property of HRH Prince Philip for a time.

Tragically, in 1962 David Ogle died at the wheel of an SX1000, effectively ending the company's manufacturing life. Direction was taken over by Tom Karen, an innovative Czech-born designer. He was responsible for some effective designs, most significantly the Reliant Scimitar GTE sports estate.

The tangerine bug
The car of which Karen was most proud was the 1970 Bond Bug, a highly individual-looking three-wheeler based on a Reliant chassis. In many respects it was ground-breaking with its hinging canopy, its fixed, moulded-in seating, its use of aircraft-style black decals. Intended as a cheap fun car, it was available in only one colour – bright tangerine! Despite this, several thousand were sold.

Perhaps Ogle's most ambitious project was an Aston Martin DBS-based

sportscar created for the 1972 Montreal show. This sharply styled coupé featured much Triplex Sundym (tinted) glass, a green corduroy-and-leather interior with seating for three (the rear passenger sited diagonally behind) and brushed-steel highlight panels. Most remarkable of all was the rear-lamp panel, which had 22 circular lights. Many of these were sequential indicators, which flashed outwards in the direction you were turning; six others were for braking, the severity being indicated by the number of lamps lit.

Ogle went on to design a number of further one-offs such as the Princess 10-20 Glassback, the Mogul (which was a full-size version of a child's toy car Ogle had already designed), a modified Vauxhall Astra and various taxi projects.

Ogle Design's automotive work gradually dwindled away into occasional ventures such as the Project 2000 and a proposal for an updated three-wheeler to celebrate 21 years of the Bond Bug. Today, Ogle's car connections are at best tenuous as it concentrates on other industrial design work.

■ ABOVE *The Bond Bug was the most characterful of all Ogle Design's cars. A front-engined three-wheeler, it was available in only one colour – bright tangerine.*

■ BELOW *Ogle's Aston Martin DBS Special was state-of-the-art in 1972, featuring large Sundym (tinted) glass areas and brushed steel. Two examples were built.*

■ ABOVE *To get into the Bug, the roof canopy had to be lifted up, taking the sidescreens (windows) with it.*

■ RIGHT *The tail of the Ogle Aston housed no fewer than 22 lamps for braking, reversing and rear lighting.*

PEUGEOT

■ LEFT *Peugeot's best-known dream car is the Oxia, and not without reason. Its low, wide face was distinctively Peugeot.*

With Paul Bracq at the helm, Peugeot has had an illustrious design influence. Its true dream-car programme began with the Quasar at Paris in 1984. Based on the 205 Turbo 16 rally car, it was a formidable compact mid-engined sportscar with four-wheel drive and 200bhp. Its styling was light and forward-thrusting, its interior dramatically encased by a red roll cage.

The spectacular Oxia

Without a shadow of doubt, Peugeot's most important ever show car was the Oxia, first seen in 1988. Unlike many other dream cars, the Oxia was a fully-functioning prototype, quite capable of stunning levels of performance, as Peugeot proved during numerous well-documented test runs.

In its looks, too, the Oxia was absolutely spectacular. It was designed in-house by Gerard Welter and incorporated such Peugeot elements as low-cut headlamps, horizontal grille and rampant lion badge. The flamboyantly rakish and wide shape was realized in lightweight carbonfibre, and was topped off by an adjustable rear spoiler to help stability.

On a high-tech menu to set technophiles' palates slavering were a four-wheel steering system with variable weighting (variable assist), permanent (full-time) four-wheel drive (via a Ferguson viscous coupling), six-speed gearbox, anti-lock brakes, electronically controlled axle differentials and automatic

■ LEFT *With a turbocharged race-spec engine developing 680bhp, Peugeot was justified in claiming a top speed in excess of 200mph (322kph).*

■ BELOW *Based on the rallying Peugeot 205 T16, the mid-engined Quasar not only looked purposeful, it had the power and punch to carry out that purpose.*

■ ABOVE *The 1984 Quasar demonstrated that Peugeot's in-house design team had plenty to offer.*

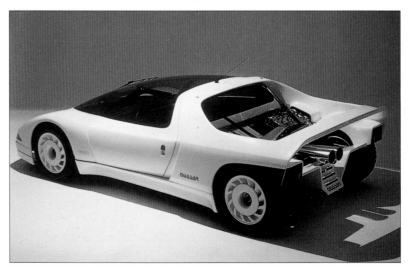

■ LEFT *The sculpturally engaging Proxima of 1986 was a formidably light and powerful sportscar concept.*

■ ABOVE *Opening the Proxima's roof canopy revealed an uncompromisingly scarlet cockpit.*

tyre-pressure monitors. Inside, traditional leather blended with solar-powered air-conditioning, a personal computer, a sound system described as "intergalactic" and a navigation system.

The basic engine was Peugeot's familiar 2.85-litre V-six but monstrously modified to full race specification with twin turbochargers to develop no less than 680bhp. Peugeot claimed – with justification – that the Oxia was capable of a top speed of 205mph (330kph).

Ion, Asphalte and Touareg

At the 1994 Paris Salon, Peugeot presented the Ion, an urban study vehicle powered by electricity. Only 11ft (3.3 metres) long, its monobox style was compact and modern, yet could fit four adults. Perhaps the main novelty was the total absence of door handles; to get in, you pressed a sensitive area on the rear wing – with your hip if your arms were full – and so released the locks. The same system worked for the large rear hatch.

"Crazy" was how some professionals described the extraordinary 1996 Paris Salon debutante called the Asphalte. The front-end picked up Peugeot design themes – wide snout, narrow headlamps – but toward the back-end things got very strange. The rear track was extremely narrow, so that from the side it looked like a three-wheeler with a pinched-in tail. The ultra-smooth topless profile promised sizzling performance, but strangely Peugeot opted to install a mere 1.6-litre engine and an automatic gearbox.

The Touareg off-road buggy stood out because of its mighty, even frightening wheels, straight off a science-fiction film set. One interesting quirk was its choice of power: four electric motors, one for each of those Tonka-toy wheels.

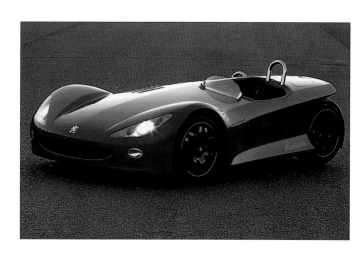

■ ABOVE *All attention focuses on the moon buggy wheels and tyres with Peugeot's 1996 Touareg concept car.*

■ LEFT *Although it looks like a three-wheeler, the Asphalte in fact had a pair of rear wheels, which were very narrowly set.*

PININFARINA

■ BELOW *Pininfarina has always been one of the great Italian coachbuilding names. This is a 1949 design based on a Cadillac chassis.*

At only 5ft (1.5 metres) tall, Battista Farina's nickname of Pinin – "kid" – is altogether fitting; so much so in fact that the name stuck and late in life he changed it officially. He founded a design centre of true genius, which his son Sergio continues to run from Turin, the capital of Italian and indeed world car design. He is among the great names of car design.

The pinnacle of car design

To cast back over the company's long list of production greats confirms the consistency of quality and proportion that distinguishes his work. From the

revolutionary 1945 Cisitalia (displayed in the New York Museum of Modern Art) to present-day Ferraris (which, since 1952, have almost exclusively carried the Pininfarina badge), the mark of genius is evident in the little blue 'f' badge with a crown on top. In between are dozens of designs for Alfa Romeo, Fiat, Peugeot, Honda, Rolls-Royce and many others.

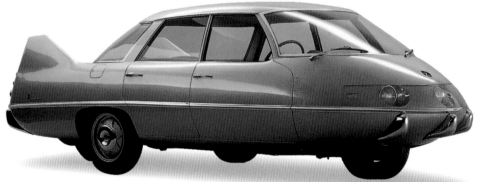

■ ABOVE *Farina's fascination with aerodynamics was evident in the extraordinary PFX prototype of 1960. Its diamond-wheel footprint helped reduce frontal area and thus drag.*

■ BELOW *The 1968 Ferrari P6 Berlinetta Speciale looked beautiful from all angles and became the point of departure for the Berlinetta Boxer.*

■ ABOVE *Despite a fascination with flowing shapes, aggression had its place in Farina's school of thought, as the Can-Am-inspired 1968 Alfa Romeo P/33 shows.*

■ LEFT *Pure sculpture on wheels is the almost inevitable description for the extraordinary Modulo of 1970, based on a Ferrari 512S.*

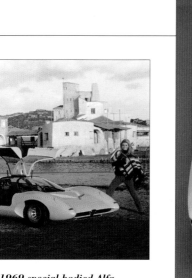

■ ABOVE *The 1969 special-bodied Alfa Romeo 33 was one of the great shapes of the 1960s, inspiring a generation of supercars.*

Pininfarina's dream cars are united by one theme: a flowing shape and perfect proportions. While others explored geometric shapes, Farina was inspired by the way snow in the Italian mountains was shaped by the winds, and the wind-cheating shapes of all his cars owe something to this stimulus. Others claimed that Farina said his ground-breaking stimulus came from well-formed female shapes.

The art of aerodynamics
Pininfarina was one of the first companies to install a wind tunnel (in 1972). A direct result of testing in this environment was the PF-CNR family-size car, which achieved a world record Cd figure of 0.161 and had a curious banana-shaped form: Pininfarina proved it could be practical by creating a version with air intakes, lights and mirrors (though the Cd figure increased to 0.23).

Not that aerodynamics was a new art-form, as the 1960 PFX proved. This extraordinary befinned, egg-shaped car even used a diamond-shaped-wheel footprint in its search for wind-cheating efficiency. A seminal aerodynamic study was the 1967 Dino 206SP, based on a racing Ferrari. It featured adjustable front and rear spoilers and gullwing doors. In the 1960s, Pininfarina experimented with some wild shapes, yet none of them had the glitzy fripperies of American show cars. Farina's designs were always classically elegant. One of the most influential was undoubtedly the 206 Dino and later Ferrari 365 P Special Berlinetta, which led directly to the Dino production car.

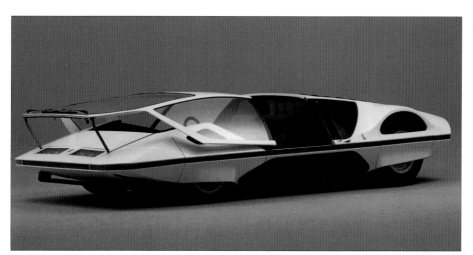

■ ABOVE *The Modulo had enclosed wheels and a canopy, which slid and cantilevered forward, drawing attention to what was in fact a brilliantly simple shape.*

■ RIGHT *One of Pininfarina's most admired production designs was the Fiat 130 Coupé. Here is the Maremma, an estate (station wagon) development study.*

PININFARINA

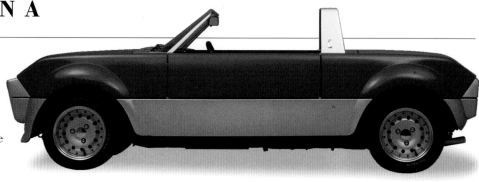

Farina Ferraris and Alfas

Pininfarina was always Ferrari's favoured couturier, not surprisingly in the light of such brilliant dream-car designs as the 250/P5 Berlinetta and the superbly clean P6 Berlinetta. Possibly the zenith of this golden era of mid-

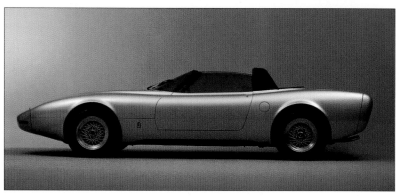

■ LEFT *A world record co-efficient of drag was recorded for this windtunnel-honed CNR – just 0.161.*

■ ABOVE *No doubt disappointed that Jaguar had failed to replace, in spirit, the great E-Type, Pininfarina produced this 1978 Jaguar proposal, based on the XJS.*

engined fantasy were the Ferrari 512 prototype and very similar-looking Alfa Romeo 33 prototype, whose exquisite sculpted sides, gullwing doors and ultra-low profile clearly inspired the Boxer and Countach of the following years to come.

Exploring the wedge school of design was the 1968 Alfa Romeo P/33 Roadster, based on the mid-engined racing 33. This was intended for impact, as evidenced by the row of six headlamps, front stabilizing fins, cut-down wind deflector (airdam) and prominent rear spoiler.

With the 1970 Modulo, based on the ultra-rare Ferrari 512S racer, the very extremes of sportscar design were explored to the absolute limit. Its very low bodywork formed an almost flat, almost symmetrical arc and was made by joining separate upper and

lower halves together. The prominent waistline strip – so low that it could almost be called an ankle-line – was allowed to run uninterrupted right around the car, including the wheels. These were covered with spats (skirts) which incorporated cut-outs in their tops. To allow entry, a one-piece canopy cantilevered forward.

Honda, Peugeot and Jaguar

Equally dramatic was the 1984 Studio HPX, a mid-engined supercar using a 2.0-litre Honda Formula 2 V-eight engine. Its striking shape was highly aerodynamic, partly owing to ground effect technology and the curious extended canopy (a Cd figure of 0.25 was claimed).

■ LEFT *Ferrari was always the keenest on Pininfarina's shapes, and the Turin design house pushed the boat even further with this supremely elegant Pinin prototype of 1980.*

■ ABOVE *Honda is another firm with a long association with Pininfarina. This Honda HPX had an extended glass canopy for optimized airflow.*

■ RIGHT *The 1985 Peugeot Griffe 4 was a good example of Pininfarina's restrained good taste, even in its show cars.*

Widely admired for its simplicity was the 1976 Peugette, an exercise in virtual symmetry of form. In fact the front and rear bodywork sections were completely interchangeable, and hinged up in identical fashion. The lights were housed in the bumpers, and the interior was marvellously unadorned. Its mechanical basis was the Peugeot 104.

The 1978 XJ Spider showed what the fabled Jaguar E-Type might have become. On the basis of a Jaguar V-twelve engine, a timelessly elegant body was created, picking up the E-Type themes of an oval front air intake and a profile, which bulged over the front and rear wheels. Jaguar's boss Sir John Egan fell in love with the XJ Spider and even developed its themes with the intention of launching an F-Type Jaguar. This was scotched, but it's enlightening to see how the current XK8 picks up many of the XJ Spider's details.

Perhaps even more elegant than the Jaguar study was Farina's Ferrari-based

study for a four-door car of two years later, called simply Pinin. In proportion it was supremely correct, and its sharp yet soft-edged style predicted the way many cars would be designed in the late 1980s. Ferrari never officially made a four-door car, and after seeing the Pinin many observers felt they ought to have done so.

Mythos, Chronos and Ethos

After doing several relatively "sensible" concept cars (such as the 1988 HIT based on Lancia Delta HF mechanicals), it was time in 1989 to try something more ambitious, and the Mythos was the result. The designers at Pininfarina based the car on the Ferrari Testarossa.

■ ABOVE *The HPX was typically clean but atypically geometric in its wedge-shaped profile.*

■ BELOW *Disguising the extreme girth of the Ferrari Testarossa was a challenge that the 1989 Mythos addressed.*

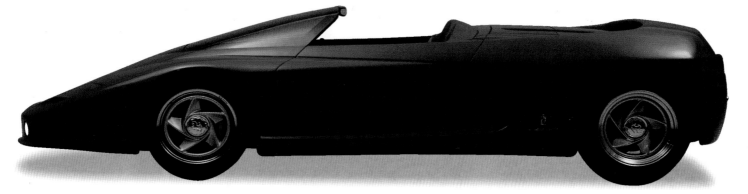

PININFARINA

■ RIGHT *Showing an originality of thought, the remarkable thing about the Ethos roadster was that at one stage Honda seemed likely to put it into production.*

■ ABOVE *To fit six people in the Ethos III, two rows of three seats had to be installed.*

The 1991 Chronos was a serious stab at a two-seater coupé based on Lotus Carlton/Omega running gear. Pininfarina wanted to persuade General Motors to go into production with the Chronos but ultimately did not succeed, probably because the shape was slightly disappointing for a Farina.

The same cannot be said of the 1992 Ethos, which also seemed capable of becoming a highly significant production car. It used an Australian-made Orbital 1.2-litre two-stroke engine mounted amidships and a sequential five-speed gearbox.

The Ethos body was penned by Stephane Schwarz, and was a steeply raked pure sportscar with deeply indented sides, virtually cycle-type rear wings, head fairings and a bold, stark interior with twin silver bars for a dashboard. At one stage, Honda looked likely to produce the Ethos, but the Orbital two-stroke engine unfortunately suffered many delays and the project faltered, despite the appearance of an Ethos II coupé.

The Ethos III of 1994 attempted to reinvent the city car. Into a body barely longer than a Fiat Cinquecento, Pininfarina managed to squeeze six seats – two rows of three with the middle seat offset. Crucial to the compact dimensions was the tiny 1.2-litre

■ ABOVE *The Ethos III was another extremely clever design. The body was smaller than virtually any car on the market, yet it could seat six people.*

■ BELOW *Argento Vivo is Italian for "quicksilver", and this Honda-based study was certainly mercurial in character. It combined "retro" and hi-tech themes.*

three-cylinder Orbital two-stroke engine. Lightweight aluminium kept the weight at 1720lb (780kg) and helped create 63mpg (100kpg) fuel economy.

Honda and Fiat

A 16-year co-operation with Honda was finally cemented in 1995 with the Argento Vivo sportscar concept. This was a power-top roadster with striking polished aluminium boot and bonnet (trunk and hood), blue bodywork and wide use of plywood. It was notable for a folding transparent roof, which could also be left in a targa position. Unfortunately, Honda was already developing a similar car in the SSM, and the Argento Vivo remained a scintillating prototype.

For the 1996 Turin show, Fiat asked various stylists to come up with ideas on its Bravo/Brava. Pininfarina's concept was the Song, a compact MPV with a multi-adaptable interior and more than a hint of off-road influence in its roof rails, clipped overhangs and chunky wheels. At the same show was the Eta Beta, powered by a hybrid petrol/electric (gasoline/electric) system and featuring a tail section extendable by 8in (20cm) for extra carrying capacity.

In 1997 Pininfarina continued its rich tradition as the world's leading design house; its advanced Nautilus saloon (sedan) car concept for Peugeot proved that it was still very much on the leading edge of car design.

■ RIGHT *As a fully functioning project using Honda Vigor and NSX components, the Argento Vivo might have made a practical production proposition, but Honda had irons in other fires.*

■ LEFT *The cleverest feature of the hybrid/electric Eta Beta was rear bodywork that could fold out to increase luggage capacity.*

■ BELOW *Farina's concept car for 1997 was the Nautilus, an extremely handsome four-door saloon (sedan) based on Peugeot components.*

RENAULT

The largest French car-maker founded its fortunes on comfortable, conventional and often rather boring family cars. It certainly did not go in for outlandish styling concepts and dream cars, preferring merely to hint at a little chic in its road-car offerings, which were deliberately designed for the masses.

That old attitude changed dramatically with the arrival of Patrick Le Quément as head of design in 1987. "We sell to people, not the masses" he said, and Renault's approach to its

■ ABOVE *Renault was one of the great show-car exponents. Here is an impressive selection of concept cars, starting with the 1990 Laguna (front right) and ending with the 1995 Initiale (second car in, top right)*

■ LEFT *The Zoom's headlight shows Renault's attention to stylized details.*

production car design was transformed with such innovative cars as the Twingo and Mégane Scenic.

Le Quément cleverly instituted a policy of producing show cars – and names – which clearly predicted future production Renaults, a trick he picked up during 17 years with Ford. In this way a lot of publicity was gained for Renault's show cars and the public was prepared for the revolutionary shapes and ideas of the next generation.

Le Quément banished the ghosts of such uninspiring experimental Renaults as the Vesta 1 and 2 (both super-economy cars) and the Eve Plus, an

■ ABOVE *Created by Renault-owned Matra, the tiny Zoom was a vision of a future electric city car.*

■ RIGHT *The Zoom's party piece was an ability to fold its rear under, shortening its overall length by 21.5in (55cm).*

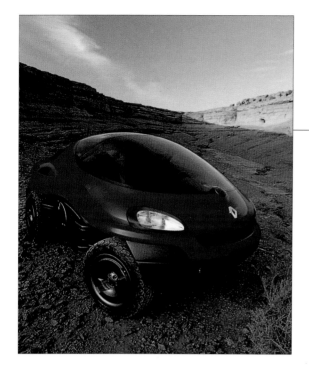

■ LEFT *The moon-buggy Racoon was a go-anywhere vehicle in the widest sense: it could also take to the water!*

■ ABOVE *The Scenic concept car of 1991 (left) led directly to the production Mégane Scenic car (right).*

aerodynamic efficiency saloon (sedan). The first project he oversaw was the 1988 Mégane, an elegant three-box saloon with such essential 80s equipment as four-wheel steering, intelligent suspension and a turbocharged engine. It was highly aerodynamic, notching up the very impressive Cd figure of 0.21.

From Twingo to Zoom

A tremendous exponent of the one-box design embodied by Renault's Espace, Le Quément's team created the much-vaunted Twingo, having earlier shown a larger one-box design called the Scenic at the 1991 Frankfurt show. This evolved into the production Mégane Scenic of 1996, a car that can genuinely

be said to have revolutionized one segment of car design.

In 1990, Renault first used the name Laguna on an ultra-sporty open two-seater dream car. Underneath the swoopy shape lay a mid-mounted two-litre engine (210bhp), and the cockpit could be covered by a solid tonneau. The concept of a completely open mid-engined sportscar obviously struck a chord at Renault because, some five years later, the very similar Sport Spider actually entered production.

Renault's subsidiary, Matra, developed the 1992 Zoom prototype, a startling electric two-seater. Quite apart from its arresting egg-like appearance and scissor-type opening doors, the

Zoom could amaze onlookers by pulling its rear wheels in and under its body, shortening the overall length from 104.3in to 82.7in (265cm to 210cm) – handy for parking in that tight Paris spot.

From Racoon to Initiale

Renault described its adventurous 1993 Racoon concept car as "an amphibious go-anywhere vehicle". It had four-wheel drive, hydraulic jacks to elevate ground clearance, a watertight body and completely amphibious capability. Its mechanical specification was not retiring either: a twin-turbo 262bhp V-six engine and six-speed gearbox.

Equally striking was the Twingo-based Argos roadster of 1994. This show

■ RIGHT *Launched at the 1994 Geneva Motor Show, the Argos was a startlingly original design from design chief Patrick Le Quément. The "piano lid" is actually the hinging boot.*

■ FAR RIGHT *Argos details: retractable screen, doors and mirrors, exposed rivets and a single rear seat with hi-fi gear.*

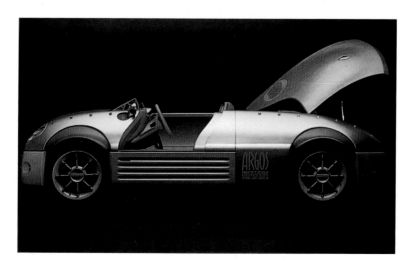

RENAULT

car really gave rein to Le Quément's vision of breaking with the "organic" shapes of the early 1990s. The Argos was full of industrial, Bauhaus-style detailing and little technological tricks such as ignition-activated swivelling door mirrors, drop-down doors, a folding 1920s aeroplane-style windshield and a piano-like opening rear lid. Interior textures in shades of green, cork and silver made a visual feast.

If anyone thought one-box design was

■ ABOVE *The 1995 Initiale was a projected future Renault limousine of superb elegance and, thanks to a detuned Formula 1 engine, deeply impressive performance.*

■ LEFT *Hard edges and soft curves balanced the Initiale's presence superbly.*

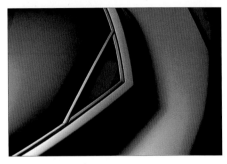

■ ABOVE *Avant-garde detailing from the rear end of the Initiale.*

■ BELOW *The Modus and Ludo were Renault's 1994 vision of electric-powered city transport of the future.*

the only way to go, then Renault banished that idea with the Ludo concept car at the Paris Salon in 1994. The two-box Ludo had a very adaptable interior with foldable, removable seats and a huge interior volume; it anticipated similar treatment for the 1997 Renault Clio.

With the elegant Initiale (1995), Renault signalled a way ahead for luxury cars, and stole some of the thunder of Ford's edge-design programme. The Initiale was a super-saloon (high-performance sedan) powered by a detuned Formula 1 engine (claimed top speed was 190mph, or 306kph), yet had accommodation for four people. The tapered nose and tail recalled the style of the 40CV, Renault's prestige model in the 1920s.

Fiftie and Pangea

To celebrate 50 years of the highly successful Renault 4CV, Renault's design team produced the Fiftie for the

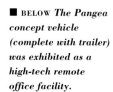

■ ABOVE *Novel interior treatment in the Fiftie included wickerwork (woven) trim and curious stacks at either end of the dashboard.*

■ RIGHT *Retro and resolutely modern influences met in the Fiftie concept car of 1996.*

Geneva show in 1996. This was a concept car out of the normal stream. Certain elements of the 4CV were recognizable – the curved roof-line, the raised bonnet (hood), the air intakes for a rear- mounted engine – but this was definitely not a retro design.

The fact was that the Fiftie had a Sport Spider chassis and was an ultra-modern two-seater. It marked the first fitment of Renault's new 1149cc engine (which would later power a revised Twingo), and was sporting in slant. The roof could be wound back and then folded down to make a virtual convertible, while the interior was a delightful blend of natural textures and curious "stacks" at either end of the dash. Particularly striking was the treatment of the lights, both front and rear, the tail-lamps "evoking waving flags," said Renault.

At the 1997 Geneva show, Renault displayed a concept van called the Pangea, which clearly predicted the shape of its forthcoming Kangoo utility/family car. In spirit, this was greeted as a revival of the long lost, greatly mourned Renault R4, as its boxy shape recalled the car that was France's best-selling machine of all time. Again this was no throwback, however, but was resolutely looking forward – like all of Renault's concept machines.

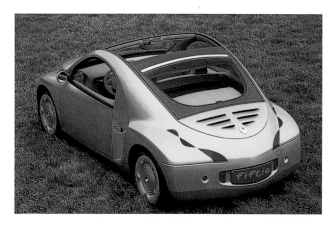

■ LEFT *The Fiftie's roof slid back and then down on to the rear deck. Note the rear lights – evocative of flags waving in the wind, said Renault.*

■ BELOW *The Pangea concept vehicle (complete with trailer) was exhibited as a high-tech remote office facility.*

RINSPEED

Based in Zurich, Switzerland, Rinspeed's main stock-in-trade has always been outrageously fast and furious conversions based on regular production performance cars. It started out turbocharging Volkswagen Golfs, then moved on to Porsches, with which it really made its name. One of its most celebrated conversions was a "droop-snoot" front-end on a 911, a style that Porsche itself later adopted for its own car designs.

Usually Rinspeed altered the aesthetics of its base cars, typically upgrading wheels and tyres, adding a body kit, installing pop-up or high-intensity headlamps, injecting leather and wood into the interior and stacking up a monster hi-fi system.

Eventually, it also turned to other, even more exotic projects. The Veleno was a mutated, 550bhp nitrous-oxide-injected Dodge Viper, for example, while Rinspeed also modified a Bugatti EB110 visually and mechanically.

Then, at successive Geneva Motor Shows, it surprised and occasionally

■ LEFT *Swiss specialist Rinspeed founded its fortunes on Porsche 911 conversions such as this Speedster-style car.*

shocked the world with its avant-garde dream cars. Unusually, these design extremes were actually offered for sale in series (regular production) at stupendously high prices, admittedly, at last offering some home-grown

competition for the king of automotive couture extraordinaire, Lausanne-based Franco Sbarro.

This achievement was realized by teaming up with American operations TLC and Panoz, which actually

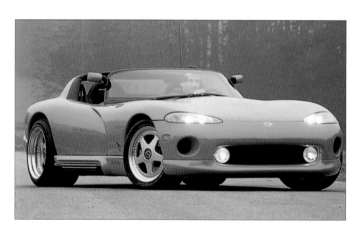

■ LEFT *Called the Veleno, this heavily modified Dodge Viper looked different and – thanks to a nitrous oxide-charged 550bhp – felt quite different too.*

■ LEFT *The Roadster was a sportscar in the old-fashioned sense of the word. Note the strange "eyes-on-stalks" headlamp treatment.*

■ ABOVE *Fitted with a Ford Mustang V-eight engine, with up to 305bhp on offer, the Roadster was a very rapid machine.*

■ ABOVE *The Yello Talbo was inspired by the classic 1930s Talbot-Lago but brought kicking and screaming into the '90s – hence the association with electro band Yello.*

manufactured the cars; Rinspeed was responsible for the outlandish additions to the coachwork.

Stars of the Geneva show

The first of the Geneva series was the 1995 Roadster, a sort of updated Lotus 7/AC Cobra cross-over with tiny doors, a narrow windscreen, separate wings and evocative roll-over hoops. It was the nose that grabbed all the attention: extraordinary "eyebrows" sprouted from either side of the jut-forward snout, housing compact, underslung double headlamps and indicator units sited on their tips. The impression was of the

face of some wild banshee, an effect augmented by the colour of the show car – bright orange!

Powering the Roadster was a five-litre Ford Mustang engine, available in two states of tune. The R version had 218bhp while the ferocious SC-R got 305bhp. Rinspeed claimed performance figures of 160mph (258kph) and 0–60mph (96kph) in 4.4 seconds for the faster SC-R version.

The following year (1996), Rinspeed presented the Yello Talbo, whose name derived from TLC's existing Talbo model in the USA and the urban/electro-pop music group Yello, which endorsed the

car. Inspired by a 1938 Talbot-Lago 150SS design by Figoni & Falaschi, the Yello Talbo resolutely brought the shape into the 1990s. Its supercharged V-eight engine developed 320bhp.

In 1997 came the strangest Rinspeed yet, the Mono Ego. Many questions were raised at its Geneva show debut. If this was a Yankee-style hot rod, why did it have a Hyundai engine (an "experimental V-eight") and Hyundai Coupé lights? Why one seat? Why was a famous French fashion designer involved? No satisfactory explanation was received, but that was in a way the point: a total defiance of logic.

■ RIGHT *An implausibly long bonnet (hood) covered an equally implausible engine – a V-eight from Korean company Hyundai.*

■ ABOVE *No one was quite sure what to make of the Mono Ego, a bizarre mix of haute couture fashion and American hot rod.*

SBARRO

Franco Sbarro is an Italian who emigrated to Switzerland in the 1950s and went on to become that country's most famous car-maker and one of the design world's most adventurous figures. His extraordinary work ranges through tiny electric cars, exquisite replicas of great classics, racing-cars, imaginative one-offs and innovative supercars.

He shot to fame in 1969 when he transformed a Lola T70 racing-car into the world's fastest road car, but his name

■ LEFT *Franco Sbarro's extraordinary dynasty kicked off with exquisite replicas such as this Bugatti Royale, which used two Rover V-eight engines joined together to make a V-sixteen.*

■ ABOVE *The Super Twelve may have looked like a hatchback with a simple paint job, but underneath it all lay two Kawasaki motorcycle engines making a 12-cylinder unit.*

became widely known through a string of replicas, including BMW 328, Bugatti Royale and Ferrari P4.

His "Super" series was particularly headline-grabbing. Its least spectacular members were the Super Eight, which looked like a VW Golf but had a Ferrari 308 chassis and engine, and a Porsche 928-engined Golf. The first of the series, the 1982 Super Twelve, was simply outrageous: an unassuming hatchback with two Kawasaki six-cylinder motorcycle engines joined together amidships for a single engine developing 240bhp.

Another project in a similar vein was the Robur, a very compact, 130in (330cm) long car with a 200bhp mid-mounted Audi turbo engine and a fifth wheel, which proved useful for pulling the rear-end into tight parking spots.

The Challenge came close to being a mass-production car by Sbarro's standards, since seven have been built to date. This uncompromising wedge-shaped car, first seen in 1985, looked like a slice of Gruyère cheese and was

■ ABOVE *Looking like a slice of Swiss Gruyère cheese, the Challenge was a very rapid sports coupé offered with Porsche or Mercedes engines.*

■ BELOW *The Challenge may not have been particularly handsome, but it was dramatic in every way.*

■ RIGHT *Sbarro's unconventional approach to improving engine access is plain for all to see in the Chrono.*

claimed to have a Cd figure of just 0.25. The doors folded forward for entry. Initially the Challenge was offered with a twin-turbo Mercedes V-eight engine, but later cars had Porsche engines mounted in the rear. All were capable of storming speeds – up to 180mph (290kph) was claimed.

"Throw out the hubs!"

Proving that extremes did not have to relate to speed alone, Sbarro's 1987 Monster G was a phenomenal all-wheel-drive concoction. It was not the four-wheel drive but the wheels themselves that impressed: they were taken from a Boeing jet! These made the Monster sit

some 7ft 5in (2.3 metres) tall, and the 350bhp Mercedes-Benz 6.9-litre V-eight was needed to get those wheels moving.

"Throw out the hubs!" exhorted Franco Sbarro at the 1989 Geneva show when he released on to the world a major innovation: the hubless wheel.

The concept of a wheel without a centre to it had a sound theoretical basis, as Gordon Murray confirmed. The idea was that the wheel rotated around bearings actually in the rim. Having the drive and braking applied directly to the rim meant greater rigidity, less weight, less

■ ABOVE *The Astro was relatively toned down by Sbarro's standards. It had a Ferrari engine and curious little projector headlamps under the windscreen.*

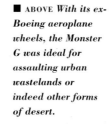

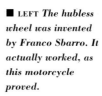

■ ABOVE *With its ex-Boeing aeroplane wheels, the Monster G was ideal for assaulting urban wastelands or indeed other forms of desert.*

■ LEFT *The hubless wheel was invented by Franco Sbarro. It actually worked, as this motorcycle proved.*

torque reaction, less axial and radial strain and perfectly vented braking. Sbarro had experimented with such wheels on a motorcycle a few years before; however, it was obvious that much more development was required, and this innovative scheme was left on the shelf.

Nevertheless, the Osmos show car, which incorporated the hubless wheel, was popular at motorshows. Cleanly styled, somewhat soberly perhaps for Sbarro, it boasted a 12-cylinder engine.

SBARRO

■ LEFT *Under the long bonnet of the concept Isatis lay a BMW 5.0-litre V-twelve engine.*

■ ABOVE *In characteristic red overalls, Franco Sbarro sits in one of his creations, the Urbi electric city car.*

Chrono, Isatis and Oxalys

The 1990 Chrono hinted at its purpose with Swiss watch badges dotted around the body. This was a car designed to go from 0–60mph (0-96kph) in the shortest possible time. Weighing just 1430lb (650kg), the same as a 2CV, yet powered by a 500bhp BMW M1 engine, it could do "the sprint" in 3.5 seconds. In a typical Sbarro touch, the whole car hinged in the middle for access to the engine.

For the 1991 Geneva show, Sbarro presented an interesting twin-chassis supercar. The V-twelve engine and gearbox, beam chassis and suspension were attached to the body by six hydraulic links. In theory, these allowed the body to be insulated from the chassis, which meant that a supremely comfortable ride was possible without sacrificing the firmness of the

suspension. The body could also be jacked up at will. Wild by anyone else's standards but shy by Sbarro's, the 1993 Isatis was based on the V12-powered BMW 750iL. The main interest lay inside, its steering wheel featuring a centre-mounted rev counter (tachometer) and speedo.

The next year came the Oxalys, an intriguing cocktail described as "designed by the young for the young". Underneath its smart exterior – designed by Espace Sbarro students – lay a 340bhp BMW M5 engine and Porsche 911 rear suspension and brakes. One novel feature of this

■ LEFT *Like virtually every Sbarro design, the 1995 Alcador was a fully functioning car capable of being driven in anger.*

■ ABOVE *With its muscular, sci-fi "shoulders" protecting the occupants, the Alcador had a 400bhp Ferrari V-twelve engine.*

■ RIGHT *With the 1996 Issima Sbarro turned his attention to an Alfa Romeo study. It was widely admired by industry professionals.*

"back-to-basics" roadster was a modern version of a dickey (rumble) seat – a convertible pair of rear seats.

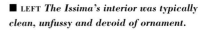

■ ABOVE *Yet another piece of radical engine surgery saw two Alfa V-six engines being joined together to create an Alfa V-twelve in the Issima.*

Issima and Ionos

The main attraction of the 1996 Issima lay under its long, Alfa-badged bonnet. Nestling there were a pair of Alfa Romeo 3.0-litre six-cylinder engines joined to make an in-line twelve with 500bhp on tap. Its smart styling was admired by Alfa's own styling boss, Walter de Silva.

According to Franco Sbarro's students, who designed the 1997 Ionos, this was how a latterday Lancia Stratos should be. Following Sbarro's joining of two Alfa engines to make a straight eight, the Ionos had two Lancia Kappa five-cylinder units joined together to make an upturned V-ten layout, with a Porsche gearbox between the banks. Transmission was Porsche four-wheel drive. The "crash helmet" window profile was reminiscent of the original Stratos.

Also at the 1997 show was a pair of sportscars called the Formule Rhin and Be Twin. They were conceived to teach rich kids how to drive and were fitted with two sets of controls. The 1320lb (600kg) Formule Rhin had a ferocious 200bhp Peugeot 3.0-litre V-six engine behind the seats, while the Be Twin, at under 990lb (450kg), had a Lotus Elan-style backbone chassis, stressed mid-mounted engine (a 140bhp 1.6-litre unit from the Citroën Saxo Cup racer), self-ventilating disc brakes and double-wishbone front suspension.

■ LEFT *The Issima's interior was typically clean, unfussy and devoid of ornament.*

■ LEFT *The 1997 Ionos was Sbarro's view of a latter-day Lancia Stratos.*

■ BELOW *Sbarro founded a design and engineering school, and the Oxalys was just one of the projects realized by his students.*

TOYOTA

While most Japanese firms turned to European design houses for their innovative designs, Toyota struck its own course. The 1969 EX III was a case in point. Here was a sleek coupé, which advanced the dream-car ideal as much as the Europeans. Its sleek shape carried over to its ultra-smooth undertray (underbody), making it very aerodynamic.

■ ABOVE *Toyota's 1987 FXV-II prototype was typical of the characterless concepts produced by Japan in the 80s.*

■ ABOVE *It may not have been a great beauty to behold, but the 4500GT marked a brave tour de force for Toyota's design and engineering teams.*

Advanced technology, maturing design

Like most Japanese makers, Toyota's dream cars struggled to find an identity until the 1980s, when advanced technology and maturing design teams began to enhance the impact of its concept machines, such as the 1984 FX-1 with its electronic suspension, cantilevered doors and variable valve timing.

On Toyota's stand at the 1987 Tokyo show was a dream car that made it to production. The little gullwing AXV-II reappeared two years later as the Sera. It may only have been a Starlet underneath, but its character was made stimulating by its expansive glass bubble top – the glass in the doors curved round to form part of the roof.

One of the greatest technical *tours de force* of all time was the verdict on the 4500GT show car of 1989. Its Lexus-based V-eight engine had five valves per cylinder, the gearbox had six speeds, the suspension was variable and the run-flat tyres had pressure sensors on board.

■ ABOVE *Born out of the AXV-II prototype, the Sera was a rare example of a concept car making it into production.*

■ BELOW *The point of the AXV-IV was to reduce weight, and its advanced construction meant a total mass of just 990lb (450kg).*

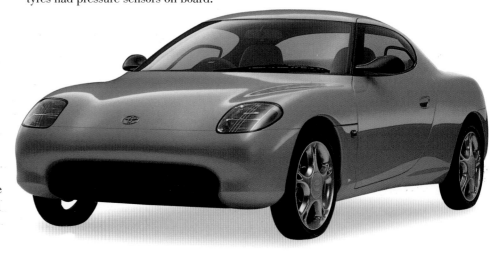

■ ABOVE *With a Cd figure of just 0.20, the AXV-V had an aerodynamic profile equivalent to that of an aeroplane.*

■ RIGHT *With suspension that was adjustable on each side (and even a half-track option instead of wheels), the Moguls turned mountains into molehills.*

Novelties included LCD shutters for the vertically stacked headlamps and sun visor, ultra-sound wing mirrors to clear water droplets and a Noise Canceller, which emitted signals of opposite phase and amplitude to eliminate noise "booms". Although the 4500GT may not have looked very pretty, all five that Toyota built were fully sorted road-going machines.

Concepts of all sizes

The AXV III concept car was merely a taster for the forthcoming Carina, while the 1991 AXV-IV was far more interesting, mainly for its construction, in ultra-lightweight aluminium,

magnesium and carbonfibre; even the springs were plastic. Immensely strong yet incredibly light (just 990lb or 450kg), the little coupé-style commuter car was fitted with a 64bhp two-cylinder 800cc two-stroke engine.

Mega Cruiser is not a subtle name, but then this was not a subtle car. Presented at the 1993 Tokyo show, it was a monstrous off-roader, 16.4 feet (5 metres) long, with a 4.1-litre truck engine. Following a good reception, it actually made it into production as one of the world's widest cars – all 7ft 1in (2.17 metres) of it.

The AXV-V of 1993 combined aerodynamics with advanced direct-

injection engine technology. Toyota claimed a Cd figure of just 0.20 – equivalent to an aeroplane – which helped to give it remarkable fuel consumption. Other technological innovations included air suspension, an anti-collision automatic brake system, touch-shift transmission and LCD monitors.

In response to a new wave of roadsters from MG, Fiat and BMW, Toyota unveiled its MRJ prototype at the 1995 Tokyo show. Actually designed by Toyota's Brussels design office, it was the company's first-ever open mid-engined car. The roof was a so-called "aerocabin" hardtop, which retracted electronically at the flick of a button.

■ ABOVE *Over 7 ft wide (2.1 metre), the four-wheel-drive, four-wheel-steer Mega Cruiser was actually sold on the Japanese market as the most expensive car around (costing 20 million yen).*

■ ABOVE *The very pretty MRJ was a mid-engined styling exercise and Toyota's first-ever open mid-engined car. It paved the way for a future generation of convertible MR sportscars.*

VW

One of the most vaunted of all 80s concept cars was Volkswagen's Futura, created by Professor Ulrich Sieffert. A one-box Golf-sized car – years before the Mégane Scenic made the genre popular – it was full of ideas.

The car that parked by itself

The gullwing doors were purely for show effect, of course: the notion of two-piece doors, of which the upper half were gullwing and the lower half dropped into the sills, was hopelessly impractical.

■ RIGHT *If the gullwing doors of the Futura were perhaps gimmicky, even more so was its ability to park itself via electronic monitors.*

■ BELOW *The idea behind the Vario was that any body could be fitted on to a common platform. This is the Vario I open four-seat buggy.*

The mostly glass upper dome was equally striking.

More significantly, the direct-injection petrol (gasoline) engine was years ahead of its time. Aided by a G40 supercharger, the 1.7-litre engine was very economical and very clean.

The Futura's main party piece was its four-wheel steer system. Based on a Golf rear axle turned through 180 degrees, it provided plenty of fun when you wanted to park. Thanks to sensors fitted for restricted visibility and electronic throttle and transmission, the Futura could wriggle into a parking space all by itself, manoeuvring back and forth on its own.

Another novel city car proposal was the three-wheeled Scooter of 1986. Based on a Polo drivetrain, it was a lightweight, good-looking shuttle capable of 125mph (201kph). The two-seater interior included a dash-mounted briefcase!

At the 1991 Geneva show, VW presented another new concept called Vario. Two styles were displayed, to show how different the bodywork could

■ BELOW *The Vario II was an alternative bodywork proposal created by design students for VW.*

■ LEFT *VW explored new territory with the Chico, a city car capable of being propelled by a variety of power sources.*

■ ABOVE *A commuter car with three wheels? The Polo-engined Scooter actually made a lot of sense, and was quick into the bargain.*

■ LEFT *Nothing less than the rebirth of the Beetle was how Volkswagen presented the Concept 1, styled by VW's California studio.*

be on the same platform. VW actually planned to sell a platform (based on a lengthened Golf Synchro 4x4) on which specialists could create their own bespoke (dedicated) bodies. However, VW's own efforts – admittedly designed by VW students – were uninspiring, and, not surprisingly, little more was heard of this novel idea.

The Beetle reborn

It was a design nucleus in VW's studio in California which created the car that stole all the thunder at the 1994 Detroit show – nothing less than the rebirth of

the legendary Beetle. Called Concept 1, it took the rounded themes of the 60-year-old Beetle and brought them into contemporary fashion, with bold Bauhaus curves and giant wheels.

The technology under it was modern, too, deriving from the Polo, and that meant front-wheel drive (or even four-wheel drive) and a front-mounted engine. The reaction to the Concept 1 (and its convertible brother, which

appeared at Geneva three months later) was so overwhelmingly positive that VW took the bold decision to engineer a production version for 1998. The shape and dimensions were changed and the basis (mechanicals) switched to the Golf MkIV, but in spirit and broad brush strokes the new Beetle was essentially a concept car born in the flesh.

Following up that media event was always going to be difficult, and efforts like the Noah gullwing MPV study, while striking, have not had such an impact.

■ RIGHT *A handsome Cabriolet (convert-ible) version of the Concept 1 was displayed at Geneva in 1994 and looked equally likely to enter production.*

ZAGATO

■ LEFT *The Alfa Romeo-based Zeta 6 was a high point for Zagato: well proportioned, smooth and purposeful in appearance.*

Zagato belongs to a select band of Italian coachbuilder dynasties. It is one of the oldest of all, founded by Ugo Zagato in 1919 in Milan, and has an illustrious past. Its heyday undoubtedly came in the 1950s and 60s when it created superb coachbuilt bodies for Ferrari, Alfa Romeo, Fiat, Maserati, Aston Martin, Bristol and Lancia.

Brothers Elio and Gianni Zagato set up a new factory in 1962 and eventually expanded into other areas such as electric and armoured cars. A unique Zagato characteristic is the "double-bubble" roof, originally intended to clear the heads of passengers in its very low bodies, but this has since become an

■ ABOVE *The Zeta's cowled instruments were in deference to the traditional Alfa Romeo style.*

■ LEFT *The undoubted beauty of the Zeta 6 impressed Aston Martin enough to commission Zagato for one of its own projects.*

From Zeta 6 to Raptor

The 1983 Zeta 6 can be singled out as perhaps Zagato's best recent design. This two-plus-two coupé was based on the 2.5-litre Alfa Romeo GTV-six. Chief stylist Giuseppe Mittino extracted a classically graceful style from this project and gave it the Zagato trademark of a distinctive double-bubble roof. It was this car, seen by Aston Martin's director Victor Gauntlett at the 1983 Geneva Motor Show, which led directly to the Aston Martin Zagato project.

Zagato started to go off the boil in the late 1980s. First it presented a vision of a future Aston Martin Lagonda called the Rapide, which was so poor that Aston Martin boss Victor Gauntlett took the unusual step of distancing his company from anything to do with it. Then came the Stelvio AZ1 project for

unmistakable trademark. By the 1970s, Zagato's importance had faded somewhat but its fortunes revived with the 1986 Aston Martin Zagato project, the Alfa Romeo SZ, Lancia Hyena, Nissan Autech Stelvio and series production of the Maserati Biturbo.

Zagato's self-financed dream cars have been relatively rare and rather inconsistent in their level of satisfaction. Alongside such sublime pieces as the Zeta 6, there have been some real disasters like the Stelvio and Lagonda Rapide. Zagato was forced to reform for the 1990s as SZ Design with Andrea Zagato at the helm.

■ LEFT *Basing the extremely compact Hyena on Lancia Integrale components gave it performance credibility. This model was sold on a special-order basis.*

Autech, a subdivision of Nissan. Unveiled in 1989, it was a two-plus-two coupé seemingly designed from the wing mirrors out (the front wings bulged out to accommodate them). Incredibly, it actually reached series production for the Japanese market. Zagato followed this exercise up with the more acceptable Gavia, Bambu and Seta projects, plus a Testarossa-based supercar called the Z93.

Perhaps marking a rebirth of the Zagato (or SZ Design) name was its 1996 Geneva showing and possible production model, the Raptor – its name recalling one of the villains of Steven Spielberg's dinosaur epic, *Jurassic Park*. Its proportions were exactly right, its Lamborghini Diablo V-twelve engine and four-wheel-drive system suitably exotic and its flop-forward double-

bubble canopy scintillating enough to engage the imagination. It justifies a link with the early, classic Zagato designs that make this *carrozzeria* a legend in car design.

■ ABOVE *For a powerful supercar, the Raptor succeeded in looking light and purposeful.*

■ BELOW *The Raptor revived Zagato's tradition of a prominent double-bubble roof. The car was based on Lamborghini parts.*

■ ABOVE *Zagato was effectively reborn in the 1990s. Its most promising project was the Raptor, developed for the 1996 Geneva Motor Show.*

■ OPPOSITE *The Hyena's hunched haunches gave a hint of high performance.*

INDEX

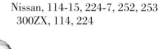

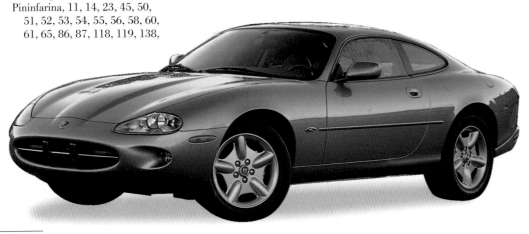